COLONIALISM

AND AGRARIAN

TRANSFORMATION

IN BOLIVIA

Colonialism and Agrarian Transformation in Bolivia

Cochabamba, 1550-1900

BROOKE LARSON

PRINCETON UNIVERSITY PRESS

PRINCETON, NEW JERSEY

Contents

LIST OF ILLUSTRATIONS

vii

LIST OF TABLES

ACKNOWLEDGMENTS

Authors of first books should be allowed to celebrate the rites of passage—not by passing through the process of tenure review, but in song, dance, and festivity. If this were a venerable academic ritual, my fiesta would take place on the alpine slopes of El Tunari, overlooking the fertile Valle Bajo, where I would toast the scores of friends, colleagues, and archivists who contributed to this project during its various phases.

In lieu of that happier alternative, I am forced to express but a few sober words of gratitude to all the people and institutions that helped me to carry out and complete this study. Perhaps my first intellectual debt is owed to my undergraduate professors in Latin American history, Ralph della Cava and Magnus Mörner, who opened up the field of Latin American history to me, encouraged me to pursue it, and gave me the courage to follow my star in spite of the bleak prospects of academic employment. I also want to warmly acknowledge the intellectual support and continuing encouragement of Herbert Klein and Karen Spalding, with whom I worked in graduate school. In spite of the fact that I did not take his advice to "publish the dissertation quickly," Herbert Klein never entirely lost faith in me—especially after I overcame my instinctual distaste for statistics, mastered SPSS, and processed a thousand punch cards on *alcabalas*! Karen Spalding, on the other hand, wasn't so interested in alcabalas, but she did stretch my horizons in Andean ethnohistory and anthropology, and she has been an unending source of inspiration and support over the years. In addition to my intellectual patrons, I wish to express my gratitude to my graduate-school *compañeros*—particularly Antonio Mitre, Adrian deWind, Carmen Ramos, Steven Volk, Elinor Burkett, and Elizabeth Dore—for their contributions to the early phases of this study and with a certain degree of nostalgia for more exciting political times. Numerous colleagues and friends have given me the benefit of their thoughts and criticism on various drafts of this book; in particular, Steve Stern, Antonio Mitre, Tristan Platt, Enrique Tandeter, John Murra, and Nicolás Sánchez-Albornoz were generous with their time and interest. I also appreciate the support I have received during the past three years from Barbara Weinstein and others of my colleagues at the State University of New York at Stony Brook.

During the course of my field research, I incurred many intellectual debts and received wonderful hospitality in Bolivia, Argentina, and Spain. I owe thanks to all the unsung employees of archives who carried dusty files to me day after day. I also am indebted to Gunnar Mendoza for his support and guidance during my work in the Archivo nacional de Bolivia. A host of people from Cochabamba offered me generous assistance, moral support, and warm hospitality. The municipal authorities responsible for opening the Cochabamba archive to me in 1974 (and, later, for the first time, to the public at large) should receive special mention. I will always be grateful to the Mitre family of Cochabamba for their loyal friendship, generosity, and hospitality. I also have had the good fortune of learning about various aspects of contemporary Bolivian society from several colleagues and friends over the years. I am especially grateful to Tito Jiménez, Jorge Dandler, Rosario León, Xavier Albó, Nancy Velarde, and Cassandra Torrico.

Of course, the project could never have been completed without the generous financial support I received from several institutions. An initial Foreign Area Field Program Fellowship from the American Council of Learned Societies and the Social Science Research Council allowed me to spend eighteen months in archival research. A Williams College faculty summer grant, an award for recent recipients of the Ph.D. from the American Council of Learned Societies, and a grant from the Inter-American Foundation allowed me to return to Bolivia for parts of several summers to expand the scope of my dissertation. I am also grateful to the Centro para el estudio de la realidad económica y social (CERES) for support enabling me to participate during the summer of 1981 in a collaborative project on the peasant economy of Cochabamba.

I wish to thank all those people who contributed to the laborious tasks of typing and editing drafts of this book. María Onestini, Carmen Díaz, Julie Franks, and Marie Murray deserve special mention for their work, as does my illustrator, Lisa Tingey Davis. I was most fortunate to have Robert A. Feldmesser as the book's copyeditor. His exacting criticism and valuable suggestions contributed in important ways to the final outcome. I am also indebted to the editor in chief of Princeton University Press, Sanford G. Thatcher, for his encouragement and support over the past several years.

Another part of the social infrastructure lies closer to home. As any woman (or man) involved in a high-pressured, two-career family can testify, the magnitude of the tasks of research and writing becomes clear only when parenting suddenly has to be balanced against all the rest. It has been possible for me to find joy in both work and family because Carter Bancroft has shared so fully and happily in the responsibilities of child raising, and because two wonderful grandmothers have always been there when needed. To them, and to Josh and Devon, who put it all in proper perspective, I owe more than I can ever say.

ABBREVIATIONS

AGI   Archivo General de Indias (Seville)

AGN   Archivo General de la Nación (Buenos Aires)

AHMC Archivo Histórico Municipal de Cochabamba (Cochabamba)

ANB   Archivo Nacional de Bolivia (Sucre)

BN   Biblioteca Nacional del Perú (Lima)

EC   Expedientes y Correspondencia (pertaining to the manuscript collections catalogued as Tierras e Indios and as La Audiencia de Charcas in the ANB)

EP   Escrituras públicas

f., ff.   *folio, folios* (front side of page of archival document)

ML   Mata Linares manuscript collection of the Real Academia de Historia

RAH   Real Academia de Historia (Madrid)

COLONIALISM
AND AGRARIAN
TRANSFORMATION
IN BOLIVIA

Introduction

This book traces the evolution of agrarian society in the region of Cochabamba, Bolivia, between the sixteenth and nineteenth centuries. It explores the long-term impact of colonial rule upon the formation and development of agrarian class relationships that were defined by European principles of property ownership and reinforced by Spanish imperial rule. The central aim of the study is to show how the pressures and contradictions of colonialism and class gradually gave rise to a distinctive Indian and mestizo peasantry that eventually became a powerful protagonist in regional society. The study also explores the consequences of the emergence of this peasant sector for the nature and balance of local class relations, for peasant-state relations, and for the regional economy as a whole in the late colonial and the postcolonial periods.

The region with which the study is concerned is the former colonial province of Cochabamba, which was incorporated into the vast intendancy of Santa Cruz de la Sierra in the late eighteenth century. Located to the east of the *altiplano* (high plains) at about the seventeenth degree of south latitude, this geopolitical space had no physiographic uniformity. It represented a cross-section of the vertical Andean landscape that swept down from the snow-capped peaks of the Cordillera Oriental, bordering the eastern edge of the altiplano, past the ancient lake basins and plains lying at middle-range altitudes of some 8,500 feet above sea level, to the eastern lowland fringes of the tropical frontier. In spite of the region's ecological diversity, it was known for its fertile, temperate valleys that caught the waters tumbling down from glacial lakes in the mountain chains to the north and west. A cluster of three contiguous valleys composed the unifying feature of the region (see figure 1). Their extraordinary fertility attracted Andean cultivators from the western *puna* who sought warm, moist soil to cultivate maize and other crops that

Figure 1   The Region of Cochabamba

did not thrive in the harsher alpine environments. Later, Europeans discovered the broad expanse of irrigated bottomlands and rich pastures in these central valleys. Although the region was always strongly oriented to the western altiplano, before and after the European arrival, it gained a territorial integrity and geohistorical identity of its own over the course of the colonial centuries.

The agrarian history of Cochabamba is no more representative of broader socioeconomic trends than any other Andean region. It is not my intention to project regional patterns onto the larger canvas of colonial Peru or Alto Perú. Rather, this study is focused on three specific aims. The first is to examine the region's strategic importance in the larger context of Tawantinsuyu and later of Alto Perú. The region's unique ecological endowments in the southern Andean landscape made it a vital area of surplus grain production for the Incas and the Spanish colonizers. In the late sixteenth century, Cochabamba was famous for the maize and wheat it shipped to the silver mines of Potosí. In some ways, the region became a classic agrarian hinterland of a dominant export sector.[1] Even as its functional role of granary in Alto Perú diminished over time, the region did not lose its importance as grain supplier to the cities and mines across the altiplano. In the late eighteenth and nineteenth centuries, Cochabamba's grains still supplemented the tuber diet of highland Andean peasants and provisioned some of the cities of the altiplano, particularly in times of drought and dearth. Moreover, Cochabamba became an important area of Spanish, mestizo, and Andean settlement in its own right. Intensive agriculture on the bottomlands sustained a relatively dense concentration of people who lived and worked in a network of towns, haciendas, and villages that crisscrossed the central valleys and hugged the banks of the western river valleys. But for a variety of reasons, which will emerge in the course of this study, the region gradually came to supply the dominant mining sector with another commodity: the labor power of impoverished peasants seeking wage work in the mineral lodes around the beginning of the twentieth century. One purpose of this history of Cochabamba, then, is to show the changing nature of the region's integra-

---

1 The seminal work on the formation of the internal colonial market revolving around Potosí is Carlos Sempat Assadourian, *El sistema de la economía colonial: Mercado interno, regiones, y espacio económico* (Lima: Instituto de Estudios Peruanos, 1982). See also the important article by Luís Miguel Glave, "Trajines: Un capítulo en la formación del mercado interno colonial," *Revista andina* 1 (1983): 9-76.

tion into the larger political economy and its link to the dominant mining economy and, through it, to the world market.

The second aim of this study is to illuminate the processes of structural change over a long period of time in an area of the Andes that was thoroughly integrated into the Spanish colonial empire. Through an examination of the long-term patterns of regional change in the context of mines, markets, and state formation in Alto Perú, it reveals the powerful extraregional forces of change that seemed to suck the region into the vortex of the expanding European economy during the first century of colonial rule. But it also seeks to show how Andean people conditioned the impact of those world-historical forces and sometimes set in motion counterforces that contained or limited the erosive effects of mercantile colonial pressures at the local level; and it identifies an important source of historical change in the internecine conflicts among factions of the colonial elite, as they tried to adjust to increasing competition for Indian labor during a protracted period of economic stagnation and a weak, decentralizing state in the seventeenth and early eighteenth centuries. Thus, considerable attention is given to the processes of market and state formation during the Toledan and post-Toledan periods in Alto Perú in order to explore how Andeans and Europeans in the Cochabamba valleys responded to (and to a certain degree impinged upon) the development of mercantile colonialism in this part of the Andes.

Cochabamba is a case study of radical transformation of preconquest patterns of life and work during the first century of Spanish rule. The market economy penetrated deeply, giving rise to new forms of exploitation and compelling Andean peoples to accommodate or to find new strategies of resistance. By the beginning of the seventeenth century, enterprising Spanish landowners (*chacareros*) had extended their reach across much of the valley land and created a servile class of peasants dependent upon them for the means of subsistence.

But the analysis of agrarian change in this region does not end with the transformation of native peoples into inferior "Indian" peasants. The broad temporal scope of this study allows for an exploration of the dynamics of ethnic and class relationships long after the dramatic confrontation between Andeans and Europeans had ended. The formation of European-style agrarian classes during the first century of colonialism did not establish a local hegemonic order that was either static or immutable to social pressures from below. Contrary to popular images of passive peons and tenant farmers bent in permanent subservience before the all-powerful *patrón*, most peasants who lived on haciendas were neither immobilized by debt nor limited in their livelihood activities to the boundaries of the "great estate." The study will show how a sector of the peasantry developed strategies of subsistence that combined Andean forms of communal labor and reciprocal exchange with small-scale commodity production and marketing, and in particular how the adaptive vitality of this peasantry eroded the economic power, prosperity, and hegemony of the landed elite in Cochabamba during the late colonial and the postcolonial periods.

At the same time, the study examines the dialectical nature of agrarian social relations. For if the emergent peasant economy began to challenge the landowning class (already suffering from the deleterious effects of estate fragmentation and market contraction), the landowners deployed their own schemes and strategies of accumulation and exploitation to shore up their eroding position in rural society. One consequence was a sharpening of class tensions in the region during the Bourbon period of increased state intervention and fiscal pressures. While the Bourbon state tried to smooth the raw edges of agrarian class relations in the region, the cumulative effect of its reforms was to deepen class antagonisms, as the burdens of colonialism grew heavier. The later chapters of the book therefore focus on the intersection of class and colonial relationships in rural Cochabamba in the late colonial period.

This analysis of regional change tries to demonstrate the historically contingent and sometimes precarious nature of agrarian classes in a colonial context. It assumes that the balance of class forces was subject to the internal social tensions, ecological disturbances (such as shifts in land-to-man ratios), and cyclical crises of subsistence that plagued all preindustrial societies. It also takes into account the initiatives of local groups and their responses to the continuing impact of larger historical forces, long after the watershed events of conquest and colonization.

However, one caveat is necessary. This study of agrarian transformations neither seeks nor finds the origins of capitalist transition in eighteenth- or early nineteenth-century Cochabamba. The study describes a regional economy that was in the process of diversifying into crafts, but that never saw peasant craft activity transformed into primitive manufacturing for the domestic market of a proletarianizing labor force. The study probes into agrarian estates, but finds little evidence of landlords bent upon rationalizing their enterprises to increase productivity or simply to enlarge their estates. Nor are there clear signs of enterprising capitalist farmers, an incipient kulak class, who harnessed their small-scale enterprises to expanding markets. The patterns of social realignments in the countryside were far more subtle. Under the intensifying fiscal pressures of the Bourbon state, each group struggled to maintain or improve its bargaining position in local society as the region was gradually drained of its meager capital resources in the late eighteenth century. Processes of social differentiation within the Cochabamba peasantry would have to advance much further before social pressures and uncertainties would turn a sector of the peasantry into a migrant work force in the distant industrial mines, or before a few prospering peasants would begin to acquire titles to pieces of crumbling haciendas around the beginning of the present century. Traditional haciendas continued to coexist uneasily with small-scale commodity production. Thus, while the balance and dynamics of class relations under colonialism and neocolonialism were characterized by historical motion and contradiction, the agrarian class structure in the Cochabamba region proved remarkably resilient throughout the late eighteenth, the nineteenth, and the early twentieth centuries.[2]

2 My interest in the development of agrarian class relations reflects, in an indirect way, some of the controversy among historians of early modern Europe over the relative autonomy of class and class conflict as forces of change. At issue, essentially, is where to locate the "motor force" of change in the gradual, uneven, and nonlinear process of transition toward capitalist relations of production: in the Malthusian dynamics of demographics; in the growth of trade and commercial capitalism; or in the internal class conflicts and contradictions embedded in the organization of production. Among Marxists, the issues of the debate were crystallized succinctly in the 1950s in a series of essays later gathered in Rodney Hilton, ed., *The Transition from Feudalism to Capitalism* (London: New Left Books, 1976). The debate was rekindled and broadened in the late 1970s with the publication of Robert Brenner, "Agrarian Class Structure and Economic Development in Pre-Industrial Europe," *Past and Present* 70 (1976): 30-75, and the subsequent commentaries under the same title by M. M. Postan and John Hatcher, *Past and Present* 78 (1978): 24-37, and Rodney Hilton, *Past and Present* 80 (1978): 3-19. Two additional Marxist essays on this "transition debate," which argued for the analytical primacy of class and class relations in the study of Eastern Europe and of Third World areas that were subordinate to, or penetrated by, European commercial capital, redirected the debate toward the world-systems approach to historical change; see Robert Brenner, "The Origins of Capitalist Development: A Critique of Neo-Smithian Marxism," *New Left Review*, no. 104 (1977): 25-92, and Aidan Foster-Carter, "The Modes of Production Controversy," ibid., no. 107 (1978): 47-78. A major object of their critique was, of course, Immanuel Wallerstein, *The Modern World-System: Capitalist Agriculture and the Origins of the European World Economy in the Sixteenth Century* (New York: Academic Press, 1974).

The third major aim of this study is to analyze patterns of agrarian change over the long term in comparative regional terms. The extraordinary cultural and social diversity of Andean rural societies, even after several centuries of colonial domination, dictates against insular approaches to regional history. Social historians and ethnohistorians have shown, in recent research, the persistent variation in social and economic organizations in Andean regions which, over five centuries, were subjected to common successive forms of political and economic domination.[3] From another angle, the ethnohistorical emphasis on the variety and adaptability of Andean forms of life and work reminds us that, in spite of the legendary wealth and world importance of Potosí, the market economy had an extremely variegated and uneven impact on southern Andean communities. Many Andean peoples managed to shield themselves against the most divisive effects of mercantile colonialism, sometimes through strategic engagement with the market or colonial state for purposes of preserving some semblance of economic autonomy and subsistence security.[4] The incursion of market forces (and of the colonial

3 David Lehmann, "Introduction: Andean Societies and the Theory of Peasant Economy," in David Lehmann, ed., *Ecology and Exchange in the Andes* (Cambridge: Cambridge University Press, 1982), 1-2. The ethnological literature on Andean diversity is too abundant to inventory here. For a succinct overview of recent research, see Frank Salomon, "Andean Ethnology in the 1970s: A Retrospective," *Latin American Research Review* 17 (1982): 75-128.

4 For contemporary ethnographic studies of Andean societies and of the interpenetration of reciprocal and market relations, see, for example, Billie Jean Isbell, *To Defend Ourselves: Ecology and Ritual in an Andean Village* (Austin: University of Texas Press, 1978); Barbara Bradby, " 'Resistance to Capitalism' in the Peruvian Andes," in Lehmann, ed., *Ecology and Exchange*, 97-122; Olivia Harris, "Labor and Produce in an Ethnic Economy: Northern Potosí, Bolivia," in ibid., 70-97; and Tristan Platt, "The Role of the Andean Ayllu in the Reproduction of the Petty Commodity Regime in Northern Potosí (Bolivia)," in ibid., 27-69. Ethnohistorical studies on the patterns and consequences of Andean market participation under colonial rule include John Murra, "Aymara Lords and Their European Agents at Potosí," *Nova Americana*, no. 1 (1978): 231-244; Thierry Saignes, "De la filiation à la résidence: Les ethnies dans les vallées de Larecaja," *Annales E.S.C.* 33 (1978): 1160-1181; Jorge Hidalgo Lehuedé, "Ecological Complementarity and Tribute in Atacama, 1683-1792," in Shozo Masuda, Izumi Shimada, and Craig Morris, eds., *Andean Ecology and Civilization: An Interdisciplinary Perspective on Andean Ecological Complementarity* (Tokyo: Tokyo University Press, 1985), 161-184; Karen Spalding, "Kurakas and Commerce: A Chapter in the Evolution of Andean Society," *Hispanic American Historical Review* 53 (1973): 581-599; Steve Stern, "The Struggle for Solidarity: Class, Culture, and Community in Highland Indian America," *Radical History Review*, no. 27 (1983): 21-48; and several of the essays in Olivia Harris, Brooke Larson,

state) was necessary, but certainly not sufficient, for the disintegration or erosion of Andean ethnic economies. The region of Chayanta, contiguous to Cochabamba, was but one area where Indian ethnic groups held on to their traditional lands and reproduced their social organization, with significant modifications, to withstand the pressures of colonialism.[5] The contrast in the colonial experience of the two regions, Cochabamba and Chayanta, stands as a vivid reminder of the differential impact of mercantile colonialism on Andean rural societies even in the economic heartland of Alto Perú. Furthermore, we need only recall that, at the birth of the Bolivian republic, some 70 percent of its Indian population still lived in autonomous communities to put the Cochabamba region into proper perspective, at least in the context of the southern Andes.

More than most regions of Alto Perú, Cochabamba experienced the economic and cultural shocks of European colonization. In contrast to Chayanta and many other highland areas, Andean peoples of the valleys were unable to contain the divisive forces of class within their communities or to slow the advance of Spanish land ownership. The challenge, therefore, is to determine the reasons why Andean peoples in Cochabamba succumbed so early to the European forms of domination, even as the Toledan state mounted its apparatus of indirect rule. Toward this end, it is necessary to explore the patterns and consequences of the unfolding struggles, conflicts, and alliances among and between Andeans and Europeans in the critical years between 1550 and 1600. The ethnic rivalry and disunity that weakened Andean resistance to European encroachment on valley land were similar to those that have been described for several other Andean regions in the same period.[6] But equally important was the peculiar legacy of late Incaic rule in the Valle Bajo of Cochabamba. Once the local Incan agrarian regime was shattered by the Spanish Conquest, Europeans could sift through some of the shards and piece together their own agrarian enterprises geared to the emerging market of Potosí. In this way, the deep imprint of particular precolonial state and social structures in Cochabamba created opportunities for

and Enrique Tandeter, eds., *La participación indígena en los mercados surandinos: Estrategias y reproducción social, siglos XVI-XX* (La Paz: CERES, 1987).

5 See Tristan Platt, *Estado boliviano y ayllu andino: Tierra y tributo en el Norte de Potosí* (Lima: Instituto de Estudios Peruanos, 1982), chaps. 1 and 2.

6 See, for example, Steve Stern, *Peru's Indian Peoples and the Challenge of the Spanish Conquest: Huamanga to 1640* (Madison: University of Wisconsin Press, 1982) and Thierry Saignes, *Los Andes orientales: Historia de un olvido* (Cochabamba: CERES, 1985).

European colonizers to engage in more extensive restructuring of patterns of production and exchange than was possible in many other Andean regions.

The study of regional change is approached here from several conceptual angles. Because the origins and evolution of this rural colonial society cannot be understood simply in terms of historical processes at the regional level, Cochabamba must be studied in the context of mercantile colonialism in Alto Perú. The early chapters of this book therefore approach regional history "from the outside." Necessarily, they chart broad patterns of change rather than the fine-grained detail of rural life. Chapters 1 and 2 locate the region in the larger colonial formation during the early period and consider the processes by which Europeans subordinated Andean traditions to their own economic, political, and ideological imperatives (which were not always congruent). Chapter 3 provides an overarching interpretive framework within which to trace secular trends over the course of the seventeenth and early eighteenth centuries and to explore the interaction between these trends and patterns of regional change. They seek to show how rural society in Cochabamba both adapted to and, in some measure, shaped the larger patterns of Andean population decline and dispersion, mineral decline and slow recovery, and political fragmentation in the period before the Bourbon reforms.

The later chapters narrow the temporal scope to the late colonial period in order to take a closer look at regional change. Chapters 4 through 8 explore various aspects of regional society and economy from the perspective of ethnic, class, and colonial relationships. Most of the data pertain to regional society during the second half of the eighteenth century, for which period there exists a wealth of quantitative and qualitative material on Cochabamba. But, as indicated earlier, the decision to focus on the internal dynamics of class and ethnicity in this period was motivated by more than simply pragmatic considerations. The eighteenth century seemed to be a period when regional patterns of landholding, agricultural production, and marketing began to configure and crystallize in forms that would endure well beyond the colonial period. Furthermore, the pressures of political reform in the late eighteenth century magnified the tensions intrinsic to peasant-landlord relations and threw into bold relief the social contours of class in this region.

Chapter 4 focuses on demographic characteristics and social relations in the Andean villages that were subject both to continuing encroachment from outside and to internal pressures and divisions.

In particular, this chapter studies the ways in which class differentiation in the village of Tapacarí created a crisis of authority for the caciques. Chapter 5 broadens the analysis to include the majority of the region's peasant families: those who lived outside the village on parcels of hacienda land, on small plots of their own, and on the outskirts of Spanish towns. It explores the nature and implications of peasant subsistence strategies, partly based upon small-scale commodity production and exchange. The next two chapters, 6 and 7, shift the analysis to the landed elite, who developed defensive strategies against the incursion of peasant smallholders, but who in turn contributed to their own declining position in rural society. These chapters explore the limits of reformist initiatives and the structural constraints that forced landlords to find rentier forms of income. Chapter 8 again enlarges the picture to examine the impact of the administrative reforms introduced by the Bourbons on the deterioration of the regional economy at the end of the colonial period.

Finally, chapter 9 draws together the various strands of analysis to show the principal currents of change in the region over the course of the colonial period. Beyond this synoptic overview, the chapter explores the legacies of colonialism and class in Cochabamba in the nineteenth century and indicates the ways in which the acceleration of social differentiation in the valleys toward the end of the century both strengthened the peasant family economy in the region and simultaneously created the basis for peasant migration and proletarianization. The agrarian crisis and change in Cochabamba around the turn of the twentieth century had roots that lay deep in the subsoil of the colonial past.

Along the Inca Frontier

The traveler in the sixteenth century who set off southward from the shores of Lake Titicaca on a journey through Alto Perú (today Bolivia) left behind him one of the world's most arresting lacustrine landscapes. Pausing a moment in the hot morning sun to contemplate the landscape, a European traveler must have been struck by the lake's vast expanse and deep blue waters set off by the golden reeds that rose from the shallow waters near the shore. He saw great herds of alpaca and llama grazing on yellow-green pastures, and peasants planting quinoa and potatoes on hillsides sloping gently down to the lake. Across the inland sea to the northeast rose glaciered peaks that formed part of the endless eastern cordillera flanking the lake and the *altiplano*. Those mountains formed a topographic barrier between the dense human settlements around the lake and the vast, tropical frontier stretching eastward across the upper Amazonic basin. In the afternoons, the peaks vanished in white clouds that welled up from the tropical jungle beyond the cordillera, as if beckoning people of the high, arid plains to venture across the mountains into the steamy lowlands. From the altiplano, at 12,000 feet above sea level, the foreigner could feel the effects of the dry, "thin" air that seemed to lend an extraordinary luminosity to the landscape. The sun's warmth was deceptive, for the temperature would plummet to near freezing on most clear nights. The Aymara peoples who inhabited the high plains harnessed the extreme diurnal temperature contrast to make "freeze-dried" potatoes (*chuño*), a major source of their stored energy, and to preserve other staples. But for the European, the altiplano was bleak and inhospitable country.

Continuing southward, the sojourner encountered the bitter wind that scoured the high plains during the winter months, portent of a harsher climate. The southern reaches of the altiplano, near the towns of Oruro, Poopó, and Potosí, were considerably more arid and

13

cold than the lake region or points north.[1] Farther south, in the desolate territory of the Lipez, it was said that during the winter months the cold split stones and shrank the facial muscles of the dead, leaving ghostly smiles on their frozen, withered faces.[2] It was strange landscape, where shallow lakes were really salt marshes and where it was impossible to judge distance across the high plains to the next *tambo* or town. The luminous air seemed to play dangerous games with European perceptions of space.

The Southern Landscapes

Continental mountain chains border the altiplano on its western and eastern sides, so that in reality it is a series of high intermontane basins that formed a corridor of highland movement and settlement along a north-south axis between Cuzco and southern Alto Perú (see figure 2). To the west, the Cordillera Occidental juts sharply upward from the altiplano, its peaks reaching heights of 15,500 feet. A few rivers originate in this volcanic belt and flow westward toward the sea; the vertiginous western slopes drop off into the Atacama desert region bordering the sea. Mountain passages are few and treacherous, but the descent into the desert is the only outlet to the sea and the world beyond.

Crossing the eastern mountain chain, the Cordillera Oriental, the sixteenth-century traveler encountered a rugged, corrugated landscape that seemed more vertical than horizontal. Three or four days on muleback would bring the traveler through mountain passes near the snow line (at 15,000 feet) and across slopes and high pastures, where llamas grazed on *ichu* grasses, to cultivated fields where peasants planted tubers, barley, and perhaps some European wheat, at altitudes ranging from about 11,400 to 13,800 feet.[3] The puna lands

1 David Browman, "El manejo de la tierra árida del altiplano del Perú y Bolivia," *American indígena* 40 (1980): 145; Wendell C. Bennett, "The Andean Highlands: An Introduction," in J. Steward, ed., *The Handbook of South American Indians*, (Washington, D.C.: Smithsonian Institution, 1946), 2: 17.

2 Tristan Platt, "The Ayllus of Lipez in the Nineteenth Century" (paper presented at the Congress of Americanists, Manchester, England, September 5-10, 1982), citing Bernabé Cobo, *Historia del nuevo mundo* (1653) (Madrid: Atlas, 1956).

3 See Platt, "Role of the Andean ayllu," 30-31. For a discussion of agricultural tiers in the region, see Stephen B. Brush, "Man's Use of an Andean Ecosystem," *Human Ecology* 4 (1976): 147-166; and Olivier Dollfus, *El reto del espacio andino* (Lima: Instituto de Estudios Andinos, 1981).

Figure 2 Ecological Zones of Bolivia
Source: E. Boyd Wennergren and Morris D. Whitaker, *The Status of Bolivian Agriculture*, p. 20. © 1975 Praeger Publishers. Reprinted by permission of Praeger Publishers.

were cold, but every so often the sojourner would come across a warm, sheltered valley that had a microclimate allowing peasants to cultivate less hardy crops than the tubers. This mountain range was wider than the western cordillera, and its tortured landscape sometimes seemed impenetrable, but actually these mountains were less hostile. Volcanic lakes fed streams that plunged into the cordillera and carved out rugged gorges and crevices. In the dry winter months, mountain streambeds became passageways into the warmer lowlands. There, the weary traveler at last began to feel at home: the *kichwa* region, ranging from 6,500 to 11,000 feet, was a temperate zone where European crops flourished alongside native ones. European colonists compared the valleys favorably to their own homelands in Spain.

In this longitudinal slice of the eastern cordillera, three broad intermontane basins created important agricultural regions in the kichwa ecological tier. Of the three valleys—Cochabamba, Chuquisaca, and Tarija—the northernmost, Cochabamba, was the largest and probably the most fertile. It consisted in turn of three contiguous, connected valleys, each with its own ecological characteristics (see figure 1).[4] The central valley, called the Valle Bajo or Lower Valley, was blessed with moist, alluvial soil deposited by a mountain river (known today as the Rocha River) that ran the length of the valley and spilled into the next, smaller valley, called Sacaba. In the richest lands, especially in the western reaches of the Valle Bajo, where the basin began to twist southward through the cordillera, peasants planted maize continuously on irrigated lands. There was no need to let the lands lie fallow where the alluvial soil was so deep and water readily available. A passage through a small mountain chain at the eastern end of the Valle Bajo led to the larger, higher, and more arid valley of Cliza. During winter months, its dry, dusty fields had none of the charms of the moister lands in the Valle Bajo or the Sacaba Valley, but its fields provided good pastures for European stock and pockets of moist soil that might be planted with maize and potatoes.

Though they opened on to each other, these central valleys of Cochabamba (as we shall refer to them) were fairly contained geographically. The cordillera rose sharply on all sides of the three valleys, isolating them from the altiplano and from other large settlements or valley regions. To the north and east, the rugged land jutted upward toward the sky, barricading the valleys from the tropical frontier on the other side of the eastern escarpment. South of the Cliza Valley, the landscape erupted in dry, jagged mountains that cut off the valley region from the southern intermontane basins and the large settlements of Chuquisaca and Tarija. The central valleys of Cochabamba were not cul-de-sacs; it was possible to travel eastward across the valleys and then, turning south, to follow winding mountain trails to the southern towns. But like most settlements in the warm kichwa tier along the eastern escarpment, the towns and villages of Cochabamba were off the beaten track—situated far from

4 See chap. 5 for a detailed description of the different zones in the late colonial period.

the altiplano and perched on the eastern edges of the colonial frontier, where the land dropped off precipitously into the untamed tropical expanse. The most heavily traveled routes followed the Arque and Tapacarí rivers in the western territory of the Cochabamba region through the cordillera to the altiplano.

The bleak puna and sharp, broken landscape of the cordillera that vexed and tortured Europeans provided an extraordinary variety of ecological niches which Andean peoples harnessed in precolonial times. The Aymara tribes, which inhabited the southern Andes long before the arrival of even the Incas, adopted pastoral and agricultural strategies that took advantage of the variations in climate and flora in the distinct ecological zones, often widely dispersed in space.[5]

The Aymara people implanted their core settlements in the bleak lands of the altiplano and puna. Highland settlements could take advantage of the tough grasses to graze their cameloid animals, chiefly llamas and alpacas. With careful planning and frequent rotation, tuber crops and quinoa also thrived in higher altitudes, where rainfall provided the only water. And the cold, dry climate proved ideal for preserving for ten or twelve months the vital foods that could supplement the consumption of chuño, which highlanders sometimes stored for years on end.[6] However harsh and forbidding the puna might seem to Europeans, it was the heartland of the domesticated cameloids and tubers that provided the staples of life for most Andean peoples. Furthermore, the puna tier was a strategic location for Andean communities. It usually formed a "middle ground" between the upper alpine pastures, too cold for even the hardiest crops to be sown, and the lower valleys and slopes in the kichwa zone. More important, puna settlements could be fortified more easily than villages nestled in remote valleys at lower altitudes.[7] But the

5 Carl Troll, "The Cordilleras of the Tropical Americas: Aspects of Climatic, Phytogeographical, and Agrarian Ecology," in Carl Troll, ed., *Geo-Ecology of the Mountainous Regions of the Tropical Americas*. (Bonn: University of Bonn Geographical Institute, 1968); John V. Murra, "El 'control vertical' de un máximo de pisos ecológicos en la economía de las sociedades andinas," in Iñigo Ortíz de Zúñiga, ed., *Visita de la provincia de León de Huánuco en 1562* (Huánuco: Universidad Nacional Hermilio Valdizán, 1972) 2: 429-476, as reprinted in John V. Murra, *Formaciones económicas y políticas del mundo andino* (Lima: Instituto de Estudios Andinos, 1975), 59-116 (citations refer to the reprinted edition).

6 John V. Murra, "Rite and Crop in the Inca State," in Stanley Diamond, ed., *Culture in History* (New York: Columbia University Press, 1960), 393-407, as translated and reprinted in Murra, *Formaciones económicas*, pp. 46-47.

7 Harry Tschopik, Jr., "The Aymaras," in J. Steward, ed., *Handbook of South*

puna not only nourished its inhabitants; it also formed the battle-grounds where rival Aymara kingdoms or clans engaged in ceremonial and real warfare. Small wonder that the Aymara word for highlands, *urco*, also connoted "virility associated with violence." In contrast, the warm, fertile lowlands were associated with feminine qualities, and valley settlements were considered to be subordinate to the core ethnic group of the puna.[8]

Life and agriculture at altitudes of 12,000 feet above sea level were fraught with uncertainty. Communities on the shores of Titicaca had the benefit of that large, deep body of water, which tempered the cold, dry climate of the altiplano. But most Aymaras lived with the expectation that frost, drought, or hailstorms would cut deeply into the harvest about three out of every five years.[9] It was not enough that abundant rain fell near harvest time if mild drought struck in the crucial months of September, October, and November, when highland peasants planted precious potato seed in the thin topsoil of the puna. And no season was free of the threat of frost; it could strike at any moment, sometimes claiming an entire harvest as winter approached.[10] Even under optimal climatic conditions, cultivators had to manage puna resources carefully, allowing their fields to rest— sometimes as long as twenty years—between crops. Highland peasants rotated potato, another tuber called *oca*, and the barley-like quinoa among multiple, dispersed plots of ground where the angle of the slope, patterns of light and shade, altitude, and soil condition combined in different ways to produce varied ecological conditions within the puna zone. In that way, cultivators didn't upset the delicate ecological balance, and they hedged their bets against natural calamity in any one locality.

Strict ecological constraints and the risks involved in puna agriculture impelled the highland communities to reach out to distant lands in the east. The moist lands in the kichwa zone meant that highland people could complement their everyday diet of potatoes,

American Indians, 7 vols. (New York: Cooper Square, 1963), 2: 547; Brush, "Man's Use of an Andean Ecosystem," 160.

8 Thérèse Bouysse-Cassagne, "L'espace aymara: Urco et uma," *Annales E.S.C.* 33 (1978): 1061 and 1063.

9 Juan Polo de Ondegardo, "Informe . . . al Lic. Briviesca de Muñatones sobre la perpetuidad de las encomiendas en el Perú" (1561), *Revista histórica* 13 (1940): 168.

10 R. Brooke Thomas and Bruce P. Winterhalder, "Physical and Biotic Environment of Southern Highland Peru," in P. Baker and M. Little, eds., *Man in the Andes* (Stroudsburg, Pa.: Doudon, Hutchinson, and Ross, 1976), 21-59.

chuño, and oca with such exotic products as maize, chili peppers (*ají*), and squashes. Without large-scale public works to terrace hill-sides and build irrigation systems, valley agriculture remained small-scale, dispersed, and secondary to highland subsistence agriculture.[11] But scattered parcels of irrigated land in the river valleys of Cochabamba might yield maize crops large enough to allow some to be stored in communal silos against future emergencies—when, for example, drought in the *temporal* lands of the puna diminished the community's potato harvest. More than simply insurance, maize had symbolic value as a ceremonial crop, to be consumed (often in the form of *chicha*, or beer) at holiday festivities, work parties, or life-cycle rituals. It was a food of the gods as well as of the peasant family. Thus, rich maize fields in the eastern valleys provided precious resources to highland communities with which to appease the local deities and to guard against the frequent harvest failures.

Like most of the Andean peoples that inhabited the highlands south of the Cajamarca region, Aymara communities assured themselves of a stable source of subsistence through their control of multiple ecological tiers. At the local level of the *ayllu*, an extended kin group, this "vertical control of the ecology" might simply take the form of crop diversification across different microclimates located at great distance from one another. Even today in many parts of Bolivia, Aymara kin groups collectively control high pastures where came-loids and sheep are reared as well as crop land scattered throughout the puna and in the tucks and folds of the warm valleys, several days' journey away.[12] Murra's pathbreaking ethnohistorical study of the Chupaychu and Lupaqa kingdoms in the sixteenth century revealed extensive networks of "vertical control" that interlaced multiple settlements along the eastern and western cordilleras and nuclear political and kin groups in the highlands.[13] These ethnic kingdoms

11 Murra, *Formaciones económicas*, 47-48.

12 See Tristan Platt, "Espejos y maíz: El concepto de yanatín entre los Macha de Bolivia," in E. Mayer and R. Bolton, eds., *Parentesco y matrimonio en los Andes* (Lima: Universidad Católica, 1980), 139-182; Platt, "Role of the Andean ayllu"; O. Harris, "Labor and Produce"; Olivia Harris, "Ecological Duality and the Role of the Center: Northern Potosí," in Masuda, Shimada, and Morris, *Andean Ecology and Civilization*, 311-336; Joseph W. Bastien, *Mountain of the Condor* (St. Paul, Minn.: West Publishing, 1978); and Josep M. Barnadas, *Los Aymaras dentro de la sociedad boliviana* (La Paz: Centro de Investigación y Promoción del Campesinado, 1976).

13 Murra, " 'Control vertical.' " See also his articles " 'El archipiélago vertical' Revisited" and "The Limits and Limitations of the 'Vertical Archipelago' in the

created "peripheral islands" of kinsmen in fertile pockets in the eastern kichwa regions, on oases along the Pacific coast, and on the edges of the tropical frontier. The inhabitants of these satellite communities, who were called *mitimaes*, cultivated coca, maize, ají, and cotton; they gathered guano along the seacoast to be used as fertilizer in the highlands; and they sent tropical fruit up from the *yungas*, the eastern mountains of the tropical zone. The same settlement pattern obtained for the Aymara kingdoms located far to the south of Lake Titicaca, though their vertical orientation was perhaps more eastward toward the kichwa lowlands.[14] This "archipelago" pattern of territoriality, so different from European nucleated settlements and contiguous territorial control, required kinsmen to trek many days through diverse landscape and "foreign" territory to their outlying colonies. Once they left behind their fortified core settlement in the highlands, they moved from ethnic island to island, navigating their way through neutral or enemy territory. A bird's-eye view of the eastern cordillera and intermontane basins would reveal a mosaic of multiple (often competing) hamlets, sealed off from their neighbors but bound tightly through kin ties and ideology to their distant ethnic "headquarters" in the highlands. Thus were Andean polities able to harness the ecological diversity of the vertical landscape and ensure their social reproduction, even in the face of high-risk puna agriculture, without embarking upon the indigenous development of a market system for the exchange of specialized or surplus products.

Yet, as Murra conceptualized it, "vertical control of the ecology" cannot be reduced simply to a model of ecological adaptation. "Verticality" was also an "ideal" that shaped the social relations of production and exchange within Andean society and formed an integral part of an ideology and world view.[15] In principle and in practice,

Andes," in Masuda, Shimada, and Morris, *Andean Ecology and Civilization*, pp. 3-14 and 15-20, respectively.

14 On the Aymara nations of the southern Collasuyu, see the testimony of Charcas Indians in Waldemar Espinoza Soriano, ed., "El memorial de Charcas: Crónica inédita de 1582," *Cantuta: Revista de la Universidad Nacional de Educación* (Chosica, Peru, 1969): 1-35.

15 For a discussion of the verticality model as an Andean ideal, see Olivia Harris, "Kinship and the Vertical Economy of the Laymi Ayllu, Norte de Potosí," *Actes du XLIIe Congrès International des Americanistes* (Paris: Société des Americanistes, 1976), 4: 165-177. For an exploratory essay on the concept of complementarity as applied to Andean societies, see Frank Salomon, "The Dynamic Potential of the Complementarity Concept," in Masuda, Shimada, and Morris, *Andean Ecology and Civilization*, 511-532. See also the important essays by Murra, " 'Archipiélago vertical' Revisited" and "Limits and Limita-

vertical control implied the existence of a communal tradition and ideology that bound people together in a web of mutual rights and responsibilities. Through reciprocity and communal labor, people coordinated their efforts to minimize and pool subsistence risks and ensure the social reproduction of their community or kindred. In its purest form, the principle of reciprocity involved the exchange of equivalencies, mediated by kinship and ritual kinship relations. As anthropologists have long argued, however, reciprocal relations may take a variety of forms, some symmetrical and some not, so that the term refers only vaguely to a relationship defined by a process of advances and restitutions over time.[16]

What was crucial in the precolonial Andean context, however, was that kinship provided a language and an ideology defining and legitimating patterns of give and take, at both the ayllu and the state level, which gave a certain cohesion and unity to kin groups scattered widely across space. In Andean societies, kin groups were bounded units composed of an extended network of households. Households were joined together to form larger, nested groups such as the ayllu, the lineage, and the community, tribe, or ethnic lordship (*señorío*). The ayllu, the cell of Andean society, was theoretically an endogamous lineage that traced its origins to a common ancestor. Ayllus were nested in extended lineages which, in turn, claimed descent from a mythical ancestor-god. These "confederated lineages" formed a half-dozen or so polities embracing thousands of households and extensive "vertical archipelagos." Before and after Incaic penetration, the Colla and Lupaqa kingdoms of the lake district, the Pacajes peoples south of the lake, and, to the far south, the Charcas, Caracaras, Chuyes, and Chichas all identified themselves

---

tions." A more critical view of "verticality" may be found in Rodrigo Sánchez, "The Model of Verticality in the Andean Economy: A Critical Reconsideration," *Actes du XLIIe Congrès International des Américanistes* (Paris: Société des Américanistes), 4: 213-226.

16 On the concept of reciprocity as a process of "advances and restitutions," see Claude Meillassoux, *Femmes, greniers, et capitaux* (Paris: Maspero, 1975). For critical discussions of the concept as applied in the Andean context, see Nathan Wachtel, "La reciprocidad y el estado inca: De Karl Polanyi a John V. Murra," in his *Sociedad e ideología* (Lima: Instituto de Estudios Peruanos, 1973), 59-78; O. Harris, "Kinship and the Vertical Economy," 172; Bradby " 'Resistance to Capitalism,' " esp. 114-115; and Benjamin Orlove, "Inequality among Peasants: The Forms and Uses of Reciprocal Exchange in Andean Peru," in Rhoda Halperin and James Dow, eds., *Peasant Livelihood: Studies in Economic Anthropology and Cultural Ecology* (New York: St. Martin's, 1977), 201-214.

as cultural groups distinguished by their Aymara dialects, styles of dress, music, weaving, and local rituals and deities (see figure 3).[17]

To realize the ideals of self-sufficiency and community, extended kin groups vested authority in an elaborate hierarchy of chieftains, including *mallkus*, or superior lords, and *hilacatas*, or secondary chiefs who governed at the level of the ayllu or moiety. These lords and chiefs symbolized the unity, common interests and identity of the ethnic group at the highest levels of social organization.[18] Vertical control of the environment thus implied a centralized political system which reproduced its own political, ideological, and religious power through the mobilization of peasant labor.[19] Theoretically, the contradiction engendered by the ideals of verticality and community, on the one hand, and the appropriation of surplus by ethnic elites, on the other, found its resolution in the services and gifts the mallkus (or *kurakas*, as they were called in the Quechua language) offered to the community at large or to individual kin. At all levels of the ethnic hierarchy, the principles of reciprocity and redistribution governed the social relations between direct producers and their lords. Andean chiefs gained authority and legitimacy by serving the

17 An important survey of Aymara peoples is the classic study by Luís G. Lumbreras, *The Peoples and Cultures of Ancient Peru* (Washington, D.C.: Smithsonian Institution Press, 1974), esp. 200-213. See also John Hyslop, "An Archeological Investigation of the Lupaqa Kingdom and Its Origins" (Ph.D. diss., Columbia University, 1976). On Aymara kinship organization, see Freda Y. Wolf, "Parentesco aymara en el siglo XVI," in E. Mayer and R. Bolton, eds., *Parentesco y matrimonio en los Andes* (Lima: Universidad Católica, 1980), 115-136, and Xavier Albó and Mauricio Mamani, "Esposos, suegros, y padrinos entre los Aymaras," in ibid., 283-326. Two recent regional approaches to Andean social relations and ideology, both of them focused on the central highlands of Peru, are Karen Spalding, *Huarochirí: An Andean Society under Inca and Spanish Rule* (Stanford, Calif.: Stanford University Press, 1984), esp. chap. 1-3; and Stern, *Peru's Indian Peoples*, chap. 1.

18 In his study of the Lupaqa on the western shores of Lake Titicaca, Murra identified two kings who reigned simultaneously around the time of the Spanish Conquest. This dualistic political organization, which split Lupaqa settlements into moieties, was a common Andean pattern which survived, at the local level, the transition to colonial rule. But it seemed to be particularly marked among some Aymara polities, which were also segmented in their political and social spatial organization. See John V. Murra, "An Aymara Kingdom in 1567," *Ethnohistory* 15 (1968): 115-151, as reprinted in Murra, *Formaciones económicas*, 207-209; Bouysse-Cassagne, "Espace aymara," 1058-1059; O. Harris, "Ecological Duality"; and Platt, "Espejos y maíz."

19 See Bradby, " 'Resistance to Capitalism,' " for a discussion of vertical control as a social relation.

Figure 3 The Aymara Kingdoms
Source: Thérèse Bouysse-Cassagne, "L'espace aymara: Urco et Uma, *Annales E.S.C.* 5-6 (1978): 1059. Reproduced by permission.

collective interests. They protected and maintained the community's property and norms; generously feasted laborers working on communal projects; coordinated the production, storage, and redistribution of products among ayllus and across the vertical archipelago; mediated disputes and rivalries so as to preserve the group's solidarity; interpreted and appeased the gods and the sacred ancestors; and defended community interests against outside threats. Above all, they guaranteed to all kin who shared communal responsibility a minimum of subsistence security and a cushion against natural disaster.

Ethnohistorians who have reconstructed the social organization of

Andean societies prior to the European intrusion have found under-currents of conflict and contradiction that animated these societies and often pulled them in opposite directions. While they have not agreed on the course these societies might have taken had the European invasion not arrested their development, most Andean ethno-historians take pains to demystify *lo andino*—the "Andean way"— as an egalitarian utopia or ideal.[20] Whether we are dealing with the powerful Aymara kingdoms of the southern steppes or the Andean tribes of the central sierra, power and access to resources were dis-tributed unequally. Furthermore, the internal dynamics of com-munal organization that supported a powerful, often bellicose ethnic elite sharpened the contradictions within local Andean society and probably widened the gap between Andean ideals and social reality. Communal forms of work and life contained the germs of class dif-ferentiation; the ideology of reciprocity often masked relations of po-litical domination and surplus extraction; and the ideal of vertical control intensified ethnic rivalry among polities struggling to extend their reach into the maize valleys.[21]

The crucial point, nevertheless, is that the ideals of verticality, community, and reciprocity established the ideological boundaries within which people defined and articulated social norms, created standards of justice and social legitimacy, and interpreted their world and cosmos. These principles formed the basis of "moral econ-omy" that to a greater or lesser degree governed social relationships, bound together kinship and social hierarchy, and strengthened com-munal solidarity.[22] They endowed everyday subsistence activities

20 See esp. Murra, " 'Control vertical' "; Spalding, *Huarochirí*, chap. 2 and 3; Stern, *Peru's Indian Peoples*, chap. 1; and Nathan Wachtel, *The Vision of the Vanquished: The Spanish Conquest of Peru through Indian Eyes, 1530-1570* (New York: Harper and Row, 1977).

21 Stern, *Peru's Indian Peoples*, chapter 1; Bradby, " 'Resistance to Capital-ism' "; Murra, " 'Control vertical.' "

22 Historians and anthropologists who study change in traditional societies within the framework of "moral economy" are not concerned simply with the apparent "objective" conditions of life and work within precapitalist agrarian or-ders. Rather, they emphasize the pattern of moral rights and expectations that both governed social behavior within a kin group or ethnically bounded commu-nity and provided the normative order or standards by which people judged their own behavior and that of outsiders. In many traditional agrarian societies, that moral order revolved around the shared expectation of distributing risks and scarce resources among members of the community in a way that guaranteed some form of subsistence to all members engaged in communal activities. Tra-ditional ideals of reciprocity also governed relations between peasants and their

and labor prestations with symbolic, even religious, meaning. They gave peasants the right to call on their mallkus or hilacatas for assistance or generosity in times of need. On a broader level, the ideals of verticality, community, and reciprocity gave social cohesion to the Charcas or Caracaras who were scattered in isolated hamlets across a tortured landscape, because those ideals legitimated and preserved their moral claim to "subsistence rights" no matter what ecological niche they inhabited in their polity. Thus, while Andean societies may have been marred by social differentiation and accumulative processes, the normative order mandated a degree of social control that placed structural limits on the exploitation of the poorer peasants. The dominant ideology thus blunted the cutting edge of class formation based on property relations.

Yet the communal tradition and ideology had a double edge. It provided an overarching unity, but it could be manipulated in a way that had a disintegrating effect on the whole. Thus, for example, while Aymara lords could ensure the group's self-sufficiency and material well-being, and while they had to uphold minimum standards of justice and equity, they could also invoke the communal tradition to militarize their societies. Aymara lords of the Collao were famous for turning their peasants and herders into professional warriors. When the Incas expanded their empire into the southern Andes during the fifteenth century, the Quechua-speaking invaders began to appreciate the power and authority that Aymara lords wielded in their ethnic kingdoms and to turn it to their own imperialist ends.

___

Incaic Inroads

Under the emperor Pachacuti (1438-1471), Inca warriors from the north pushed their way into the rich, populous kingdoms of the Collao, the region around Lake Titicaca. The invaders from Cuzco encountered bitter resistance, but they finally managed to impose imperial control over the Aymara dynasties of the lake district. During two successive administrations, the Incas consolidated their rule over the Aymara nations, absorbing them into the Collasuyu "quarter" of the Incaic empire of Tawantinsuyu. The emperor Yu-

___

overlords and other members of the ruling group. On the politics of "moral economy," see Edward P. Thompson, "The Moral Economy of the English Crowd," *Past and Present*, no. 50 (1971): 76-136. On the moral tissue of peasant societies and the logic of reciprocal relationships, see James Scott, *The Moral Economy of the Peasant* (New Haven: Yale University Press, 1976), and Barrington Moore, Jr., *Social Origins of Dictatorship and Democracy: Lord and Peasant in the Making of the Modern World* (Boston: Beacon, 1966), esp. 453-483.

panqui (1471-1493) settled ethnically alien populations among the recently subdued natives, constructed a network of roads and tambos, and began to recruit Aymara warriors for his own imperial armies. As the Incas advanced the northern frontiers of their empire, they drew more heavily on the loyal Aymara, Pukinas, and Uru nations of the southern highlands for their soldiers. Military recruitment intensified under Huayna Cápac (1493-1527), as he elevated the status of certain Aymara groups to serve as his professional warriors. Many years later (in 1582), in litigation aimed at recovering some of their former privileges and status, the Charcas, Caracaras, Chuyes, and Chichas proudly described themselves as "soldiers of the [Incan] emperor," who had "fought and conquered the Chachapoyas, Cayambis, Canares, Quitos, and Quillaycincas, who are the [tribes] of Guayaquil and Popoyán." The Aymara warriors furnished the shock troops on the northern edges of the empire, and the Incas also stationed soldiers from the "four nations" along the southeastern escarpment to fortify their territory against the unconquerable Chiriguanos, who inhabited the tropical lowlands beyond the imperial frontier.[23]

The Incas' ability to mobilize Aymara troops to fight their own expansionist wars a thousand mountainous miles from the soldiers' homeland provides a striking example of indirect rule. The Incas grafted extractive institutions onto local ones and worked through the existing ethnic hierarchy, allowing the ayllu and the ethnic polity to retain considerable autonomy under their rule. Peasants had to contribute their labor to cultivate state and religious lands, but they did so in much the same way as they participated in ayllu tasks and in obligations to their ethnic lords and community. Tribute obligations to the state therefore overlapped and blended with communal obligations, without eroding the subsistence base of the local group. The Incan state skillfully manipulated the norms of vertical complementarity, reciprocity, and community to "absorb the surplus production of a self-sufficient population."[24]

In the case of the Aymara warriors, of course, the stakes were

---

23 Espinoza Soriano, ed., "Memorial de Charcas," esp. 24-25.

24 John V. Murra, "On Inca Political Structure," in Ronald Cohen and J. Middleton, eds., *Comparative Political Systems* (New York: Natural History, 1967), 357. See also John V. Murra, *La organización del estado inca* (México City: Siglo XXI, 1978); Franklin Pease, "The Formation of Tawantinsuyu: Mechanisms of Colonization and Relationship with Ethnic Groups," in George Collier, Renato Rosaldo, and John Wirth, eds., *The Inca and Aztec States, 1400-1800* (New York: Academic Press, 1982), 173-198.

higher: tribute was paid in blood. Precisely for this reason, the Incan emperors cultivated the allegiance of the Aymara chiefs, who mobilized the troops and ensured their effectiveness and loyalty. Invoking the principle of recriprocity, the emperors showered status, privilege, and wealth on the Aymara groups who contributed their young men. The "generosity" of the Inca was expressed not merely in the usual way of feasting those in the service of the state, though the emperor's soldiers did receive special rations of maize beer, quinoa flour, meat, and other valuable items. The Charcas, Caracaras, Soras, Quillacas, and Carangas were also rewarded with grants of precious maize land in the eastern part of the Valle Bajo; moreover, as the Aymaras pointed out in a petition to the Spanish king in 1582, the emperors had exempted them from all other tributes and "personal services such as guarding the [royal] herds . . . serving in the *mit'a* [a system of rotative forced labor] in the . . . court of Cuzco . . . weaving *cumbi* and *abasca* cloth, and . . . serving as . . . field hands [on state lands.]."[25] Perhaps they exaggerated Inca beneficence, since they were seeking to recover some of the status and privileges they had enjoyed under the Spaniards. But their sense of indignation and abuse under the newly arrived overlords, and their collective testimony to Incaic generosity, bespoke the special relationship the Incas established with certain Aymara chiefs. The Incas depended upon them as crucial allies who could marshal the most valiant soldiers in Tawantinsuyu, and Cuzco demonstrated its trust, esteem, and alliance by enhancing the power, status, and probably even personal wealth of Aymara lords.

It may well be that this relationship of "reciprocity" between the Inca state and the ethnic elites of the far south created problems *within* Aymara societies. The Incas depended upon the loyal leaders of the Charcas and their neighbors to defend the Collasuyu against the European invaders.[26] But the shadowy underside of the alliance with Aymara lords was that—although it took young men away from their kinsmen and fields only periodically, in turns—it nonetheless sapped the community of its youth and vitality, leaving the old people to tend the herds and crops of their absent relatives.[27] The

25 Espinoza Soriano, ed., "Memorial de Charcas," 21 and 24.

26 For contrasting cases in the central highlands of Peru, where the Inca policy of assimilation was less successful in forging interelite alliances, see Stern, *Peru's Indian Peoples,* 22-23, and Spalding, *Huarochirí,* chap. 3.

27 John V. Murra, "La guerre et les rébellions dans l'expansion de l'état inka," *Annales E.S.C.* 33 (1978): 931.

Incas were wise not to burden those ayllus with any more obligations.

The Incas' conquest of the southern Andes gave them access to stratified societies rich in herds, lands, mines, and laborers. The Collao must have seemed like a treasure trove to the invaders from Cuzco. But the Incas also displayed imagination and initiative as they began to explore the sparsely settled kichwa frontier. There, on the edges of their empire, near the eastern precipice and the tropical lowlands, the Incas discovered the fertile, temperate valleys of Cochabamba. Within two generations, they mounted a state agricultural project of unprecedented scope. Wachtel's recent study of sixteenth-century litigation over *mitmaq* lands (i.e., the lands of the mitimaes) in the Cochabamba valleys and the publication of a portion of the trial records bring into focus an extraordinary example of direct colonization by the Incas and the collectivization of agriculture under state auspices.[28]

The appearance of the Incas in the fertile valleys of Cochabamba foreshadowed momentous change. Túpac (Emperor) Yupanqui swept through the valleys in the late fifteenth century, uprooting the indigenous Sipesipes, Cotas, and Chuyes. The first of these groups was allowed to remain in the Valle Bajo, as subjects of the Incan emperor. But Yupanqui transplanted the Cotas and Chuyes to Incaic fortresses along the eastern frontier in Mizque and Pocona, where they served as guards against the "barbarians" of the tropical lowlands. Yupanqui's "clean sweep" of the Valle Bajo left him free to claim its lands. However, the Incas' earliest annexation of the valley apparently was limited to the eastern zone, called (to this day) Calacala. Túpac Yupanqui knew little of "farming matters," preferring instead to carve out a small patrimony in a fertile corner of the valley.[29]

The human landscape began to change rapidly when Huayna Cápac appropriated extensive lands in the central valleys for state purposes. He assembled a mosaic of ethnic islands, adopting the model of the vertical archipelago and recasting it for purposes of political control.[30] He created maize-cultivating colonies of Charcas, Cara-

28 Nathan Wachtel, "The *mitimas* of the Cochabamba Valley: The Colonization Policy of Huayna Capac," in Collier, Rosaldo, and Wirth, *Inca and Aztec States*, 199-235; and *Repartimiento de tierras por el Inca Huayna Cápac* (1556) (Cochabamba: Universidad de San Simon, 1977). The subsequent discussion draws heavily on both these sources.

29 *Repartimiento de tierras*, 25, and Wachtel, "Mitimas," 201.

30 Murra distinguishes between the ancient model of vertical complementarity,

caras, Soras, Quillacas, Carangas, Urus, and other ethnic groups of the puna. In addition, he imported Plateros, who originated on the desert coast near Ica, and mitimaes from other distant lands. The central valleys were checkered by distinct ethnic mitmaq colonies, some cultivating state lands, others tending the fields of their own nuclear groups rooted in the puna.

Huayna Cápac did more than cluster mitmaq colonies in the maize valleys. Under his administration, the Incas assembled the pieces of an elaborate state enterprise which "rationalized" the large-scale production and distribution of maize and turned the Cochabamba region into a major exporter of that crop. The state annexed the western half of the Valle Bajo and stamped the valley floor with an intricate landholding grid. Westward across the valley from Quillacollo were five adjacent grain farms, or *chácaras* (as Indians later described them to Spanish magistrates), each of which was quartered and distributed to an ethnic group. The Soras, Collas, Quillacas, and Carangas each received land in one of the quarters of the chácara. Within each quarter, land was subdivided into long strips, which were distributed to different subtribes of the group. Wachtel's analysis of land tenure reveals that the Soras cultivated the largest number of strips, followed by the Quillacas and Carangas, and then by the Collas.[31] Except for one of the five chácaras, the fruits of the land were earmarked for the state. Harvests from the smallest chácara went to feed the field hands and state workers who inhabited the valleys. In this way, the Incas "reciprocated" by providing for the subsistence needs of their laboring tributaries.

The cultivation of maize on irrigated land, which sometimes yielded several crops a year, required intensive labor. People were needed to fertilize the soil, maintain the elaborate system of irrigation, plant and harvest the crop, and transport it to the royal warehouses both in the valley and in the highlands near Paria and points north. The Incas called upon two types of laborers. The Sipesipes tended the royal llama herds which grazed in the rich uplands at the southwestern end of the Valle Bajo (the *cabecera del valle*). The mitimaes who resided in the valleys were assigned strategic or skilled tasks, and others were entrusted with guarding the royal granaries. Though they worked on the "state project," under the authority of Incan governors, the mitimaes still owed their primary allegiance to

---

an ideal and a form of ecological control, and the Incas' use of mitmaq colonies—in a kind of political archipelago pattern radiating from Cuzco—to extend control over their vast empire; see Murra, " 'Control vertical,' " 109-112.

31 Wachtel, *"Mitimas,"* 210-211.

their own mallku or kuraka and their ethnic "family." The field hands, however, were corvée laborers brought into the valley for three months of intensive physical labor. In assigned groups, these Soras, Carangas, Quillacas, and Collas migrated from their puna settlements across the altiplano and down through the mountains to the Incas' chácaras. There, under the supervision of their own leaders and Inca overseers, they produced the empire's maize crop. After the harvest, these seasonal agricultural laborers (*mittayoc*) returned en masse to their highland ayllus. Thus, the Incan m'ita set in motion one of the largest seasonal migratory flows in Tawantinsuyu. The trial records give some indication of its magnitude: they mention a laboring population of 14,000, though not all were seasonal migrants.[32] But the seasonal influx of migrant workers, fresh from their highland ayllus, kept alive separate ethnic identities and reinforced the kinship ties that still bound the sedentary mitimaes in the valley to their distant highland communities. Collectivization of agriculture under the Incas did not homogenize the cultures of the valley peoples. On the contrary, it relied heavily upon Aymara kin groups and elites to coordinate the flow of labor prestations to the state's maize lands. While there existed signs of incipient class divisions within the collective enterprise, patterns of social differentiation were expressed primarily in ethnic terms.

Huayna Cápac's agrarian reform turned the Valle Bajo into Tawantinsuyu's principal cereal region. In volume of maize production, the valley was rivaled perhaps only by the richest, irrigated valleys along the seacoast.[33] Recent archeological research on the Inca's system of grain storage in the valley provides clues to the scale of production. Perched safely upon the plateau of Cotapati, overlooking the Valle Bajo, stood row after row of round stone silos, in which it is estimated that at least 9,600 tons of maize could be stored.[34] The Incas built more grain depositories on this site in the Valle Bajo than in the entire valley of Jauja, which was once thought to have been the granary of Tawantinsuyu. This stored grain was in addition to the quantity of maize exported to warehouses in Paria and other highland sites. In fact, most maize was expropriated by the state for redistribution in far-flung corners of the empire. Carangas Indians who

32 *Repartimiento de tierras*, 28; Wachtel, "*Mitimas*," 214 and 219.

33 John Murra, "Rite and Crop," 55.

34 Geraldine Byrne de Caballero, "La arquitectura de almacenamiento en la logística incáica," *Diario*, Nov. 30, 1975, 2.

recalled earlier times when they worked in the Incan maize fields mentioned the destinations of Cochabamba's superior quality crop: "In the chácaras of Potopoto, Yllaurco, Colchacollo, Anocaraire, and Viloma, they harvested the crop and carried it by llama caravan to the tambo of Paria and from there to Cuzco."[35] But if Cuzco's nobility consumed the finest quality maize, the bulk of it went to feed the emperor's soldiers. Maize nourished "all the nations of Indians who marched in the Inca's army, alongside Huayna Cápac."[36]

This analysis of the policies that were designed to assimilate the peoples of the southern Collasuyu into the rapidly expanding empire of the Incas has shown that they operated in two ways. Through methods of indirect rule and strategic alliance with powerful Aymara lords in the highlands, the Incas drained off young men to stock their imperial armies with tribesmen known for their skill and valor in warfare. In return, the emperor granted the ethnic lords lands, personal retainers (*yanaconas*), and special privileges, in the process probably buttressing the lords' power and prestige within their own societies. In contrast, the kichwa valleys afforded entirely different opportunities, which the Incas exploited with remarkable success. They focused their collective efforts on the fertile valleys of Cochabamba, where they vastly expanded the empire's maize production. Unlike the case in the puna, where the Incas ruled in subtle, almost invisible ways through ethnic intermediaries, the Incaic presence in the valleys loomed large. The state intervened in the productive process, shaping economic life in the valleys partly in accord with traditional principles of reciprocity and ethnic communalism but turning it toward new, imperialist ends. The imperatives of the state's agricultural project also required massive coordination and control over migrant laborers. It was this very enterprise that provided the surplus with which to mount the military machine on the shoulders of the highland peoples. Whether as soldiers of the emperor, or as migrant field hands who harvested the crop that fed those soldiers, the peoples of the altiplano bore a heavy burden of empire under the Incas.

Transition to Colonial Rule

The peoples of the Collao who had sacrificed their youth to the imperial armies of the Incas had every reason to ally themselves with

---

35 *Repartimiento de tierras*, 24.

36 Translated from the Spanish quotation in Wachtel, "*Mitimas*," 214.

the earliest European invaders who ventured into the southern high-lands. Like the Lucanas peoples in the central highlands of Peru, the Aymara lords might have seized the moment of political crisis that gripped the Inca state in the 1530s and joined in military alliance with the small band of Europeans to challenge Incaic rule.[37] Yet when the moment arrived, the warrior-subjects stood fast against the plundering Europeans and their native allies. Proclaiming their loy-alty to the emperor Manco Cápac and his brother Paullo, the Lu-paqas and Pacajes of the lake district and then the confederation of Charcas, Caracaras, Chuyes, and Chichas waged a bitter defensive war against the white invaders.

The valleys of Cochabamba were the battleground for the final confrontation between the Europeans (and their allies) and the con-federation of Charcas. Native warriors mobilized their troops in the fortified region of Pocona and ambushed the Europeans in the maize valleys. After weeks of fierce warfare, the Europeans finally defeated the Incas' loyal warriors in 1539 and established tenuous control over the "nations" of the Collasuyu.[38] It was a crucial victory, for despite the harsh and alien landscape of the altiplano, the Europeans soon realized that the dense native communities and rich mineral deposits in this southern zone offered extraordinary opportunities for commercial exploitation. Of immediate strategic importance was that the Europeans had succeeded in isolating the peoples of Charcas (as the territory became known) from the rebel forces of Cuzco and the Vilcabamba River valley, who continued to resist European rule. But the final battle deeply scarred the human landscape and tempo-rarily turned the cropland of Tawantinsuyu into a wasteland. Native and European soldiers alike pillaged the royal granaries and de-stroyed the herds, crops, and irrigation works, flooding the fallow lowlands that had once yielded the Incas' richest maize harvest. The mittayoc and many resident mitimaes were gone, having abandoned the royal maize valley to return home to their highland ayllus all across the altiplano.[39] Amidst the turmoil, small mitmaq commu-nities still clung to the tucks and folds of the sierra and valleys and continued performing the daily tasks of subsistence. But life would never be the same. As we shall see shortly, the collapse of Incan state

37 See Stern, *Peru's Indian Peoples*, 30ff.

38 Espinoza Soriano, ed., "Memorial de Charcas," 25-26; John Hemming, *The Conquest of the Incas* (London: Sphere, 1972), 245-247.

39 *Repartimiento de tierras*, 21; Wachtel, "Mitimas," 220.

power in the Cochabamba valleys—indeed, the very legacy of Incan colonization of Cochabamba—created a social vacuum in the post-conquest period which would soon be filled by a new set of historical actors locked in a power struggle over the valley's resources.

The Europeans in Alto Perú focused their initial settlement efforts on the southern territory of their new subjects, the Charcas. Hernando Pizarro established the first official Spanish town, Chuquisaca (or La Plata, now Sucre), in 1538-1539, in the large kichwa valley nearest the densely populated communities of the Charcas and the scattered mineral deposits in the highlands. Soon to become the administrative center of Alto Perú, or the *audiencia* (royal court) of Charcas, the town of Chuquisaca was laid out in classic grid pattern to provide a "civilized," urban setting in a temperate climate tolerable (if not pleasing) to Europeans. But in 1540s, it was the sole colonial town in a landscape that seemed desolate and untamed to European eyes. Europeans also established footholds at two mining camps: the old, pre-hispanic mines of Porco and, after 1545, the newly discovered mines of Potosí. At an altitude that dizzied most Europeans, the bleak mining site at Potosí nevertheless began to attract large numbers of Europeans as well as natives. No gleaming white, garden town like Chuquisaca, Potosí from the beginning was a gritty mining town nestled at the base of the Cerro Rico, where puna Indians, but not Europeans, felt at home in the harsh climate. Yet even as the Chuquisaca-Potosí axis of settlement grew in the 1540s, the first Europeans in Alto Perú felt vulnerable, isolated in the mountainous interior of the southern Andean zone, far from Lima, Cuzco, Arequipa, and other centers of colonial power and cut off from the sea links to Europe (see figure 4). Travel northward across the altiplano to the transit town of La Paz (and from there down to the seaport of Arica) seemed treacherous to most Europeans, because they would have to pass through Charcas, Caracaras, Carangas, and Pacajes territory before reaching the next "safe" city.[40]

The Europeans soon began, however, to alter the world they had conquered. Their first step was to parcel out the spoils of conquest: The king of Spain bestowed *encomiendas*—grants of native communities together with their inhabitants, who were obliged to pay the grantees tribute—on the privileged few deemed worthy of such rewards. (Hernando Pizarro was the first of these *encomenderos*.) The earliest of the encomiendas, or *repartimientos*, as they were also

---

40 Josep M. Barnadas, *Charcas, 1535-1565: Orígenes de una sociedad colonial* (La Paz: Centro de Investigación y Promoción del Campesinado, 1973), 34-39.

Figure 4 Cities and Towns of Alto Peru
Source: Peter Bakewell, *Miners of the Red Mountain* (Albuquerque: University
of New Mexico Press, 1984), 27.

known, grouped the Indians in units (ayllus, moieties, and confederated lineages) that corresponded loosely to pre-Hispanic ethnic and
kin patterns, and the caciques (as the Spaniards called the kurakas),
and the mitimaes subject to them, remained with their units.[41] But
soon after, expediency and European ignorance wreaked havoc on
Andean social patterns and notions of territoriality (with a few notable exceptions). The Europeans began to fragment, disintegrate,
and rearrange the ethnic kingdoms of the south. As they stamped
large, contiguous administrative districts onto the Andean landscape, they arbitrarily severed ethnic confederations, split apart

41 Thierry Saignes, "Políticas étnicas en Bolivia colonial, siglos XVI-XIX," *Historia boliviana* 3 (1983): 5-6.

moieties, and truncated the ethnic "archipelagos." Even the territorial-administrative division between Peru proper and Alto Perú sliced the Aymara-speaking world into two parts. Where Aymara peoples saw in the deep, blue waters of Lake Titicaca a sacred, unifying force, the natural center of the cosmos, the Europeans saw a natural boundary dividing, along an east-west axis, the heartland of the old Inca empire from the southern district of Charcas. Ethnic lords saw their señoríos shrink and their coastal or kichwa islands of mitimaes placed under the jurisdiction of different kurakas and their encomenderos. Thus, for example, the Lupaqa lords of the lake district lost their mitmaq colonies in the valleys near Arequipa to the local encomendero and caciques until Juan Polo de Ondegardo—a prominent jurist, an encomendero, and a student of Andean cultures, who understood the importance of the pattern of verticality—arranged for their return to their ethnic homeland.[42] As we shall see, the Charcas and other highland peoples were dispossessed of their mitmaq lands and colonists in the Cochabamba valleys. Though colonial policy did not at first institutionalize the rupture of kinship ties binding mitimaes to their distant highland homelands, the imposition of European models of territoriality set into motion a protracted process of fragmenting ethnic señoríos into localized units more easily administered by colonial authorities.[43]

As already mentioned, the Spaniards initiated their colonial exploits in Alto Perú in the highland regions, where repartimientos were rich in tributaries. At first, private encomenderos enjoyed unlimited authority over their tributaries, but in October 1550, the audiencia of Lima made the first attempt to assert royal control over encomenderos by legitimating and regulating the amount and kind of tribute they could demand. Whereas the Europeans had laid the foundations of early colonial rule on the basis of precolonial extractive institutions, the new tribute requirements, and the very circumstances under which tributaries had to meet their new obligations, forced the native peoples to alter their lifeways. The new overlords asked caciques to commandeer peasant laborers for their own small

---

42 Polo de Ondegardo, "Informe . . . al Lic. Briviesca de Muñatones," 177.

43 In a report prepared for a research planning meeting on Andean ethnohistoriography, held at the Social Science Research Council, New York, in October 1981, Murra proposed this issue of the transformation of ethnic señoríos into "Indian communities," with a gradual loss of rights, as an important line of future investigation. See Spalding, *Huarochirí*, and Saignes, *Andes orientales*, for recent studies of precisely this process.

enterprises, but—unlike the Incan emperor, who expected to be paid only in labor power—the encomendero demanded tribute in labor, kind, and increasingly in money. It was no longer enough for the Carangas or Soras to send off a small band of their kinsmen to work for a season in the distant maize fields of the Incas, knowing they would be amply fed while they were gone. Furthermore, the Incas would reciprocate in material and spiritual ways for the labor rendered. Now, tributaries required to deliver a certain quantity of maize to their encomendero had to reallocate their valley lands and cut into their own subsistence in order to meet their new obligations. More ominous, new tribute requirements in fixed amounts of products threw the burden of agricultural risk onto the backs of the producers themselves. Where the Incan emperor used to absorb the loss of crops from a severe drought or sudden frost, ethnic communities now confronted an unbending encomendero who required payment in crops no matter how wide the fluctuation of agricultural yields in the puna. Tributaries also had to deliver wheat, sheep's wool, and other products introduced into the Andes by Europeans and added to the tribute lists by encomenderos. Small wonder that most Andean peoples began to complain of tribute dues and of the social changes they wrought in their communities.[44]

The seven ethnic nations of the south suffered a particularly sharp rupture with the Incaic past. The proud Charcas and their ethnic neighbors saw their status diminished and their identity as privileged warriors lost under the strictures of early colonial rule. Subordinated to encomenderos, they no longer sent warriors or claimed exemption from ordinary tribute dues. Like other "vassals" of the Spanish crown and encomienda "Indians," they had to deliver specified amounts of eggs, maize, honey, woolen garments, and workers to their appointed "lords." Moreover, tribute requisitions were increasingly skewed by commercial considerations. A case in point is Pedro de Hinojosa's repartimiento of Macha and Chaqui, in what would become the province of Chayanta. Platt's study of this encomienda in the pre-Toledan decades reveals the extent to which encomienda tribute was becoming commodified in the early 1550s.

Hinojosa, whose encomienda was one of the richest in Alto Perú, required tributaries to provide labor services, but the vast bulk of

44 For three regional studies of early colonial relations and, in particular, the transformation of tribute institutions under colonial rule, see Spalding, *Huarochirí*, chap. 4 and 5; Stern, *Peru's Indian Peoples*, chap. 2 and 3; and Wachtel, *Vision of the Vanquished*, 98-139.

encomienda tribute was paid in products that could be marketed in Potosí, Chuquisaca, and Porco. His tributaries were required to deliver annually 1,200 *fanegas* of maize (probably harvested from non-ayllu lands) and another 20 fanegas of maize and wheat planted on communal lands to the three towns. (A fanega is equivalent to 1.6 bushels.) Hinojosa also claimed the right to collect tribute in mineral ore. Caracaras of Macha and Chaqui mined ore deposits throughout their territory and probably in Potosí, and then exchanged the metal in the *qhatu* (open-air metal market) of Potosí for pesos *ensayados y marcados* (assayed and stamped under royal authority). They paid their encomendero the enormous sum of 27,300 pesos in 1559. Tribute exactions in crude ore reflected the fact that the Caracaras inhabited a region rich in mineral deposits, just as the Lupaqas' wealth was concentrated in herds. But in 1550, royal authorities sanctioned the commercialization of specie by requiring Indians to pay their dues in imported pesos.[45] The Caracaras were not alone. All across Alto Perú's highlands, the new tribute arrangements accelerated the commodification of indigenous staples and drew ayllu Indians into the developing commercial orbit of Potosí.

Yet it would be a mistake to assume that encomenderos, even the likes of Hinojosa, unilaterally extracted surplus from Indian subjects. After all, encomenderos still could not call upon the state to enforce extraction or the commercialization of indigenous products. Although the presence of royal authority was manifest by 1550 in the first ordinances regulating tribute, the colonial state was still inchoate and weak. Furthermore, encomenderos who received repartimientos in the highlands had to harness the labor power of peasants who belonged to strong, unified ethnic polities which still managed to preserve group self-sufficiency. Even many years after military conquest, the encomenderos were confronted with Aymara lords who still controlled the basic processes of production and distribution within Andean societies. The Spaniards depended upon the persisting ability of those lords to command the labor and loyalty of ayllu peasants and to channel the flow of tribute to the "outsiders." If the system of decentralized, indirect rule was to function smoothly, Europeans had to take care not to push ethnic lords too far, lest they violate the social norms and traditions that governed relationships in Andean society and transgress the acceptable bounds of their authority. For while in the short term a despotic

45 Tristan Platt, "Acerca del sistema tributario pre-Toledano en el Alto Perú," *Avances*, no. 1 (1978), esp. 34-39.

chief might squeeze his people enough to satisfy tribute requirements, such behavior would eventually sacrifice their social trust,
jeopardize his own ability to govern, and risk open rebellion. As
Stern has shown in vivid detail for the Huamanga area in the 1550s
and 1560s, encomenderos had to establish alliances, however uneasy, with native lords. In the process, they manipulated and negotiated with "their caciques," but they also devised strategies to enforce their compliance and obedience. This mixture of force,
negotiation, and alliance that characterized the early relations in the
highlands reflected the Europeans' heavy reliance on the traditional
power and prestige of native chiefs.[46]

In sharp contrast to the situation in the highlands, Andean tradition had little bearing on the relations and balance of power that obtained between encomenderos and caciques in the valleys of Cochabamba. When the crown created four or five repartimientos of native
inhabitants scattered throughout the region, it dispersed the broken
pieces of the Incas' state agricultural project. The collapse of the precolonial state, the mass exodus of agricultural laborers, and the sack-
ing of granaries and waterworks left the region relatively impoverished, at least for a time. Encomenderos of valley repartimientos
inherited only vestigial mitmaq communities, which now fell under
the jurisdiction of local caciques. There was no dominant ethnic
group in the region, no powerful ethnic lords who, in their role as
stewards of community norms and resources, could mediate labor
relationships. The Europeans who were granted repartimientos in
the valleys had to appoint caciques in the expectation and hope that
they would channel the flow of tribute and labor to their overlords,
even in the absence of Incaic state rule and the legitimacy of their
own power.

In the early 1550s, encomiendas were granted to Rodrigo de Orellana and Juan Polo de Ondegardo.[47] Together, these encomiendas included former Inca lands (the chácaras of Potopoto, Yllaurco, Colchacollo, Anocaraire, and Viloma) and all the mitimaes placed in the
valleys by the Incas to cultivate Incaic maize fields. Orellana's holdings included parcels of land toward the eastern end of the Valle Bajo,
some of which the Incas had appropriated for themselves. His encomienda, known later by the name Tiquipaya, incorporated miti-

---

46 See Stern, *Peru's Indian Peoples*, 28-35, and Carlos Sempat Assadourian,
"Dominio colonial y señores étnicos en el espacio andino," *HISLA*, no. 1 (1983):
7-20.

47 See Wachtel, *"Mitimas,"* 202 and app. 2; also *Repartimiento de tierras*, 26.

maes of the Quillacas, Carangas, Chilques, Chiles, and Collas of Azángaro (see table 1). Polo's encomienda, El Paso, included Carangas, Urus, Soras, Caracaras, Charcas, and Yamparaes.[48]

In establishing these encomiendas, the crown placed them under the authority of the caciques Gerónimo Cuyo and Diego Tanquiri in El Paso and Hernando Cuyo in Tiquïpaya. They were charged with assigning the mitimaes to cultivate the lands that had once belonged to the Incan emperor. These caciques did not readily command the respect and labor of their charges, since they did not belong to the same ethnic family. It is true that Tanquiri was the son of a former Inca governor in the valley, but his ability to capitalize on that kin relationship was doubtful now that he was collaborating with the enemy and was seen as a traitor to the neo-Inca state struggling to survive in the Vilcabamba backlands. This dilemma was shared by all native elites whose newly found status and position in colonial society derived primarily from their collaboration with the imperial power. Their legitimacy was defined in colonial terms and their authority rested precariously on the support and patronage of their

Table 1. The Encomiendas of Cochabamba

	Precolonial Land Use	Predominant Ethnic Groups	Caciques	Encomenderos
Tapacarí	Mitmaq colonies; pasture, maize	Moyos, Soras, Carangas, Aullagas, Quillacas	—	Alonso Pérez de Castillejo; Gómez de Solis; Hernando Zárate; Marqués de San Germán; Juan de Mendoza
Sipesipe	Cabecera del valle; royal pastures and maize lands	Soras, Yungas, Cotas, Chichas, Caris, Urus, Chuyes,	—	Hernando de Silva
El Paso	Royal maize fields	Chichas, Urus, Soras, Charcas, Caracaras, Yamparaes	Gerónimo Cuyo; Diego Tanquiri	Juan Polo de Ondegardo; Gerónimo de Ondegardo
Tiquipaya	Personal lands of Yupanqui and Huayna Cápac	Carangas, Quillacas, Charcas, Chiles, Chilques, Collas	Hernando Cuyo	Rodrigo de Orellana; Francisco de Orellana
Capinota	Mitmaq colonies; rich maize lands	Carangas, Soras	—	—

Sources: *Repartimiento de tierras*; "Tasa de la visita general del virrey Francisco de Toledo," AGI, Contaduría, Leg. 1786; Nicolás Sánchez-Albornoz, *Indios y tributos en el Alto Perú* (Lima: Instituto de Estudios Peruanos, 1978).

48 Wachtel, *"Mitimas,"* 202 and 230.

overlords. Unlike their Aymara counterparts, who bargained from a position of relative strength, the valley caciques leaned heavily on their European patrons to enforce their own authority over the disparate colonies of mitimaes. This became all the clearer during the 1550s and 1560s, when Aymara lords began to challenge the rights of valley caciques and encomenderos to rule their former mitmaq colonies that remained in the valleys.

For twenty years, the Caranga, Quillaca, and Sora Indians of the highlands waged a judicial struggle against Orellana and Polo and their caciques over land rights in Cochabamba. In 1556, one Hernando Asacalla, principal cacique of the highland repartimiento of Paria, petitioned the audiencia of La Plata for the return of "certain lands" in the Valle Bajo that had been granted to his people by Huayna Cápac and his governors. The Carangas, Quillacas, and Soras claimed as their own those parcels of land (*suyos*) in the chácaras of Yllaurco, Colchacollo, Anocaraire, and Viloma which they had received from the Incas at the time of the great land reform under Huayna Cápac. They rested their court case on the weight of pre-Hispanic tradition, elaborating in fine detail the distribution of valley land and tributary labor under the Incas. Their rich oral testimony, together with other records, provides the evidence from which Wachtel was able to reconstruct with such precision the extraordinary colonization project in the valley.[49]

The king's inspector (*visitador general*), Francisco de Saavedra Ulloa, corroborated their testimony with further details about the Incas' agrarian regime in Cochabamba, and he concluded that the parcels of land granted to the caciques and Indians of the Carangas, Quillacas, and Asanaques should be returned by royal edict to the highland peoples. But his argument did not rely simply on tradition and customary right. Saavedra appealed to the crown on pragmatic and humanitarian grounds as well. Valley lands ought to be granted to the highland Indians, he seemed to reason, because the lands were abundant and the highland peoples were in need of them. Through his European eyes, the lands of his native clients appeared "very sterile, producing little food," while the temperate valleys were lands of

---

49 The litigation records are located in the AHMC. Wachtel's pioneering article, "*Mitimas*," is based on these records; an appendix to his article contains excerpts from a document of 1560 in which Polo defended his encomienda against the highlanders. Fragments of other trial records and reports have been published in *Repartimiento de tierras*. Unfortunately, the latter is poorly assembled and allows only a glimpse of the arguments and counterarguments of the litigants.

abundant harvests. Further, the puna Indians had sustained them-selves with maize, which they were now forced to purchase in the valleys. "At the time of harvest, for two or three months each year, more than 600 . . . Carangas, Quillacas, and Asanaques [descend into the valleys] looking for food."[50] Saavedra suggested that they might populate a town in the valley, so that they could cultivate maize and supply their highland communities. Besides, he added, they could receive religious instruction in the valleys. Thus, he argued his case along both European and Andean lines. But while he hoped the crown would return mitmaq lands in the maize valleys and partially reconstitute the "vertical archipelago," and while he justified native demands on the basis of Incaic tradition in the valley, Saavedra fo-cused on the periodic subsistence crises facing puna Indians who had lost their peripheral islands in the valleys and had therefore resorted to seasonal migrations. After all, how could elusive wanderers be properly converted to Christian ways or, for that matter, be taxed by encomenderos?

Faced with such powerful testimony, the valley caciques and en-comenderos closed ranks and united in opposition to the threat. In a report submitted on behalf of this coalition, the visitador Diego Nú-ñez rejected the claims to the *suyos* based on grants from the Incas. These grants did not constitute property rights, he argued, but only usufruct rights in return for tributary labor on state land in the val-leys. Lands were not granted as personal possessions, but only to en-able tributaries to sustain themselves while they cultivated the state lands. "The Indians had to sustain themselves," he reasoned, "since they were not permitted to take food from the [state] lands they cul-tivated and since they did not bring, nor could they bring, food [with them]."[51] He wondered where they would have found their suste-nance had they not been granted lands by the Incan emperor, and he argued that once the Indians ceased to farm the Incas' lands they forfeited their rights to the suyos that had provided for their subsist-ence during their tributary season in the valleys. It was an astute argument, which evoked the principle of reciprocity that supposedly governed relations between the Incaic state and its mitimaes and

50 *Repartimiento de tierras*, 29. Other contemporary observations of migration of puna Indians are Polo de Ondegardo, "Informe . . . al Lic. Briviesca de Muña-tones," 177, and Diego Cabeza de Vaca et al., "Descripción y relación de la ciu-dad de La Paz," in Marcos Jiménez de la Espada, ed., *Relaciones geográficas de Indios: El Perú* (Madrid: Atlas, 1965), 350.

51 *Repartimiento de tierras*, 30.

mittayoc. But more than that, Núñez declared that the highland caciques had no legitimate rights to valley lands, because most mitimaes had fled the valleys at the time of the Spanish Conquest and
had not returned to settle in the lowlands for some forty years since
their exodus. The Carangas appeared from time to time, but only for
purposes of barter.[52]

Who, then, did have legitimate claims to valley resources? Núñez
admitted that the Sipesipes did, for they were autochthonous peoples
predating the Incas. So did those mitimaes who had remained behind
in the valleys after the Spanish Conquest. Yet even many of those
people, Núñez argued, had not received land grants from the Incas.
They had held more privileged positions under the Incas, as loyal
guardians of the maize granaries. But since they had chosen to settle
in the valleys and thereby had ruptured their ties to their "natural
kin groups" in the distant highlands, they surely had acquired subsistence rights in their adopted region. And besides, Núñez added,
they had acute economic needs, precisely because they had lost their
links to highland communities and resources.[53]

The conflict over land rights in Cochabamba unfolded slowly over
the 1550s, 1560s, and early 1570s; native litigants discovered how
tedious and labyrinthian the colonial juridical process could be. This
particular dispute was finally resolved by Viceroy Toledo in the mid-
1570s in favor of the Carangas and their allies, who received parcels
of land in the valleys. In a small irony of history, the viceregal decision was issued at just the time when Toledo was preparing to im-
plement his massive resettlement plan, which would irrevocably alter the social landscape in accordance with European spatial patterns
(and which will be discussed later).

This judicial conflict threw into bold relief the shaky, vulnerable
ethnic hierarchy that existed in the valleys. Caught on the defensive,
the valley caciques had to enter into an alliance with their encomenderos to stave off their highland rivals and strengthen their control
over mitimaes in the valleys. They were in an extremely ambiguous
situation, since precolonial land tenure in the Cochabamba valleys
was unique, and even traditional ethnic mitmaq colonies had been
displaced and re-created by the Incas. The very meaning of Inca land

52 Polo de Ondegardo testified in 1560, many years before the Nuñez report
(which was probably issued in the mid-1570s) that Urus had started to filter into
the valleys to cultivate fields during the previous three or four years. Wachtel,
"Mitimas," app. 2, 234.

53 *Repartimiento de tierras*, 29-31.

grants to ethnic groups was now subject to interpretation and rein-
terpretation in the colonial context.

And yet, while Cochabamba was a special case, the emergence of
interethnic rivalry over former mitimaes and valley resources in the
eastern cordillera was not specific to that region. To the south, Lupaqa, Pacajes, and other Aymara lords hoped to recover the warm
lands and the colonists they had lost to the valley caciques and encomenderos. Saignes has studied the unraveling of the ethnic affiliations that had tied colonists in the eastern valleys of Larecaja to the
distant highland polities on the shores of Lake Titicaca and the ethnic conflict that accompanied that process.[54] Though still relatively
unexplored by historians, the enduring rivalry between highland ethnic lords and valley caciques over mitmaq colonies and land rights
in the kichwa region created a deep fault line in Andean society,
which judicial maneuvers could not conceal. Colonial policies that
territorialized ethnic groups along European contours only sharpened the endemic rivalry and competition among puna communities, which extended into distant kichwa pockets where other groups
also claimed resources. But this rivalry was carried into the colonial
courts in the 1550s and 1560s not merely as a way of recovering
communal rights to mitmaq lands. It reflected one strategy of communal defense and survival, among several, that Andean people of
both puna and valley seized upon as the economic pressures of colonialism began to bear down harder and as the opportunities for bargaining within the colonial judicial system began to open up.[55]

Mining and Commercial Capitalism in Early Potosí

As early as 1551, the eyes of colonial entrepreneurs were on Potosí—
"the key to all Peru," as an enthusiastic friar described the mining
town to the members of the Council of the Indies.[56] Traders, merchants, miners, and royal administrators all saw a bountiful future
in the rich silver veins that etched the interior of the Cerro Rico. In
the 1560s, the distinguished jurist Juan de Matienzo compiled the

---

54 Saignes, "De la filiation à la résidence," 1174-1175. See also Espinoza Soriano, ed., "Memorial de Charcas," for the petition of the Confederation of Charcas for land grants in Cochabamba.

55 See Stern, *Peru's Indian Peoples*, chap. 5, for a fascinating analysis of "judicial politics" and relations between Europeans and ethnic groups and among
ethnic groups in the Huamanga region.

56 Quoted in Barnadas, *Charcas*, 514.

first comprehensive report on Potosí. An *oidor* (judge or magistrate) of the audiencia of La Plata, Matienzo frequently traveled upland to the cold mining town to make his observations and gather his statistics.[57] As he looked closely at the mining enterprises, he was rather disturbed to find that Andean people actually controlled production. It was true that many Europeans held titles of ownership to slices of silver vein which they could exploit with minimal capital investment. But their enterprises were thwarted by heavy royal taxes and high labor costs.[58] Furthermore, Andeans controlled the refining of the mineral. Employing traditional metallurgy techniques, the skilled miners cut crude ore from the rich surface lodes, ground it in their simple stone mills, and smelted it in small clay furnaces (*huayras*), which caught the cold wind of the puna that fanned the fires built from dried ichu grasses and llama dung. It was this group of Indian miners, not the European titleholders to mines, who controlled the distribution of the finished product.

Under the circumstances, Europeans found themselves in a peculiarly weak bargaining position. To get the Indian smelters to take their crude ore, Europeans sometimes had to sell it to them, at prices representing only a fraction of the value of the ore's metallic content.[59] Furthermore, the yanaconas who dominated the refining also could organize the extractive activities, thus extending their control over the entire productive process. The Europeans, on the other hand, had difficulty mounting mining enterprises of any scale. Mine ownership was of little benefit at a time when mineowners were unable to hire workers simply because capitalist labor relations—the separation of workers from the means of production and development of a proletarianized work force—were still virtually nonexistent. Furthermore, the enforcement of seasonal migration of peasants to the mines and the distribution of corvée workers among selected mines were impossible as long as the colonial state sanctioned private encomiendas and failed to centralize and coordinate

57 Juan Matienzo, *Gobierno del Perú* (1567) (Buenos Aires: Cía. Sud-americana de Billetes de Banco, 1910).

58 David Brading and Harry Cross, "Colonial Silver Mining: Mexico and Peru," *Hispanic American Historical Review* 52 (1972): 552-554, and Carlos Sempat Assadourian, "La producción de la mercancía dinero en la formación del mercado interno colonial: El caso del espacio peruano, siglo XVI," in Enrigue Florescano, ed., *Ensayos sobre el desarrollo económico de México y América latina* (Mexico City: Fondo de Cultura Económica, 1979), 223-292.

59 Barnadas, *Charcas*, p. 366.

tribute to the advantage of the mineowners. Of course, mineowners could capture labor from the Lupaqa or Macha Indians who traveled to Potosí to deliver their dues or to find temporary work in order to pay off their monetary debts. But the chronic labor shortage and the inability of Europeans to enforce labor prestations sharply limited the scale of mining enterprise and relegated mineowners to a marginal, dependent position. For the time being, economic autonomy rested with a sector of the yanaconas of Potosí.

Matienzo's alarm at the strong position of Andean miners also suggested the internal dynamics of commercial accumulation at Potosí during the first "silver cycle" (1545-1570). He realized that as long as production was in the hands of Indians, Europeans had to rely upon commercial distribution and exchange for their profits. The old maxim urged buying cheap and selling dear, and this would be easier if Europeans could monopolize the supply of, say, woolen garments, or speculate in advance purchases of grain, and it would be still better if they could dispense altogether with "buying cheap" by commodifying tribute in kind. Potosí, after all, offered extraordinary commercial opportunities even in the early years. Demand seemed always to outstrip supply (at least until the economic slump of the late 1560s and early 1570s), and inflation was spiraling upward. In 1561, Polo de Ondegardo commented on the inflationary tendency in the audiencia of Charcas, such that "a llama once worth but a peso now sells for 12 or 15."[60] Like Polo, Matienzo realized the potential for commerce in indigenous articles of consumption. At Potosí, trade in native goods was essential to the accumulation of metallic money. Spaniards exchanged coca, maize, chuño, and cloth for silver; and the more commercial opportunities increased, the more power Europeans had to obtain refined silver from the Andean producers. "The more Indians at Potosí and Porco," Matienzo wrote, "the more silver they will mine; as their numbers increase they will consume more coca and bread and wear more garments, and thus they will have to mine more silver from the hills."[61]

60 Polo de Ondegardo, "Informe . . . al Lic. Briviesca de Muñatones," pp. 144-145. Polo de Ondegardo's statement neglects the fact that the prices of some goods had previously declined. For example, a random sample of forty-six sales of coca leaves at Potosí during the decade of the 1550s reveals that the average price per cesto (a basket containing about twenty pounds) declined from eighteen pesos in 1549 to six pesos in 1559. In subsequent years, the price stabilized at about four or five pesos. ANB, EP, Juan Luís Soto, 1549; Gáspar de Rojas, 1550, 1553, and 1555; Lázaro de Aguila, 1557, 1558, and 1559.

61 Matienzo, *Gobierno del Perú*, 73.

46

Matienzo's logic reveals the extent to which Potosí engendered commercial capitalism in the emerging political economy of Alto Perú even before the advent of Toledo's reforms. Assadourian's analysis of the early economy of the mining town also reveals the intense and wide circulation of indigenous commodities at Potosí, where almost 90 percent of imports were native products.[62] Even trade among Europeans themselves frequently involved transactions in indigenous articles. In 1549, one merchant of Potosí paid a debt of 10,000 pesos to another Spanish trader by delivering maize, coca, chuño, and native textiles.[63] During the first decade of mining at Potosí, it was commonplace for Europeans to form trading companies and partnerships with itinerant traders who set off into the countryside for months, sometimes for several years on end, and to establish commercial contacts with willing caciques, encomenderos, or other Europeans. The webs of trade they spun across the land created the commercial channels through which commodities could circulate and gravitate toward Potosí.[64]

Thus, Polo and Matienzo, who recorded their astute observations in the 1560s, only two decades after Andeans had stumbled upon the rich lodes of Potosí, witnessed the formation of a commercial economy in a remote part of the world where markets and commodity exchange were virtually unknown before the European intrusion. Almost instantaneously, the discovery and commodification of silver ore set into motion the commodification of native subsistence goods, from cumbi cloth and coca to chuño and oca. Telescoped into two decades was the transformation of basic subsistence goods, traditionally exchanged outside the domain of the market, into commodities that fetched inflationary monetary prices in the strange, bustling qhatu of Potosí. In that brief span, Andeans saw special, ceremonial crops like maize and coca become items of mass consumption in the mining town; they found themselves planting European wheat and hauling it by llama caravan across the mountains to the mines; and they experienced new pressures and hardships in producing the quantities and types of goods that now were demanded of them, simply because the products had acquired exchange value at the mining town.

62 Assadourian, "Producción de la mercancía dinero," 231ff.

63 ANB, EP, Soto, July 3, 1549.

64 The notarial records of Potosí provide detailed information about early commercial companies, long-distance trade, and wholesale transactions; see ANB, EP, esp. Rojas, 1550; Aguila, 1559.

Some natives adapted their ways in order to exploit the new commercial opportunities at Potosí. Several recent studies have documented the commercial engagement of Aymara chiefs in the lake district.[65] Some of these lords were able to channel their capital in ways that benefited the entire community. In other instances, commercial success led Indians to break their social commitments to the ayllu in their pursuit of profits. But by and large, the intensity of commercial exchange at Potosí and the great effective demand for food crops and special items like coca prompted many Indians to redirect the flow of goods and labor outward, toward the mining town. The shift in the balance between agrarian production for subsistence and for commercial exchange frequently had drastic consequences for the well-being of the social whole.

The disintegrating effects of agricultural commercialization were felt most acutely in those regions where coca could be produced by migrant encomienda Indians.[66] Coca was highly marketable in the early years of Potosí; the soldier and chronicler Pedro de Cieza de León speculated in 1553 that "there has never been in the whole world a plant or root . . . aside from spices . . . that is so highly valued [as coca]."[67] Matienzo reported that coca had even become a medium of exchange at Potosí.[68] But even the highland peoples on their "sterile lands" could not escape the incursion of commercial capitalism, as long as encomenderos could capitalize on the Potosí market and as long as colonial policies eroded the basis of "social insurance" that traditionally had buffered Andean communities from subsistence crises.

As early as 1550, the royal authorities formulated policies designed to mediate the relationship between private encomenderos and their repartimiento Indians. Pedro de la Gasca, president of the audiencia of Alto Perú (1547-1550), ordered inspectors to survey the

65 See Murra, "Aymara Lords"; Silvia Rivera, "El mallku y la sociedad colonial en el siglo XVII: El caso de Jesús de Machaca," *Avances*, no. 1 (1978): 7-27; and Roberto Choque, "Pedro Chipana: Cacique comerciante de Calamarca," ibid., 28-32.

66 See the published report of 1557 on the repartimiento of Pocona for descriptions of the "mass production" of coca for export to Potosí and its impact on native communities: "Visita a Pocona," *Historia y cultura* (Lima), no. 4 (1970): 269-308.

67 Pedro de Cieza de León, *The Incas*, ed. Victor W. von Hagen and trans. Harriet de Onis (Norman: University of Oklahoma Press, 1976), 260.

68 Matienzo, *Gobierno del Perú*, 90.

human landscape to ascertain the distribution of resources.[69] Anticipating the great royal *visitas* (inspections) under Toledo and his successors, La Gasca introduced reforms that would "rationalize" tribute collection even in private encomiendas. To some extent, the early efforts of royal authorities to develop institutions for the appropriation of surplus product aimed at protecting encomienda Indians from "excessive" rent. A 1551 ordinance of the audiencia of Lima was explicit on this point.[70] But La Gasca's reforms of 1549-1550 also rigidified the tribute schedule for encomienda Indians, compelling them to pay fixed rent in specified products, both native and European, and they had a negative impact on income collected over the following decade or so. Reporting in 1561, Polo de Ondegardo pointed to the decline of encomienda tribute since the reforms; and he declared that the tribute collected in his day was far less than that which Andeans had once rendered to the Incas. "The Indians are poorer in these times than they have ever been in the past."[71] But pauperization was only part of the story, in Polo's view. Increasingly, the Andean people tried to lighten the tribute burden by deceiving the royal inspectors. Ethnic lords found ways to reduce the official rent levied on their communities. Since tribute was adjusted in accordance with population counts, the Europeans were outwitted by hiding potential tributaries, keeping royal inspectors away from remote hamlets, and denying tributary status (and kinship ties) to recent migrants (*llactas runas*) who had come from distant homelands. Polo de Ondegardo advised royal inspectors to get around these subterfuges by surveying a community's cultivated fields, herds, and other resources not easily hidden from view.[72]

Political problems ran deeper, however. In the 1550s, sharp internal divisions within the colonial elite weakened the incipient state and allowed astute natives to exploit the factionalism for their own ends. As elsewhere in the Spanish colonies, encomenderos had to deal with prelates who were indignant about the treatment of natives. Conflict and rivalry over tutelage of the Indians in the southern Andes were aggravated by the coca issue. Following the First Council of Lima (1552), the church raised its voice against the commercialization and consumption of coca. Coca use was considered

69 Polo de Ondegardo, "Informe . . . al Lic. Briviesca de Muñatones," 160.

70 See Assadourian, "Dominio colonial," 11.

71 Polo de Ondegardo, "Informe . . . al Lic. Briviesca de Muñatones," 163.

72 Ibid., 161.

an evil in itself and an encouragement to paganism. Worse still, encomenderos often forced their subjects to plant coca, which they then sold to seemingly insatiable consumers at Potosí. But there was the rub. For Matienzo and other administrators soon realized that coca fetched high prices, allowing Spanish merchants and traders to accumulate enormous profits—on which the crown could levy taxes. "By means of the coca [trade], the Indians mine the greatest part of the silver which is exported and taxed each year."[73] The oidores of the audiencia of La Plata came down on the side of economics, counterbalancing the church's efforts at moral suasion.

Thus, in the two decades before the arrival of Viceroy Toledo, basic ideological issues concerning encomienda rent, the morality of coca commerce, and the legitimacy of Andean rights over former mitmaq colonies factionalized the colonial ruling elite and weakened its control over Andean peoples. The cleavages within the colonial elite afforded some leeway for Andean influence in shaping early colonial relationships. With the colonial state still in formation, the Andean peoples of Alto Perú increasingly turned to judicial procedures to test the limits of Spanish authority and to advance their collective interests. Later, when the state consolidated and began to draw the lines of colonial authority, power, and legitimacy more sharply, the Andean peoples resorted more often to clandestine, dangerous, and extralegal strategies of defense.

In the late 1560s, the alliances between some encomenderos and ethnic lords and among factions of the colonial elite were very precarious. In Madrid, far from the puna and valleys of Alto Perú and the chambers of Spanish justice in La Plata, the highest royal officials convened to consider the crisis in Peru. A millenarian movement, Taqui Ongo, which was sweeping through the mountains and villages of Huamanga, clearly posed the most immediate threat. But more ominous, perhaps, was the deterioration of silver mining at Potosí. Potosí's first cycle of silver was coming to a close: the rich surface lodes seemed to have evaporated almost overnight, and the Andean miners were vanishing. Royal expectations of unlimited supplies of specie suddenly confronted a harsh reality. From the imperial viewpoint, it was a singularly unfortunate moment for Potosí's silver enterprises to shut down. Only a few years earlier, King Philip II had been forced to default on his foreign loans, and his financial needs were growing each year. How could the king safeguard

---

73 Letter to the Spanish king from the audiencia of Charcas, Nov. 2, 1566, quoted in Barnadas, *Charcas*, p. 383.

Spain's power in Europe, fight the French, repel the Turks, and pre-
pare for war with England, if a primary source of American treasure
dried up? Taxing Castile's peasantry could yield only so much. It was
essential to revamp the tribute system in the Andes, dislodge the
private encomenderos from their position of power and privilege, and
rejuvenate Potosí's mines. In short, the crown needed to constitute
a colonial state that could serve as an agent of metropolitan interests
and a claimant on the resources of native subjects. Across the ocean,
ensconced in the Andean region, the colonial state was never to become simply a reflexive agent of the crown. But the royal impetus
for a strong colonial state beginning in the late 1560s gave to the
viceregal authority the power to intervene directly in and shape the
emerging political economy of colonialism. Viceroy Toledo would go
far toward fulfilling this mandate.

Yet on the eve of Toledo's administration, most Andeans and Europeans were too preoccupied with local struggles over lands, mitimaes, and tribute to worry about a new balance of imperial forces.
Still engaged in negotiation, bargaining, and passive resistance, the
ethnic elites of Alto Perú had no way of anticipating the power of a
strong state. In the maize valleys of Cochabamba, the caciques and
their patron encomenderos believed that it was the Carangas lords of
the highlands who posed a threat to their autonomy. But by the middle years of the 1570s, the valley caciques would witness the collapse of their alliances with encomenderos and watch the state wrest
lands away and award them to their highland rivals, and they would
discover that Spanish settlers, not Aymara lords, were the most serious threat to their lifeways.

CHAPTER TWO

The Emergence of a Market Economy

As he stepped onto the desert coast of Peru in 1569, the new viceroy of Peru, Francisco de Toledo, walked into a political and economic quagmire of impressive dimensions. Beyond the peaceful, civilized city of Lima loomed the ominous Andes, where the early colonial order had broken down and social chaos and economic decline menaced the entire European colonial project in the Andean kingdom. Insurrection was brewing in the Huamanga highlands and threatened to spread to other areas. The Taqui Ongo rebellion of the 1560s in Huamanga was dangerous enough; but worse, it exposed the fragile political underpinnings of early colonial relationships, which rested ultimately on encomendero-cacique alliances and on the ability of the traditional Andean authorities to mobilize the surplus labor of native peasants. At any moment, subversion and revolt could turn another region into a Huamanga.

But Toledo also inherited a political crisis that ran deeper than native insurrection, for it divided the colonial elite against itself and thus heightened its vulnerability. At issue was the distribution of power and the "spoils of conquest," now that a first generation of European colonists harbored expectations of prospering by means of their political or entrepreneurial pursuits in the Andes. In towns all across the Andes, merchants, mining entrepreneurs, lawyers and notaries, adventurers, friars and priests, and Spanish nobles who sought political patronage or coveted fertile lands and a servile labor force opposed the "archaic" system of extraction which gave private encomenderos a virtual monopoly over the goods and services of the Andean peoples. Not only did a small group of encomenderos exercise enormous control over the commodity market in native products, but many encomenderos actually seemed to be wreaking havoc on the very communities they were entrusted to protect. How else to explain the dwindling of tribute, the proliferation of restless and

51

rootless inhabitants, and the increasingly aggressive protests and challenges by ethnic lords? And, as if the very cosmos were warning encomenderos of the consequences of unbridled greed, successive epidemics swept over the human landscape, claiming millions of victims among the tributaries.[1] Thus, Toledo's challenge during his twelve-year administration (1569-1581) was not simply to resolve internecine conflicts but to save the Andean kingdom itself from social chaos and decline.[2]

The crisis led to the imposition of a "political economy of colonialism." Paradoxically, the Toledan reforms, which drew heavily on the policy proposals of Juan de Matienzo, were designed both to centralize state power over the Andean population and the colonial elite and to open up the potential for mercantile accumulation to a broad spectrum of that elite.[3] The first requirement was to dislodge the encomenderos from their position of privilege, even if that could not be done in a day or even necessarily in a generation. But under Toledo, the state irrevocably altered the balance of power among colo-

1 There were epidemics of measles, smallpox, and influenza in the Andes in 1524, 1531, 1546, 1558, and 1589-1591, claiming millions of victims among the indigenous peoples. See Noble David Cook, ed., *Tasa de la visita general de Francisco de Toledo* (Lima: Universidad Nacional Mayor de San Marcos, 1975), xiii-xxiv, and Noble David Cook, *Demographic Collapse: Indian Peru, 1520-1620* (Cambridge: Cambridge University Press, 1981), esp. chaps. 8-10. See also Henry Dobyns, "An Outline of Andean Epidemic History to 1720," *Bulletin of the History of Medicine* 37 (1963): 493-515.

2 Spalding (*Huarochirí*, 136ff.) analyzes the crisis of the "economy of plunder" in the 1560s, which, she argues, was "at root a crisis of production, directly linked to a demographic disaster." Stern (*Peru's Indian Peoples*, 47-71) also studies this crisis decade in detail. However, he focuses attention on the growing disillusionment of Andean peoples who had previously collaborated with the Spanish overlords, only to see those alliances deteriorate as commercial pressures and state exactions grew heavier. Stern interprets the millenarian movement of Huamanga's peoples as the culmination of this disillusionment. A third approach is that of Wachtel (*Vision of the Vanquished*, 85-139), who argues that Andean society decomposed and fragmented under early colonial pressures, so that many kurakas had forsaken their traditional roles, principles, and norms for more opportunistic and despotic patterns of behavior.

On Toledo's career and works, see Roberto Levillier, *Don Francisco de Toledo, supremo organizador del Perú: Su vida, su obra (1515-1582)*, 3 vols. (Madrid: Espasa-Calpe, 1935-1942). Toledo's writings are collected in Roberto Levillier, ed., *Gobernantes del Perú: Cartas y papeles, siglo XVI*, 14 vols. (Madrid: Sucesores de Rivadeneyra, 1921-1926).

3 See chap. 1. For a discussion of Matienzo's influence on Toledan policies, see Stern, *Peru's Indian Peoples*, 72-75.

nial factions, by denying encomenderos the right of feudal jurisdiction and by asserting its own authority over the terms and limits of exploitation of the crown's native subjects. Encomenderos could no longer expect to bequeath their legacies to their immediate heirs and beyond, and, more important, they now had to deal with officials sent by the viceroy to determine the amount and kind of tribute they could legitimately extract. The encomenderos who were granted a "reprieve" were living on borrowed time, before the pivotal moment when the state (or its representatives) expropriated tribute directly for the royal coffers. Thus would the Toledan state become a direct, autonomous claimant on the resources of Andean communities and assume responsibility for maintaining the outflow of surplus and securing control over Andean peasants and chieftains.

Under the new extractive system, private individuals theoretically had no greater access to the wealth produced by Andean communities than they had when encomenderos reigned supreme. The colonial authorities now were supposed to shield Andean communities from enterprising Europeans. But there was an important difference between the destiny of tribute extracted by the state and that of tribute collected by private encomenderos. The state allocated a share of its tributary income to subsidize members of the colonial elite. Toledo was to create an "age of opportunity" and of upward social mobility for the bureaucrat who enjoyed a royal pension and other perquisites of office, the merchant who increased his control over the commodity market in Andean goods, and the big mercury or silver mineowner who received allotments of "Indians" drafted by the state for temporary mine work. As long as the state could commandeer Andean peasants to subsidize the colonial bureaucracy and strategic enterprises, it could rely upon its power of patronage to co-opt and control members of the colonial elite. Patronage enabled the state to mediate among conflicting colonial interest groups and channel conflicts in ways that did not threaten imperial ends.[4]

4 The discussion above draws on Spalding's analysis of colonial state formation in the Andes (*Huarochirí*, 156-158). The author argues that the state's extraction of the surplus generated within Andean peasant economies and its redistribution to members of the colonial elite "preserved the power of patronage upon which the state rested." The patrimony of the Toledan state undergirded a colonial system of European absolutism that protected and subsidized aristocratic wealth and privilege under circumstances of rapid commercialization in a peasant society, where most producers were still bound up in subsistence economies. But state patrimony, under a centralizing bureaucracy, also preempted the emergence of feudal jurisdiction on the part of encomenderos. For a discussion of absolutism in sixteenth- and seventeenth-century Europe, see Perry Ander-

Toledo achieved neither instant nor lasting success. As we shall see in chapter 3, the Toledan colonial project set in motion social processes that ultimately undermined the project itself. By the mid-seventeenth century, the state no longer had the capacity to set the limits of exploitation and extraction. Rather, it was the Andean peoples themselves who, by their collective and individual action, determined the limits of state autonomy. But long after the Toledan program of political economy had ceased to function effectively, it remained the definitive model of colonialism in the Andes. Later viceroys could not avoid dealing with the Toledan myth and legacy, regardless of their own philosophical or pragmatic orientations. Even in the late eighteenth century, administrators in Alto Perú looked back to the era of Toledo for reformist ideals and inspiration. The imprint of Toledan reforms was especially deep in Alto Perú, where the viceroy rescued the mining industry from the doldrums and turned Potosí, for a short while, into the world's premier silver producer.

Potosí's Second Silver Cycle

Toledo's primary task was to modernize the mining industry at Potosí. Over the previous half-decade, the rich oxidized ores had dried up. Gone were most of the *huayadores* who had smelted the metal in their furnaces. The times of "easy metal" were over; a great deal of capital and technology would be needed to extract the lower-content ore from deeper within the rust-colored hill of silver. Reflecting back upon those days, Luís Capoche, owner of one of the silver-amalgamation mills, painted a bleak picture of a mining town where "the power of silver was diminished . . . the hill's rich ore exhausted . . . and ruin and harm were felt more each day."[5]

The problems of the decline in ore quality and of technological obsolescence in refining were compounded by an acute shortage of labor. Although we have no reliable population statistics for the pre-Toledan period, contemporary observers did remark on the scarcity

---

son, *Lineages of the Absolutist State* (London: New Left Books, 1974), esp. 33-42 and 397-431. A controversial treatment of the colonial formation as feudal is Marcello Carmagnani, *Formación y crisis de un sistema feudal* (Mexico City: Siglo XXI, 1976).

5 Luís Capoche, *Relación general de la villa imperial de Potosí* (1585) (Madrid: Atlas, 1959), 115-116; Bartolomé Arzáns de Orsúa y Vela, *Historia de la villa imperial de Potosí*, 3 vols., ed. Lewis Hanke and Gunnar Mendoza (Providence: Brown University Press, 1965), 1: 127.

of mineworkers. In 1567, Matienzo expressed concern about the inadequate and erratic supply of Indians at Potosí and said that Potosí's economic woes would continue unless ways could be found to attract more Indians to the mining town.[6] But Capoche, writing later with the benefit of hindsight, realized the labor problem was even more serious than Matienzo's remarks seemed to suggest. Capoche reported that "each day more Indians disappeared," so that by 1572 Potosí "was almost abandoned, the buildings in disrepair, and the residents empty-pocketed."[7] Capoche perhaps exaggerated this picture of a ghost town to bolster his argument that the logical and just solution to Potosí's crisis of production was a system of compulsory, rotating labor known as the *mita* (modeled, of course, on the Incaic institution). Nevertheless, he was pointing to a critical problem that plagued mining enterprises in many precapitalist economies: the extreme elasticity of the labor supply.[8] After twenty-five years of silver mining, local Europeans still had not managed to anchor a proletarianized labor force to the base of the Cerro Rico. As the problem of diminishing returns worsened in the 1560s, Potosí lost its ability to obtain or hold sufficient numbers of Indian wageworkers. Further, most miners at Potosí were peasants by origin and orientation. Even though the colonial state began to tighten administrative control over Andean communities and obstruct migratory movement, most Andean miners still found ways to escape from the mining economy as conditions deteriorated. Capoche perceived the transient, almost elusive nature of the miners: "As smelting metals dried up and it became difficult to mine ore profitably, Indians returned home to their villages; others (in still greater numbers) set off for the valleys of Chuquisaca and other temperate lands."[9] The wage incentive did not function in such a shallow labor market, where most miners retained their peasant roots and ethnic identity.[10]

6 Matienzo, *Gobierno del Perú*, 71-72.

7 Capoche, *Relación general*, 116 and 135.

8 Bakewell stresses this point, in his discussion of the labor supply in colonial Zacatecas: Peter J. Bakewell, *Silver Mining and Society in Colonial Mexico; Zacatecas, 1546-1700* (Cambridge: Cambridge University Press, 1971), 124-125.

9 Capoche, *Relación general*, 135.

10 Early literature and legends about the mita have shaped historians' assumptions about the predominant role of forced labor in Potosí's mining industry. Institutional approaches to colonial Andean history, such as the classic article by John H. Rowe, "The Incas under Spanish Colonial Institutions," *Hispanic American Historical Review* 35 (1957): 155-199, have placed heavy emphasis on the

Potosí's crisis was not confined to production. The mining slump depressed trade and the commodity market that had flourished since the late 1540s. Tributaries who once trekked for days across the altiplano to exchange their products for specie no longer bothered. They resorted to payment in kind, as cash became restricted to the highest echelons of society.[11] The economy seemed to retrogress to a "natural" one. Scarcity of silver, sluggish commodity circulation, and depressed prices all plunged the southern Andes into a recession. "The value of tribute has fallen off sharply in this kingdom," Capoche wrote. "Indians now pay tribute in llamas, maize, and crude cloth—the products of their own pastures, harvests, and looms."[12] The earlier trend toward commodification in the wider economic space was being reversed. Potosí had come to occupy a strategic site in the Andean economy, and the exhaustion of silver ore spelled ruin for the encomenderos, merchants, traders, and colonial artisans who had to acquire the currency with which to purchase European goods and invest in their future. Capoche stressed this point: "All the repartimientos . . . and cities . . . of this kingdom acquire [specie] in . . . Potosí. Potosí's market bestows monetary value on all goods, even in the remote villages whence they come. . . . Without silver or a market outlet, [native] goods fetch no price, nor bring any return." The qhatu still existed, but Andean traders who remained at Potosí

mita as the bulwark of silver mining at Potosí. See also the recent study by Jeffrey A. Cole, *The Potosí Mita, 1573-1700: Compulsory Indian Labor in the Andes* (Stanford, Calif.: Stanford University Press, 1985). Traditionally, Potosí provided a sharp contrast to Mexican mining, where forced rotational labor remained small in scale. However, recent work on southern Andean history has challenged the earlier assumptions about the mita. The recent study by Peter J. Bakewell, *Miners of the Red Mountain: Indian Labor at Potosí, 1545-1650* (Albuquerque: University of New Mexico Press, 1984), illuminates the complexities of labor arrangements at Potosí, where less than half the work force in about 1600 was classified as draft, or compulsory, laborers. The mingas, or free wageworkers, were not only numerically dominant; they also enjoyed a limited degree of leverage in their relationship with mineowners. But Bakewell also shows that it was the mita workers (mitayos), not the mineowners, who paid the material cost of the mingas' slim economic advantages, in the form of below-subsistence wages and harsh, regimented work conditions. As we shall see in chap. 3, Tandeter advances this argument even further in his study of eighteenth-century Potosí.

11 Capoche, *Relación general*, 135.

12 Ibid., 115. See also Juan Polo de Ondegardo, "Relación de los fundamentos acerca del notable daño que resulta de no guardar a los indios sus fueros" (1571), in *Colección de documentos inéditos relativos al descubrimiento, conquista, y organización de las antiguas posesiones españolas de América y Oceanía . . .*, 42 vols. (Madrid: Imprenta del Hospicio, 1872), 17: 116-117.

resorted to "ancient forms" of barter and exchange, "customs they practiced before the Europeans arrived."[13]

In an effort to revitalize the mining industry, the new viceroy, in a series of ordinances, mandated the introduction of sweeping technological reforms. Toledo imported amalgamation techniques that employed mercury and salt to separate out silver from its by-products. Although it was almost two decades before the technique was perfected at Potosí, refiners eventually used this "patio process" of refining more efficiently than their Mexican competitors. More important, the new method finally allowed mineowners to exploit the bulk of the Cerro Rico's primary ores: the hard, dark ores called *negrillos*, buried deep in the mountain. Mineowners began to sink shafts and tunnels deep into the middle zones of the Cerro. Eventually, some shafts were so deep that the workers who hauled ore and earth often spent half of their eight-hour shifts climbing rope or cowhide ladders.[14]

The technological changes produced almost immediate results. In 1576, an oidor of the audiencia of Lima issued an enthusiastic report about the early experiments with mercury amalgamation at Potosí, and he urged the crown to increase the supply of quicksilver.[15] That same year, Toledo decreed that Potosí was to be the destination of all mercury produced in Huancavelica. He already envisaged the Potosí-Huancavelica nexus as Peru's primary strategic export sector. He apparently had good reason for doing so; royal taxes on silver production had jumped from 105,926 pesos to 336,144 pesos during the first three years in which the amalgamation techniques were used (1573-1576). By the time Capoche wrote in 1585, royal *quintos*—the tax on silver production—had more than doubled again.[16] Improvements in the extractive as well as the refining processes set in mo-

13 Capoche, *Relación general*, 115.

14 Peter Bakewell, "Technological Change in Potosí; The Silver Boom of the 1570s," *Jahrbuch für Geschichte von Staat, Wirtschaft, und Gesellschaft Lateinamerikas* 14 (1977): 55-77; Brading and Cross, "Colonial Silver Mining," 547 and 554.

15 Lic. Ramírez de Cartagena to the crown, May 6, 1576, in Levillier, ed., *Gobernantes del Perú*, 7: 282ff., also cited and summarized in Silvio Zavala, *El servicio personal de los indios en el Perú*, 3 vols. (México City: Colegio de México, 1978), 1:100.

16 Capoche, *Relación general*, 177. Toledo to Juan de Ovando, Mar. 12, 1576, in Levillier, ed., *Gobernantes del Perú*, 5: 472-480; John J. TePaske, "The Fiscal Structure of Upper Peru and the Financing of Empire," in Karen Spalding, ed., *Essays in the Political, Economic, and Social History of Colonial Latin America* (Newark: University of Delaware, 1982), 86.

tion industrial changes that would allow Potosí's mineowners to accelerate production and to penetrate into the middle ore zones almost a century earlier than happened in the silver mines of Mexico. On the world market, the quantity of silver exported from Potosí would virtually eliminate the German silver mines from the European market by the end of the sixteenth-century.[17]

The imperatives of mining as "big business" shifted economic power away from the direct producers and concentrated it in the hands of the relatively few owners of mines and mills. Although in 1585 there were five hundred registered mineowners, the real power rested with some seventy-five "mercury men" (*azogueros*) who owned the great silver refineries. Behind them stood a smaller group of silver merchants who advanced cash and credit to the mineowners and the azogueros to tide them over during the frequent lulls in production and to allow them to import mercury. The silver merchants also lubricated the productive mechanism by channeling silver bar to the mint at Potosí, the final step in the production of the commodity money.[18]

This new interlocking elite that exercised control over the factors and processes of mineral production depended upon a new breed of laborer, one that was directly subordinate and beholden to the owners of mines and mills for its means of subsistence and survival. Capoche reported that, at Potosí in 1585, "in general, mine work is salaried labor; under the *jornal* [wage system], the *mitayos* [mita workers] receive 3 1/2 reales [a day] and the *mingas* [free wage earners] receive 4 reales."[19] To his way of thinking, the ideological and real distinctions between forced labor and free (wage) labor were less striking than the historical transformation of semi-independent An-

17 Pierre Vilar, *A History of Gold and Money, 1450-1920* (London: New Left Books, 1976), 125. On mineral production trends, see Alvaro Jara, "Dans le Pérou du XVIe siècle: La courbe de production de metaux monnayables," *Annales E.S.C.* 22 (1967): 590-608, and Peter J. Bakewell, "Registered Silver Production in the Potosí District, 1550-1735," *Jahrbuch für Geschichte von Staat, Wirtschaft, und Gesellschaft Lateinamerikas* 12 (1975): 67-103. On the more general impact of American silver on Europen price trends, see Fernand Braudel and F. Spooner, "Prices in Europe from 1450 to 1750," in E. E. Rich and C. H. Wilson, ed., *The Cambridge Economic History of Europe*, 7 vols. (Cambridge: Cambridge University Press, 1967), 4: 378-486.

18 Brading and Cross, "Colonial Silver Mining," 567. On the economic and social aspects of Potosí, see Arzáns de Orsúa y Vela, *Historia de la villa imperial*, and Lewis Hanke, *The Imperial City of Potosí* (The Hague: Nijhoff, 1956).

19 Capoche, *Relación general*, 144-145.

dean miners (who had once owned their own tools, enjoyed free access to perhaps one-quarter of the mines, and controlled smelting) into dependent wage laborers "deprived of their livelihood, unable to feed themselves or pay tribute except by means of wage work."[20] Though hardly disinterested, Capoche seemed to lament the passing of an age when Andean miners enjoyed a relatively strong bargaining position vis-à-vis European mineowners and a certain amount of economic integrity.

But the transition to wage labor at Potosí was neither easy nor complete during the second silver boom. The mingas who had intimate knowledge of the labyrinthian interiors of the mines, or who had established trading relationships in the city's qhatu, or who could mobilize the labor of kinsmen recently arrived from their villages—all had resources to draw upon in their struggle for a livelihood. They employed tactics that allowed them to recover some of their economic autonomy and enhance their bargaining power. As long as colonial authorities did not effectively suppress the flourishing trade in pieces of crude ore in the city's metal market, Andean miners could commodify the ore they managed to extract on their own, bypassing the wage circuit and supplementing their wages with the income derived from that ore. The miners would not work unless they were given the rights to *la corpa*, or "bonus" chunks of ore. As Capoche wrote, "to keep [the mingas] content and grateful so they will return to work each day, the mineowners allow them to take a chunk of metal, and altogether the mingas amass a great quantity of ore they sell at the qhatu." He estimated that la corpa constituted one-quarter of all the silver mined.[21] As long as miners continued to have the right to la corpa and were able to exchange it for other commodities in the city, they had ample incentive to smuggle ore out of the Cerro and evidently did smuggle large quantities of it. In effect, the institution of la corpa created a hybrid labor system that resembled sharecropping almost as much as it did wage work.

Toledo sought to resolve the conflict over the legitimacy of la corpa in favor of the mineworkers. At first sight, it seems curious that the viceroy allied himself with the refractory and lawless mingas. After all, if the state had eliminated the illicit trade in ore, it presumably would have significantly reduced production costs (the value of the crude ore the workers were allowed to take and of that

20 Ibid., 162.

21 Ibid., 154.

they smuggled out).[22] But Toledo must have accepted the custom of la corpa as a necessary evil that had to be tolerated if the mingas were to work for wages at all. Capoche suggests, in fact, that Toledo fixed the daily wage rate of four reales in full realization that mingas could not sustain themselves on such a wage. His strategy was not to outlaw the custom of issuing rights to metal, but to incorporate la corpa into the new wage system. Thus, Toledo's "wage regime" did not absolutely subordinate mingas to the owners of productive means. It left "space" wherein Andean miners could reassert control over a limited part of the production and distribution of crude ore. If Toledo's policies cut into the short-term profits of mineowners, they also provided an economic incentive for mine work on the part of workers who could still exercise other livelihood options. For the labor market was probably still rather shallow in the 1580s. Men who were wageworkers one month might vanish the next, to return to their villages at harvest time or simply to escape the harsh life of a miner. A fully proletarianized labor force, dependent upon wage work for subsistence and reproduction, was still small in scale. Under the circumstances, the state and the mineowners had to make certain economic concessions to the mingas for the sake of meeting the needs of the industry. Toledo was under no illusion, however, that these concessions would make it possible to attract and hold the much larger labor force that the new mills and mine shafts required. Labor would continue to be a major bottleneck if the big mineowners depended exclusively upon nonconscripted wageworkers. A plan was needed to harness the vast resources of Andean communities to the silver enterprises.

Toledo was not the first colonial authority to draft peasants by turns for temporary mine work at Potosí, but he was the first to use the power of the state on a large scale to enforce mass migrations of peasants to the mines. His model for the mining mita of Potosí was probably the Incaic labor drafts for maize agriculture in the Cochabamba valleys (see chapter 1). The viceroy called upon the labor power of peasants inhabiting some 139 designated villages in sixteen provinces, from Canas y Canches and Tinta in the north near Cuzco to Tarija in the south. This mita was to tap about one-seventh of the

22 Assadourian has calculated that, relative to the average value of quintos in 1580-1584, la corpa represented a cost of about 10 percent of the total value of silver output, while for the average minga, it represented an increase of 80 percent in monetary income: Assadourian, "La producción de la mercancía dinero," 269.

adult male population of those villages.[23] In all, the state drafted some 12,600 mitayos each year. Only a few southern provinces were declared "free territories": Larecaja, Tomina, Pilaya, Mizque, and Yamparaes, valley regions on the margins of the densely populated Indian highlands. Among the lowland dwellers, only Cochabamba's native inhabitants were not exempted from the mita and were forced to trek upland through the mountains to the cold puna of Potosí to serve their mita duty.

The infusion of mitayos into the silver veins and mills of Potosí increased the Indian labor force in the late sixteenth century by one-third to one-half.[24] The mitayos were assigned to the owners of the large mines and mills, except during their "rest weeks." Theoretically, only one-third of the mitayo population was subjected to the terms of the mita in any given week. Most mita recruits were permitted to hire their labor out as "free" workers during their rest periods. At close range, then, the proportion of forced workers was surprisingly small, and the boundaries between forced and free labor seemed blurred. But the institution's importance cannot be reduced simply to the fraction of the labor force that was actually under mita assignment, for it served three vital functions.

First, the mita ensured a stable, disciplined labor force that undercut the economic influence of the mingas. Fresh from the countryside, gangs of mitayos worked under the immediate authority of one of their own villagers in the assigned mines and mills. The mita system allowed mineowners to allocate labor "rationally" to the most dangerous and exhausting tasks. Furthermore, the mitayos who hauled ore up the long rope ladders or who tended the liquified metal in huge vats were less susceptible to the "corrupt western influences" that, in the opinion of local clerics and mineowners, bred violence and indolence among the mingas.

Second, the mita expanded the pool of people available for wage work in the mines. During their rest weeks, mitayos hired themselves out as wageworkers in order to support themselves during their year or more in residence at Potosí. In addition, the women and

---

23 On the mita, see Bakewell, *Miners of the Red Mountain*, and Alberto Crespo Rodas, "La mita de Potosí," *Revista histórica* 22 (1955-1956), 158-162. Zavala's monumental work, *Servicio personal*, touches on many aspects of the mita over three centuries of Spanish rule.

24 Assadourian, "Producción de la mercancía dinero," 242 and 255-257; Cook, *Demographic Collapse*, 242ff.; and Bakewell, *Miners of the Red Mountain*, esp. the conclusion.

children who accompanied the mitayos engaged in many types of economic activities in mining and petty commerce. The forced migrations therefore channeled peasant labor into both mining and subsidiary work at Potosí.

Third, and perhaps most important, the mita represented an enormous subsidy to the recipient mining enterprises.[25] An anonymous report (*memorial*) written in about 1610 presented a crude calculation of the labor costs saved by those mineowners who employed mita labor.[26] Mitayos were then apparently receiving a daily wage of four reales, half the wage of free workers. Moreover, mitayos did not enjoy any rights to bonus ore, representing a further saving estimated to average about five reales a day. Thus, a mitayo cost only about one-third as much as a minga. In addition, many mineowners received direct subsidies in the form of commutation payments from Indians purchasing their way out of forced labor. Combining the estimated value of commutation payments with the value of "lost wages" (as a result of the undervaluation of mita labor), the memorialist estimated that the mita system saved the mining industry more than 3,800,000 pesos ensayados each year. It was no trivial sum, even in those heady days.

The architects of the mining mita thus designed a labor system that drew heavily upon the resources of the ayllus and communities. It was widely recognized that the mitayo's weekly wage alone was below the minimum remuneration necessary for a peasant family to survive in the city. Even when supplemented by income earned during the rest weeks, it was still insufficient. Mitayos depended upon their kinsmen and communities to provide them with subsistence goods and with extra workers who accompanied them to the mines. The mita affected not only those who were forced to migrate to Po-

---

25 Assadourian's conceptualization of "Peruvian economic space" and of the formation of a mining economy dependent upon the coerced participation of Andean peasant labor in the internal market and the resultant subsidy to the mining industry broke new ground in the study of the complex and changing articulation of peasant subsistence-oriented economies and the mining export economy. His conceptual framework of the emergent colonial socioeconomic formation situates the peasant economy at its center, even though Potosí was the "growth pole" around which Peruvian economic space configured. See Assadourian, "Producción de la mercancía dinero;" see also his "La organización económica espacial del sistema colonial," in his *Sistema de la economía colonial*, 277-321.

26 "Discurso breve en razón de lo que pierden los indios que van a las minas de Potosí . . .," cited and summarized in Zavala, *Servicio personal*, 2: 44-45. See also Assadourian, "La produccion de la mercancía dinero," 255ff.

tosí, but also those left behind in the villages. To furnish mitayo teams with the means of survival, ayllus and villages invested several months in preparation: grinding corn into flour, reallocating community stocks, rounding up and equipping llama caravans for the long journey. Mitayo families took with them their herds, crops, and clothes.[27] Europeans who encountered mitayo "companies" en route to Potosí reported that they looked like villages in microcosm moving across the altiplano. In 1603, Alfonso Messía Venegas described 7,000 people moving south from the lakeshore villages around Titicaca. Men, women, and children accompanied an endless train of llamas carrying chuño, maize, charqui, dried fish, and quinoa flour. The mitayos themselves were only a fraction of the group.[28] If a European had stationed himself at the gates of the city and inventoried the goods that mitayos carried into Potosí, he might have been more impressed. A census of Potosí in 1603 estimated that mitayo households brought some 60,000 llamas and 40,000 fanegas of food into the city, with an estimated worth of 440,000 pesos ensayados.[29] It is unlikely that these food crops or herds were sold, except perhaps for a small proportion of the produce to raise hard currency for the mitayos' kurakas and communities. Most of the food was consumed, and eventually even the beasts of burden were eaten.

These images offer perhaps the most graphic evidence of the compulsory incorporation of the Andean peasant economy into the mining export sector. Toledo expanded and reinforced state power to coerce a surplus out of self-sufficient peasantries and to funnel massive amounts of cheap labor to the mines. Legendary fortunes made from mining enterprises were not simply the rewards of entrepreneurial success and advantageous market fluctuations; they were partially the result of the ability of the colonial state to supply the needed workers and hold wages at levels below subsistence requirements. The mita, as conceived by Toledo, was a form of subsidy to the owners of the silver mines and mills. Toledo's use of the coercive powers of the state to provide these subsidies was a response to the

27 "Discurso breve," and "Memorial que se dió a S.M. sobre el trabajo de los indios en las minas de Potosí" (1610), cited and discussed in Zavala, *Servicio personal,* 2: 44-45.

28 Alfonso Messía Venegas, "Memorial al virrey Luís de Velasco" (1603), in Rubén Vargas Ugarte, ed., *Pareceres jurídicos en asuntos de Indias (1601-1718)* (Lima, 1951), 94-115.

29 "Descripción de la villa y minas de Potosí, año de 1603," in Jiménez de la Espada, *Relaciones geográficas de Indias,* 380-382.

imperatives of Spanish imperialism and of world demand for the commodity money. The royal quintos not only filled the crown's coffers in Madrid and financed much of the cost of the swelling colonial bureaucracy, which both enforced and fed from the surplus product and labor of the native peoples; the taxes and profits from mining also lubricated the internal and overseas commodity trade. Potosí's spectacular second silver cycle was made possible by the colonial apparatus that reinforced extractive relationships and redistributed the surplus generated within the domain of Andean communities to the mining elites of Potosí.

The deployment of state power to enforce peasant participation in the colonial economy was not limited to the mining enterprises. State institutions, policies, laws, and social practices generated a complex, overlapping network of legal and extralegal levies that stimulated both the demand for and the supply of goods and labor in the colonial economy which, left to spontaneous market forces, would have remained embryonic in character and small in scale. Thus, as Spalding has argued, "the dynamism of the economy was generated not within the system of production itself but from the outside. It came through the coercive mechanisms applied by the colonial state."[30] Beyond the great silver mines, a host of private enterprises were springing up which produced commodities for Potosí and other growing towns and cities. Directly or indirectly, young commercial endeavors in the colony were tied into the network of surplus extraction. As long as the state continued to impose extractive institutions like tribute and the mita, it could offer subsidies to factions of the colonial elite. As we shall see shortly, the colonial state could also target its subsidies to strategic economic sectors and thereby exercise some degree of control over competing colonial interest groups. The state acted as an autonomous claimant on peasant resources, and its power of extraction furnished the political weaponry which enabled it to arbitrate among groups within the colonial elite.

Andean Villages and the Patron-State

If the state defined and enforced the "contributions" of Andean peoples to the colonial project, it also attempted to legitimate and protect their claims to a certain minimum of subsistence insurance.

30 Karen Spalding, "Exploitation As an Economic System: The State and the Extraction of Surplus in Colonial Peru," in Collier, Rosaldo, and Wirth, *Inca and Aztec States*, 325.

The new, intrusive economic demands of the state could be met by peasant households only if they could provide for their own sustenance and physical reproduction within the matrix of the ayllu or village economy. Toledo fully realized that the state had a vested interest in protecting the internal capacity of Andean communities to provide a basic level of social welfare for its members and to absorb the state's fiscal and labor demands. If the state was to ensure a stable source of revenue from the rural sector, to continue to drain ayllus of people for the silver mines, and to ensure some degree of compliance from its tributaries, then it would have to offer its rural subjects a bedrock of subsistence guarantees. Thus, the issue of the social reproduction of local Andean economies was inextricably linked with the enforcement of economic subsidies to strategic colonial enterprises and ultimately with the power and wealth of the state. The colonial regime not only imposed fiscal demands and set the boundaries of legitimate exploitation; it also began to reach into the very heart of Andean communities to dictate the terms of intraethnic social relations.

Among the first priorities in expanding the state's scope of extraction was to balance its levies against a population's resources and competing social obligations. In principle, the Toledan regime wanted to adjust its claims to the ability of its tributaries to pay. In preparation for the official tax assessments, colonial authorities fanned out to all corners of the kingdom to do their field research—cadastral surveys, head counts, interviews—following the example of Toledo himself, who traveled across the mountainous backlands for nearly five years. The agents were required to obtain detailed pictures of Andean villages, ayllus, and lineages. No fragment of data was lost to view. Royal inspectors were to record the expanse, quality, and variety of the dispersed crop lands and pasturage; the availability of water, salt pans, fisheries, and fertilizer; the villages' herds, silos of grain, and storehouses of cloth; and, not least, the number of Indian households. The past was considered, too; royal inspectors were to assess the amount of tribute (in labor presentations and in kind) that an Indian population had formerly paid to the Incas and to their encomendero.[31] In effect, an early form of anthropology was being put to the service of Spanish imperialism.

There was a contradiction in the Toledan policy of tax assessment.

---

31 Carlos A. Romero, ed., "Libro de la visita general del virrey Francisco de Toledo, 1570-1575," *Revista histórica* 7 (1924): 115-216; see esp. "Instrucción nueva para visitadores," 177-186. This document is also summarized in Zavala, *Servicio personal,* 2: 96-97.

The state wanted to exercise some degree of prudence in its fiscal claims so as not to erode the very tax base upon which the mercantile colonial system rested. It therefore had to intrude into local life and to map the rural Andean economies in order to determine (in accord with European preconceptions) the reproductive capacity of those economies. Yet in the process, the growing central authority of the state provided the administrative armature for tapping the resources of those communities more systematically and for reducing any slippage that may once have afforded peasants room in which to elude or resist outside claimants. State penetration into local communities, for the purpose of centralizing and rationalizing tax collection, therefore posed a threat to the well-being of those communities, for it led to a more rigid and regressive tax system. In good times and bad, an ayllu or village had to pay up; even if a peasant household eked out a living on the community's most marginal lands, it still owed a fixed head tax, unadjusted to take account of changing circumstances—and almost all tribute was now levied in silver coin. Viewed from below, the assessments threatened to impose new hardships and sharpened native perceptions of an omnipotent and intrusive state.[32]

The implications of preserving the agrarian subsistence base of the Andean communities went far beyond tax-adjustment policies. The state needed to define, legitimate, and rationalize (again, in accordance with European norms) land tenure among its native subjects. Now that private colonists were launching productive enterprises all across the Andes to capitalize on lucrative markets, they competed with each other and with Andean cultivators for access to fertile lands, good pasturage, irrigation streams, and hired field hands. How could the state protect its tributaries against the growing threats of encroachment unless it threw up legal barriers against these intruders? Furthermore, even in remote puna regions, where Europeans rarely ventured, the effort to institute centralized administration and systematic extraction mandated sweeping reforms that would regroup Indians into a network of rural communities. The dispersed and fragmented landholding patterns of the ayllus left too many spaces in which tributaries could hide from colonial authorities or slip between territorial jurisdictions. As we have seen, the pastoral-

---

32 The most extensive and detailed study through Andean eyes of the colonial system in the seventeenth century is the chronicle of Felipe Guaman Poma de Ayala, *El primer neuva corónica y buen gobierno*, 3 vols., ed. John V. Murra and Rolena Adorno (Mexico City: Siglo XXI, 1980).

ists and cultivators of the puna sought to minimize the risk of crop failure by cultivating patches of land dispersed among several different environments. Their own subsistence needs required some access to resources at lower altitudes. (To this day, many ayllus in Norte Potosí and other parts of Bolivia have access to multiple ecological zones.)[33] Thus, Andean kin groups needed to retain vertical landholding patterns. Toledo himself settled some disputes in favor of highland Indians seeking to reclaim their rights to distant valley settlements. But for purposes of tightened administration and authority over rural Andean society, the state was bent upon sharply restricting the dispersed settlement patterns. With varying degrees of success, Toledo advanced the process, begun by his predecessors, of fragmenting dispersed kin groups and destroying the vestiges of political archipelagos.[34]

Toledo's program of forced resettlement was an assault on Andean kin networks of unprecedented scope. The principle behind the plan was to designate towns and their rural surroundings as official "Indian communities" and to assign certain Indian populations to inhabit them. This meant that the viceroy's agents had to uproot many Andean peoples and sweep them into nucleated settlements. The multiple hamlets that speckled the mountain slopes and hid in deep river valleys would be "reduced" to orderly, administered towns, their sites chosen for purposes of administrative expedience and "good climate."[35]

The spatial layout of the new Indian towns revealed the degree of the state's intrusion into the everyday life of Andean people. "Orderly planning" required that the *reducciones* be fashioned after grid-patterned Spanish colonial towns, wherein a prison, schoolhouse, and parish church would flank the central plaza. There, colonial au-

33 Lehmann, ed., *Ecology and Exchange;* Dollfus, *Reto del espacio andino;* and Jürgen Golte, *La racionalidad de la organización andina* (Lima: Instituto de Estudios Peruanos, 1980).

34 John V. Murra, "Investigaciones en etnohistoria andina," in his *Formaciones económicas,* 286.

35 Levillier, ed., *Gobernantes del Perú,* 8: 330-331. See also Magnus Mörner, *La corona española y los foraneos en los pueblos de indios de América* (Stockholm: Almqvist and Wiksell, 1970) and his more recent study, *The Andean Past: Land, Societies, and Conflict* (New York: Columbia University Press, 1985), esp. 59-63; Alejandro Málaga Medina, "Las reducciones en el Perú (1532-1600)," *Historia y cultura* (Lima) 8 (1974): 155-167; and Daniel W. Gade and Mario Escobar, "Village Settlement and the Colonial Legacy in Southern Peru," *Geographical Review* 72 (1982): 430-449.

thorities could collect taxes, administer the sacraments, and instruct Indians in the lifeways of "honest and obedient Christians." Contact with the outside world could be readily monitored in such insular towns, since authorities could restrict the coming and going of Indians and outsiders. And the towns, beacons of Christian civilization, would draw solitary herders and cultivators into their orbit, removing them from their ancient and remote lands, where natural formations were imbued with strange, idolatrous spirituality and meaning. The influences of urbanization were to absorb even a community's shepherds, who would no longer remain isolated in the high pastures for more than six months at a time, so that they would not return to their rural, primitive ways. Against the strong centrifugal forces endemic to Andean society, the state designed a network of social control pivoting on the stable habitation of the Indians in their official towns.[36]

The naked force by which the state reduced Andean settlements into reconstituted Indian communities was buttressed by the viceroy's guarantees of subsistence rights for residents of the reducciones. A redistribution of land accompanied the creation of the Indian villages, such that the state legitimated usufruct rights for all Andean households whose menfolk were inscribed as tributaries and mitayos. In many instances, that meant taking land away from the host Indian community, the site of the new reducción, and parceling it out among the ayllus, *parcialidades* (moieties), or repartimiento Indians who were transplanted to the community. As Toledo noted in one of his ordinances, this policy provoked numerous land disputes and court suits. The more that royal officials infringed on Andean rights to dispersed fields, forests, and pastures and tried to create a uniform land tenure pattern, the more they had to intercede in the disputes. In principle, all resettled Indians were to be compensated with appropriate land grants, even if that meant that the crown had to expropriate lands from other (non-reducción) Indians or from Spaniards.[37]

Nor was that all. The state also moved inside the jurisdiction of the Indian towns to sanction and dictate the terms of redistribution of surplus crops. Toledo ordered communities to designate parcels of potato and maize lands as *chacras de comunidad*, whose yields were

36 Francisco de Toledo, "Ordenanzas para los indios de . . . Charcas, destinados a evitar los daños y agravios que recibían de sus encomenderos . . . ," in Levillier, ed., *Gobernantes del Perú*, 8: 304-382.

37 Ibid., 330-331 and 353-354.

to feed the poorest inhabitants. In good years, a village was to sell part of the crop and put the proceeds in its *caja da comunidad,* or community treasury. In times of dearth, the community's crop would be distributed directly to the poor and the savings in the caja would provide for food purchases to tide the people over until the next harvest. Through cultivation of communal lands and participation in the product market, the Indian community was to guarantee minimal subsistence even to the poorest peasant families. These risk-sharing mechanisms would establish some kind of social equilibrium within the village economy and presumably prevent the poorer peasants from fleeing their communities and their social obligations to the state in times of scarcity.

Thus, the Toledan state took advantage of traditional Andean norms of reciprocity and redistribution and turned them to its own ends. Even as royal authorities uprooted ayllus and drove people from their ancient lands, joining them with alien ayllus or lineages, stripping them of their traditional land rights, and subordinating them to the parish priest and the magistrate (*corregidor*) who were, for all practical purposes, in charge of the Indian town, Toledo sanctioned a normative order that absorbed elements of the moral economy that had governed social relations in Andean society. But, as Wachtel has noted, the underlying contradiction of the extractive system of exploitation was its preservation and legitimation of certain cultural traditions, customs, and norms wrenched loose from the total Andean socioeconomic formation.[38] Form without content, customs without context: the Andean cultural and ideological systems that gave meaning to kinship relationships were under assault by the very colonial policies that were theoretically meant to protect certain customs and traditions. Rituals and ceremonies that regenerated social bonds, communal commitments, and ethnic identity were eroded, though never stamped out successfully, by the religious and civil bureaucracy.[39] Often, Andean myths, rituals, and beliefs had to go underground to allow the people to seek material wellbeing and harmony from their local dieties (*huacas*) and ancestorgods.[40] And while people still expressed their norms of reciprocity in

38 Wachtel, *Vision of the Vanquished,* 85-139 and 164-165.

39 Spalding, *Huarochirí,* chap. 8; Pierre Duviols, "La represión del paganismo andino y la expulsión de los moriscos," *Anuario de estudios americanos* 28 (1971): 201-207.

40 Two recent ethnohistorical studies explore the transformation and preservation of rituals and symbolic systems among specific ethnic groups in the south-

the ideology of kinship, it was now the state which theoretically defined the outer boundaries of "community" and determined the local
ethnic map. Even at the most mundane level, the state altered Andean lifeways even as it sought to preserve them. For example, while
Indians were supposed to continue to observe their communitarian
practices of sharing scarce resources (under state supervision), they
were at the same time ordered to till their fields with oxen and plows
rather than with the traditional digging sticks.[41] With the new protection and patronage of the state came a paternalism that reinforced
its political and ideological authority over its Indian subjects. As we
shall see in chapter 3, during the seventeenth and eighteenth centuries Andean peoples increasingly challenged certain colonial authorities and found ways to loosen state control over their lives. But in
the immediate aftermath of the Toledan reforms, the colonial bureaucracy seemed to expand its scope of power and make its presence
felt in all parts of the southern Andes. The colonial leviathan appeared more omnipotent than eventually it proved to be.

In order to execute and enforce the reorganization of rural Andean
society, Toledo created an intricate, interlocking network of Andean
and European power brokers. On the European side, a hierarchy of
colonial functionaries—from corregidor and parish priest to royal
protector of Indians, jailer, and judicial officer—served as links in the
chain of command that began at the highest echelons of government.
As agents of a centralized state, they oversaw the extractive institutions, maintained the colonial order through mediation and threat,
and diffused the norms and ideology of the dominant colonial elites
among the native peoples. But if these white administrators had relied mainly on the power vested in them by the state, they would
have had little success. Instead, colonial authorities had to work
through the ethnic hierarchy in order to carry out the massive relo-
cations, enforce the extraction of tribute and labor, and ensure the
health of the village economy that subsidized the colonial enterprises, although this native hierarchy had to be carefully groomed by
the colonial state if it were to serve its new purposes. Thus, Toledo
sought to assimilate native authorities into the new power structure.
The terms under which they would be subordinated to, and co-opted

ern Andes during (and beyond) colonial rule: Thomas Abercrombie, "The Politics of Sacrifice: An Aymara Cosmology in Action" (Ph.D. diss., University of
Chicago, 1986); and Roger Rasnake, "The *Kurahkuna* of Yura: Indigenous Authorities of Colonial Charcas and Contemporary Bolivia" (Ph.D. diss., Cornell
University, 1982).

41 Levillier, ed., *Gobernantes del Perú*, 8: 333.

by, the colonial regime were the subject of much debate. Spalding writes that Toledo sought to convert the hereditary position of kuraka into an appointed office.[42] Though he did not prevail, he did manage to institutionalize state control over the succession of the kurakas. Indians could nominate a successor from among members of the noble lineage, but the nominee then had to be approved by the audiencia. This rule later provided a crucial mechanism for state intervention in the internal affairs of Indian communities in Alto Perú (see chapter 8).

Toledo also had other ways of whittling down the power and prestige of kurakas and converting them into agents of the state. One strategy was to restructure the normative order of Indian society. It was the state that now formalized and legitimated the relations between native elites and members of their own ayllu or moiety. The kurakas (or caciques), *principales* (heads of the ayllu segments within the parcialidades), and a host of secondary chiefs had formed a governing hierarchy that corresponded to the native grouping. In a series of ordinances, Toledo sought to define the status, function, and privileges of the members of this hierarchy.[43] They were to oversee the outflow of tribute twice a year and the dispatch of the mitayos. They were to track down fugitive Indians; mobilize work parties to build churches, bridges, and roads; and coordinate the traditional communal activities, such as terracing fields, cleaning irrigation works, and cultivating communal lands. And, as was customary, they were to reciprocate for labor services by offering drink, food, and seeds to their workers. They were also to distribute rights to land and pasturage, arbitrate local disputes, and mediate between the moiety or village and the colonial authorities. In return for exercising his power with prudence and in accordance with the law, the principal kuraka could call upon the community to provide him with laborers to cultivate four fanegadas each of corn and potatoes and two of wheat. A few other privileges accrued to the native notables, all spelled out in the new regulations.[44]

Thus, two principles governed the reforms that revamped the ethnic power structure. First, the state assumed the role of defining the

42 Spalding, *Huarochirí*, 220-221.

43 "De los caciques principales y lo que deben guardar por razón de sus cargos," ordenanzas 1-28, in Levillier, ed., *Gobernantes del Perú*, 8: 340-353.

44 Ibid.; Spalding, *Huarochirí*, 220-221; Waldemar Espinoza Soriano, "El alcalde mayor indígena en el virreinato del Perú," *Anuario de estudios americanos* 17 (1960): 183-300.

positions, powers, and privileges in the kuraka or cacique system (*kurakazgo* or *cacicazgo*). Second, the state sought to limit and control excesses and abuses in the system. Toledo apparently tried to walk a thin line between giving privileges to the native power brokers, on the one hand, and blocking the development of a native oligarchy which could abuse its power and prestige at the expense of the community, on the other. It was to prove impossible (see chapter 3).

The extractive system that Toledo designed sat heavily upon Indian communities throughout the highlands. The Aymara and, to a lesser extent, Quechua peoples who inhabited the puna between Cuzco and Tarija had to bear the brunt of the reforms. In the regions closer to the silver mines of Potosí, the four ethnic nations that formed the loose confederation of Charcas were the most deeply affected. These four nations—the Charcas, Caracaras, Chuyes, and Chichas (see figure 3)—were major sources of tribute and mitayos (they had had ten thousand soldiers and tributaries in the service of the Incas). The once powerful Aymara lords of the lakeshore region remained bountiful providers under the new order. Toledo's vision was focused on the potential wealth of the puna, traditionally the site of the most populous and powerful ethnic groups.

In the eyes of Aymara lords, Toledo must have seemed ruthless and unyielding: a man who took pleasure in stripping once powerful lords of their traditional sources of status, prestige, and wealth. In the span of a generation or two, the lords of the Charcas, Caracaras, Chuyes, and Chichas saw their former privileges and power wiped out by colonial law, and their ayllus forcefully dislocated and burdened with excessive tribute dues. Gone were the times of glory and pride, when the four nations enjoyed the respect and patronage of the Incas in return for their contributions to the imperial war machine. It is no surprise, then, that Toledo's reforms met with resistance. In 1582, the caciques of the Charcas confederation presented a petition to the king of Spain, listing a host of grievances against Toledo's policies, ranging from violations of the traditional prerogatives and privileges of the ethnic lords to the new economic hardships. "If, during the past seven years, repartimiento Indians have paid their tribute . . . it has been out of fear of Viceroy Toledo, because his ordinances all say that caciques who fail to deliver their full tribute quota shall be suspended from the cacicazgo and replaced by others." Impoverished, indebted, and bound to their creditors, their people were suffering under the new tribute schedule (*retasa*). The caciques, who had once enjoyed a status akin to that of Spanish dukes and counts and had ruled over as many as eight or ten thousand people, had now been stripped of the "yanaconas and services" that were appropriate to their positions.[45]

Furthermore, the lords complained, Toledan policies had led to sharp increases in the tribute rate, from four pesos ensayados to seven. The new assessments had not taken into proper account the absentee tributaries, who could no longer be counted on to contribute their share. Because of the reducciones, Indians had been herded into towns, many of them with insufficient pasturage and inadequate access to fertile land. The petition also touched on a new menace that threatened the Indian communities: Spanish colonists were beginning to occupy lands in the kichwa valleys to the east.

By the early 1580s, highland lords saw Spanish colonists as dangerous rivals in an emerging struggle over migrant Indians. If the communities were to pay their tribute in full, they needed to mobilize all their resources and distribute the tax burdens among all able-bodied inhabitants. Every absent tributary meant extra labor for others in the community. Fiscal adjustments were rarely made, so tax burdens also bore down harder on the remaining inhabitants. The leaders of the Charcas confederation therefore asked the crown to grant them jurisdiction over the cimarron tributaries who were in the "power of Spaniards: so that we may round them up and take them away from [their patron], no matter how wealthy."[46]

Another problem raised in the petition was royal toleration and legitimation of colonial land-tenure patterns. The caciques protested the right of the *cabildos* (town councils) and of the audiencia of Charcas to issue land grants (*mercedes*) to Spaniards covering traditional mitmaq lands in the eastern valleys. In particular, the lords formally requested that parcels of land in the Valle Bajo of Cochabamba be returned to their jurisdiction.[47] Presumably, they had been given hope by the earlier viceregal decision to return mitmaq lands in Cochabamba to the Soras and Carangas lords (see chapter 1).

The efforts of the Charcas peoples to recover lost valley lands was but one tactic in their struggle against a social and political system that seemed to grow harsher and more hostile every year. If they were to bear the burdens of tribute and the mita, they had to prevent economic "seepage" from their ayllus and villages. But as long as

45 Espinoza Soriano, ed., "*Memorial de Charcas*," 14.

46 Ibid., 15.

47 Ibid., 15 and 21.

Spanish colonists could accept migrants on their private domains and shelter them from most levies and from forced labor in the mines, the highland lords had little control over disaffected or defiant Indians. In the 1580s, a decade after Toledo initiated his reforms, the Charcas had identified a fatal flaw in them. The growing Spanish agrarian enterprises in the eastern valleys offered a loophole through which highland migrants might slip if they chose to escape the fiscal net that was tightening around their communities. The Aymara lords not only protested the loss of their mitmaq colonies; they also challenged the existence of the Spanish *chácaras* that were offering havens to their people.

Land and Labor in the Valleys

It was in the kichwa valleys where the advance of Spanish colonization most threatened the self-sufficiency and economic autonomy of village life. The highland lords might challenge the right of individual chacareros in distant valleys to shelter Andean migrants, but the valley caciques were plunged into a confrontation over maize lands, water, herds, and native laborers. Caught at the cutting edge of the Spanish agricultural frontier, the valley Indians braced themselves against the threat of European penetration into the heart of their rural society. The Spanish agrarian advance gained momentum during the 1570s, but to prescient observers, the threat already loomed large in the 1560s. Early in that decade, the oidores of La Plata were concerned about (though not opposed to) the growing number of Europeans who had ranches and small farms in Charcas. They believed that about a thousand Spaniards were earning a livelihood from commercial agriculture there.[48] In Chuquisaca, Tarija, Mizque, Cochabamba, Tomina, Paspaya, Pilaya, and other temperate valleys, European settlers found ideal ecological and topographical conditions for European seed, livestock, and agricultural implements. They also found that the commodity market in Potosí could bring them a handsome profit. Beyond the fertile, moist bottomlands of the Valle Bajo, where maize often yielded two harvests a year and wheat flourished in the drier parts of the valley, Europeans discovered the rich, extensive pastures of Cliza and the sheltered and fertile valley of Sacaba (to the east of the Valle Bajo). These valleys and their surround-

48 Barnadas, *Charcas*, 378.

ing mountains inevitably impressed European travelers, who compared the region favorably to Spanish climes and landscapes.[49]

In 1562, the audiencia of Charcas reported some one hundred European inhabitants of the Cochabamba valleys.[50] It was probably a conservative estimate, for only a few years later, about forty or fifty Spanish families controlled resources in the valleys.[51] One of these families was the Orellanas. Garcí Ruíz de Orellana entered the valleys in 1540, establishing a foothold in the Valle Bajo before leaving to fight against Gonzalo Pizarro in the battles of Warina and Sacsahuamán. Later, Ruíz de Orellana returned to Cochabamba, where he eventually purchased lands from the caciques of Sipesipe, in encomienda to Hernando Silva, of Chuquisaca. The fertile lands of Canata, an undulating plain south of the Sacaba River, where Inca herds had grazed and royal maize had flourished, thus passed into Spanish hands. Over the next generation, the Orellanas consolidated their holdings in the eastern end of the Valle Bajo. Rodrigo and Francisco de Orellana controlled the encomienda of Tiquipaya, once the personal possessions of Yupanqui and Huayna Cápac. Francisco also extended control over rich pasturelands in the Valle Bajo.[52]

The herds of cattle, goats, sheep, horses, mules, oxen, and other European livestock, small and large, must have increased greatly during the 1560s, with the influx of Spanish settlers from the south. Attacks by the Chiriguanos on Spanish settlers in Tarija forced many of them to drive their herds to safer valleys in the interior, away from the tropical frontier and the "savage" tribes.[53] Even before the Toledan reforms, Spanish colonizers negotiated, cajoled, and coerced Andean ethnic groups into surrendering control over their lands. Often hidden from the public eye and from royal scrutiny, a host of land transactions took place in the 1560s, amounting to a piecemeal, de

49 Antonio Vázquez de Espinosa, *Compendio y descripción de las Indias occidentales* (1630) (Madrid: Atlas, 1969), 410. See below, chap. 5, for a detailed description of the region in the eighteenth century.

50 Roberto Levillier, ed., *La audiencia de Charcas; Correspondencia de presidentes y oidores*, 3 vols. (Madrid: J. Pueyro, 1918-1922), 1: 72.

51 Augusto Guzmán, *Cochabamba* (Cochabamba: Amigos del Libro, 1972), 84-85.

52 Ibid., 81-83. Excerpts and fragments of early notarial records, including land transactions, tithes, grain sales, and wills, can be found in José Macedonio Urquidi, *El origen de la noble villa de Oropesa*, 2nd ed. (Cochabamba: Municipalidad de Cochabamba, 1971).

53 Barnadas, *Charcas*, 379-380.

facto, and often ostensibly peaceful territorial advance. Notarized land transactions from this period commonly offer Spanish explanations for native willingness to sell land. One such transaction, dated 1563, registered the purchase of maize land in the Cliza valley. Several Europeans paid 560 pesos to the Indians of Pojo (?) for land parcels, claiming that the Indians needed cash with which to buy cows, sheep, and even llamas. According to the Spaniards, the investment in llamas was part of the Indians' plan to transport coca from the yungas (probably to Potosí).[54] Thus, the alienation of native lands in Cliza was seen as a means by which Indians would invest in pack driving and take advantage of the rising price of coca. To European eyes, it was all part of the mercantilization of native-European relations.

As European land acquisitions increased, the Spanish presence began to pose a threat to social equilibrium in the valleys. The Spanish settlers sought royal sanction and an official disposition of physical space in the valleys. They were not content with extending their reach, haphazardly and somewhat tentatively, across the valleys. Prominent landholders wanted royal permission to establish a municipality that would give territorial jurisdiction to a cabildo and a corregidor. In August 1571, Toledo granted to Captain Gerónimo Osorio the right to found the town (*villa*) of Oropesa in the Valle Bajo. For the next three years, the town existed in name only: a territorial unit of municipal government was designated, but no new town was actually built. The small native village of Canata, near Sipesipe, became the site of local administration. It was not until 1574 that Oropesa appeared, at the eastern end of the Valle Bajo, where the central plaza of the city of Cochabamba is located today.[55] Oropesa, which soon came to be called Cochabamba, was laid out in the classic grid pattern, with its requisite Augustinian and Franciscan chapels, jail, hospital, and town hall flanking the central square. The Spanish presence in the valley now had official physical and political visibility.

The establishment of Oropesa symbolized the shifting balance of power in favor of the white colonizers. For the formal foundation of the town, the Spanish corregidor called together the caciques of El

54 "Compra de tierras por D. Luís Abasire," AHMC, Leg. 1195.

55 Guzmán, *Cochabamba*, 86-90. Confusion due to the lapse of time between the Toledan authorization for the founding of Oropesa and its actual establishment created a minor controversy over the date of its founding (1571 or 1574) when preparations were being made to celebrate its four hundredth anniversary.

Paso (under encomienda of Gerónimo Ondegardo) and Tiquipaya (in encomienda to Francisco de Orellana), as well as the caciques of Sipesipe, Tapacarí, Paria, Sacaba, and Pocona at the site. By their presence, the caciques were to acknowledge Spanish settlement and municipal authority, and they were to dispatch two hundred Indians to lay out and build the town. The Europeans, in turn, were to choose their house sites and eventually move off the land into the town. The chacareros were to be "reduced" from their scattered dwellings across the valley to the urban nucleus of Christian civilization. But the town's establishment represented more than a physical concentration of European culture and power, amidst the few material amenities in the village of adobe huts and chapels. The founding fathers of Oropesa sought royal sanction for the chácaras that every Spanish inhabitant (*vecino*) "has and possesses" in the valleys. Further, the town charter denied the right of Indians to challenge the vecinos' title to their lands, even when a deed could not be produced. The status of original vecino was to confer, ipso facto, landholding rights.[56] The act of foundation thus gave local authorities a device for rejecting Andean protests against Spanish land occupation.

Meanwhile, the establishment of the Indian communities placed the caciques of the Cochabamba valleys in a paradoxical position. On the one hand, the centralizing colonial state superseded the authority of local encomenderos and legitimated a set of rights and obligations (albeit quite asymmetrical) governing relations between the state and the village Indians. In the kichwa valleys of Cochabamba, state designation of Indian communties, accompanied by the forced resettlement of Andeans, theoretically worked in favor of the local caciques. The reducciónes hardened territorial boundaries and jurisdictions that undercut or weakened traditional links between valley mitmaq colonies and their distant highland ayllus. Royal recognition of Indian villages also bestowed protection against encroachment by outsiders.

On the other hand, the colonial authorities were not always scrupulous about protecting the Andean communities. In the same years that the caciques of Tapacarí, Sipesipe, El Paso, and Tiquipaya saw the scattered rural hamlets of their people reduced into one or two Indian towns and placed under religious and civil authorities (even while they remained in encomienda), they also witnessed what they

---

56 The "Acta de la fundación de la villa de Oropesa" appears as an appendix in Francisco de Viedma, *Descripción geográfica y estadística de la provincia de Santa Cruz de la Sierra* (Cochabamba: Amigos del Libro, 1969), 285-286.

believed to be a betrayal of their communal autonomy, when Toledo resolved the long, bitter dispute between the Sipesipes and the Carangas, Quillacas, and Soras over local mitmaq lands in favor of the highland Indians (see chapter 1). The state's intervention in this old rivalry was a concern to the valley caciques, for they feared that it would encourage other highland ayllus to press similar claims. Further, it weakened the ability of encomenderos to protect their Indian subjects from the aggression of outside claimants.

Nor did the state act forcefully against the rapid advance of Spanish land ownership in the Valle Bajo. Toledo's concessions to the founding vecinos in 1574 legitimated all previous despoliation of Indian land and blocked Andean challenges through court proceedings. Valley Indians could challenge *future* encroachments on their communal resources, but that was no defense against the aggressive chacareros who had already staked out pastures and fields throughout the three central valleys. Ironically, then, the Toledan policies aimed at preserving the Andean communities ended by tipping the balance of political forces against them.

The valley communities suffered the same "internal shocks" as their highland counterparts did during the years of royal inspection, reduction, and administrative reorganization. The resettlement created five Indian districts in the *corregimiento* (magistracy) of Cochabamba. Three of them—Sipesipe, El Paso, and Tiquipaya—were carved out of the Valle Bajo, on former Incaic lands where a variety of ethnic groups was clustered. Tapacarí, the largest district, stretched along the valley of the Tapacarí River and into the surrounding highlands in the western reaches of the province. The fifth district, Capinota, was situated in the warm valley of the Arque River and its nearby highlands.[57] Tapacarí, El Paso, and Tiquipaya were still tied to encomenderos (of the second or third generation). Only Sipesipe was clearly designated as a crown possession. Nonetheless, all the communities were the objects of forced resettlement. Tapacarí's forty-two scattered hamlets and ranches were reduced to two central villages; Sipesipe's fifty-odd settlements were concentrated into one main village.[58] That is not to say that the state severed all vertical kinship ties that cut across the ecological tiers. As

57 Capinota does not appear in the census taken in 1573. A report made in 1618, however, gives population figures for that year and for earlier years. For a detailed discussion of the five districts in the eighteenth century, see chap. 4.

58 Nicolás Sánchez-Albornoz, *The Population of Latin America* (Berkeley and Los Angeles: University of California Press, 1974), 46.

we have seen, Toledo himself contradicted his own policies by grant-ing landholding rights in Sipesipe and Tiquipaya to highland ayllus. Furthermore, the ayllus of Tapacarí clung to their mitmaq colonists, situated in tropical valleys in Ayopaya, well into the seventeenth century.[59] Kinship relations between Indians in Capinota and high-land villages in Paria survived until the late eighteenth century (see chapter 4). But these links were but vestiges of another age. The thrust of Toledo's reforms in the valleys was to bind together the disparate, fragmented cultural groups into "royal villages" (*pueblos reales*) beholden to colonial bureaucrats (and their native intermedi-aries) for subsistence rights.

A census in 1573 revealed the size and "carrying capacity" of the Indian communities (see table 2). Tribute was set at seven pesos en-sayados per tributary. Tapacarí's population was greater than that of the other pueblos reales, and its total tribute was correspondingly higher. But all the villages (with perhaps the exception of Capinota) confronted a tax schedule that commuted (i.e., converted from a tax in kind to a tax in money) the overwhelming proportion of their trib-ute. The maize each community was required to deliver had dwin-dled to a symbolic reminder of the past. Another relic was the labor prestations that tributaries owed in two of the villages. In El Paso,

Table 2. Population and Tribute of Indian Reducción Communities, 1573

Community	Total Population	Number of Tributaries[a]	Tribute[b]	Percentage Commuted
Tapacarí	6,014	1,173	7,733 p. e. 600 f. maize	94
Sipesipe	3,691	819	5,255 p. e. 600 f. maize	92
El Paso	3,298	684	4,460 p. e. 400 f. maize[c]	94
Tiquipaya	2,573	504	3,250 p. e. 350 f. maize[c]	84
Capinota[d]	—	419	2,926 p. e.	—

Sources: "Tasa de la visita general de Francisco de Toledo," AGI, Contaduría, Leg. 1786, ff. 26, 35, 37, and 39; for Capinota, AGN, Sala 13, 18.1.3, Leg. 43 (1612 revisita of Capinota). (A published version of the census of 1573 is in Cook, ed., *Tasa de la visita general*, 23-32.) [a] Married males between the ages of 18 and 50. [b] p. e. = pesos ensayados (1 p. e. = 12 reales). f. = fanegas. A fanega of maize was assigned a value of six tomines. [c] Plus labor prestations. [d] Data are for 1612.

59 AGN, Sala 13, Padrones, 18.1.3, Leg. 43, June 1, 1618. The census of the In-dian population of Tapacarí listed ninety-two colonists living in Ayopaya in 1618.

peasants were still required to cultivate six fanegas of maize and two fanegas of wheat for the encomendero. Tiquipaya Indians also owed personal service on a maize chácara belonging to their encomendero, Francisco de Orellana.

Times were changing, however. The remaining encomiendas were destined for transition from private to royal jurisdiction. Sipesipe, the second largest village in the region, had already passed into the royal domain and almost all its tribute was owed to the state, which channeled a small portion back to the community, to serve as a cushion against calamity. Even in those communities still in private encomienda, the colonial state claimed almost one-third of their tribute as royal income, earmarked to cover the expenses of administration, including a parish priest in each of the villages, the priests at Potosí who ministered to the mitayos and other migrants to the silver mines, and such civil officials as the "protector of Indians" and the village caciques.

The royal visitadores who moved through the valleys drastically altered the conditions of life for most Andeans. Eventually, the peasants would find ways of adjusting to, mitigating, or resisting the harsher terms imposed by the state. But the region's great loss of native population during the decades following the Toledan reforms is testimony to the deep disruption they caused.[60] Yet it was the mita that had perhaps the most wrenching effect on the valley peoples. As mentioned earlier, Toledo was inclined to exempt most of the valley Indians from the mita, apparently because he feared the devastating physiological effects of the high altitude and the frigid climate on the native inhabitants of the lowlands.[61] But Cochabamba was not so exempted, perhaps because it was the site of the original Incaic mit'a, after which Toledo had fashioned the mining mita. In any event, Toledo mandated that the five Indian villages in Cochabamba fulfill a quota of 409 mitayos each year. The burden was to be distributed among the villages in accordance with the size of their tributary populations.[62] In absolute terms, Tapacarí bore the heaviest burden of the villages. However, it is quite unlikely that the Cocha-

60 See chap. 3. Migration and population loss and dispersion had probably had a substantial effect on the size and ethnic composition of the region's Indian population already during the pre-Toledan decades.

61 The effects of the climate at Potosí on Andean inhabitants of temperate valleys was still a controversial issue in the late eighteenth century. See Viedma, *Descripción geográfica*, 180.

62 Ibid., app. 4.

bamba quota was met, after the first several dispatches of mitayos. In 1617, for example, only 218 mitayos were sent to the mines.[63] In the most extreme case, almost all the men subject to the mita had abandoned the village of Tiquipaya, leaving mostly widows and spinsters in the pueblo. Nearby there beckoned the growing town of Oropesa and Spanish fields and orchards—free territory lying outside the confines of the "obligated" village. Even the corregidor of Cochabamba grumbled about the impossible task of finding mitayos to fulfill the quota.[64]

Passage out of the Indian villages into the "free" Spanish territory made possible a number of alternative labor arrangements. In the Cochabamba region, the Toledan reforms indirectly left most valley territory open for Spanish colonization. The early vecinos, unable to rely upon agricultural repartimientos,[65] had to secure their field hands, herders, muleteers, domestic servants, and weavers from among itinerant and seasonal laborers or Indian retainers. It was not uncommon for local ayllu Indians to spend a season or more on a Spanish estate and then return to village life. Day laborers (*jornaleros*) and seasonal migrants, temporarily away from their ayllus, might fulfill the intensive labor requirements of harvest during July and August. But most enterprising chacareros and hacienda owners (*hacendados*) depended upon a core group of permanent laborers, dependent upon their landlords and masters for access to the means of subsistence. By force of circumstance or bitter choice, Andeans who had lost their means of subsistence, severed themselves from their kin groups, or sought security from labor drafts often succumbed to long-term, exploitative relationships of personal dependence and servitude. The forms and content of incipient class relationships in the early agricultural enterprises in Cochabamba probably varied considerably. Cultural and class lines had not yet hardened, and there was a fluid movement of Andeans through the region and between village and chácara, chácara and town. Spanish landlords, unable to depend on the state to provide a reliable flow of laborers and faced with keen competition for the services of the Andeans, developed strategies to bind workers to their enterprises. They combined guarantees of minimum subsistence and gestures of patronage with coercive

---

63 *Digesto de ordenanzas*, 3: 4-7.

64 Ibid.

65 Juan López y Velasco, *Geografía y descripción universal de las Indias* (1574) (Madrid: Atlas, 1971), 255.

practices to extract the maximum of labor from their Indian retainers. If the chacareros were to profit from the emerging long-distance grain trade to Potosí, they needed to anchor a labor force amidst the turmoil and change provoked by Toledo's reforms.[66]

In the Toledan and pre-Toledan decades, there was a significant group of Andean laborers whose primary official status derived from their informal bondage to Spanish landlords. They were considered to be, in some ways, "rural yanaconas"—agrarian counterparts to the permanent, independent workers in the mines of Potosí who apparently had ruptured their links to their native villages or ayllus (see chapter 1) and who were called by the term yanaconas, which had been inherited from Incan times and had become a generic term for a "detached" indian who lived near and worked for a Spaniard.[67] Matienzo's categories of yanaconas gave some functional content to the term, so that Spanish colonists began to discriminate among yanacona artisans, town dwellers, independent miners, and agricultural laborers.[68] But long before the colonial nomenclature captured some of the nuances of the multiple niches that Andeans had carved out for themselves at the bottom of Spanish colonial society, authorities used the term yanaconas to refer to those Indians who had separated from their native lands and kin groups, escaping from encomienda and mita obligations and assimilating themselves (in varying de-

66 Stern (*Peru's Indian Peoples*, 138-157 and 189-193) discusses the emerging "political economy of dependence" in the colony, as many Andean peoples lost the independent means of subsistence they had had by virtue of communal membership and participation and were reduced to servitude and dependence on individual colonists. My own thinking about the rise of private modes of exploitation in early colonial Alto Perú, based upon incipient class and property relations, owes much to Stern's conceptual framework of distinct, and contradictory, forms of extraction in the colonial social formation. For another important conceptual approach to private modes of exploitation, within agrarian enterprise, see Pablo Macera, "Feudalismo colonial americano: El caso de las haciendas peruanas," in his *Trabajos de historia*, 4 vols., (Lima: Instituto Nacional de Cultura, 1977), 3: 139-227. Important historical studies on early haciendas in the Andes are Robert G. Keith, *Conquest and Agrarian Change: The Emergence of the Hacienda System on the Peruvian Coast* (Cambridge: Harvard University Press, 1976); Keith Davies, *Landowners in Colonial Peru* (Austin: University of Texas Press, 1984); and Rolando Mellafe, "Frontera agraria: El caso del virreinato peruano en el siglo XVI," in Alvaro Jara, ed., *Tierras nuevas: Expansión territorial y ocupación del suelo en América (siglos xvi-xix)* (Mexico City: Colegio de Mexico, 1969), 11-42.

67 Murra, *Formaciones económicas*, 225-242.

68 Matienzo, *Gobierno del Perú*, book 1, chap. 8.

grees) into Spanish society. It was estimated in 1571 that the Peruvian kingdom had some fifty thousand yanaconas integrated into Spanish urban and rural society.[69] In 1574, Toledo said that there were about 5,500 *yanaconas de servicio* living on 364 chácaras of Spaniards and mestizos in Charcas. He noted that some had come from various repartimientos, while others had fled their villages or the mines of Potosí.[70] The regional distribution of that population was not ascertained. But where chácaras flourished, yanaconas clustered, and the valleys of Cochabamba were a prime area of *yanaconaje* in the late sixteenth and early seventeenth centuries. No detailed census of yanaconas had been taken at the time, but over the ten-year period from 1656 to 1665, the yanacona miners of Potosí contributed more tribute revenue than yanaconas in any other part of Charcas. Among the rural districts, the yanaconas of Cochabamba generated the most royal income (see table 3). Although they were a small portion of the region's tributary population, there were probably more yanaconas in Cochabamba than in other areas of Alto Perú where chacareros had settled.

Like the other yanaconas of the southern highlands, the Andean immigrants to Cochabamba had diverse origins. Some had followed the conquistadores into the valleys of Cochabamba, shortly after the decisive battle against the Charcas conforderation. Other had been

Table 3. Tribute Paid by the Yanacona Population of Alto Perú, 1656-1665

Province or Town	Total Tribute[a]	Percentage
Villa de Potosí	58,656	31.3
Porco	21,078	11.2
Cochabamba	30,408	16.2
Chayanta	2,392	1.3
Yamparaes	24,737	13.2
Chichas	19,909	10.6
Mizque	8,260	4.4
Tomina	13,338	7.1
Pilaya	8,715	4.6
Total	187,493	99.9

Source: AGI, Contaduría, Leg. 1818, Jan. 31, 1666.
Note: Discrepancy in total of percentages due to rounding.
[a] In pesos corrientes (8 reales each), converted from pesos ensayados (12 reales each).

69 Barnadas, *Charcas*, 296, n. 302.

70 Toledo to the crown, March 20, 1574, cited in Zavala, *Servicio personal*, 1: 92.

engaged as personal retainers of the early encomenderos.[71] Still others had moved into the region after 1550, as chácaras began to flourish and Andeans fled the harsh conditions of Potosí for rural work. Many contemporaries believed that the conditions of life and work were more tolerable on private rural estates than they were in the mines or even in the Indian communities.[72] But we still know little about labor relations or living conditions for yanaconas working in private commercial agriculture in the easter valleys. One scholar, Josep Barnardas, accepts Matienzo's judgment that the material conditions, physical environment, and work rhythms there were less alienating than the burdens that weighed on the yanacona miners. He believes that most yanaconas had adapted to Hispanicized ways by the late sixteenth century.[73] Thierry Saignes, on the other hand, questions contemporary assessments of yanacona alienation from their cultural roots or kin groups. Rural yanaconas, in particular, may have maintained ties to their ayllus over the course of a lifetime, or even across generations. Neither the ascribed, official status of yanacona, nor spatial separation, necessarily led to the complete severance of kin or cultural ties. Further, yanacona families may have woven new webs of reciprocal rights and obligations with each other, allowing them to spread risk and retain some of their traditional rituals, customs, and norms, even within the confines of the hacienda.[74] Until further research is done, we can only speculate about the labor arrangements and cultural lifeways among yanaconas on sixteenth-century chácaras. Projecting ahead, though,

71 "Juicio en grado de apelación ante la real audiencia de la Plata . . . entre d. Juan Durán y los caciques de Sipesipe . . ." (1584), ANB, EC no. 72; Franklin Pease, ed., "Una visita al obispado de Charcas" (1590), *Humanidades*, no. 3 (1969): 89-125, esp. 102-103.

72 Zavala, *Servicio personal*, vols. 1 and 2, passim, and Mario Góngora, *Studies in the Colonial History of Spanish America* (Cambridge: Cambridge University Press, 1975), 149-158.

73 Barnadas, *Charcas*, 293.

74 Thierry Saignes, "Ayllus, mercado, y coacción colonial: El reto de las migraciones internas en Charcas, siglo XVII," in Harris, Larson, and Tandeter, *Participación indígena*, 111-158; and Saignes, "Políticas étnicas," 13. Zulawski's work on the region of Pilaya y Paspaya in the early eighteenth century challenges the notion of yanaconas as relatively immobile, servile workers. She has found considerable labor mobility among a group of Indians registered as yanaconas in the censuses. Ann Zulawski, "Agricultural Labor and Social Change: Pilaya and Paspaya in the Eighteenth Century" (paper presented at the International Congress of Americanists, the Universidad de los Andes, Bogotá, July 1-7, 1985).

it is perhaps revealing that, among Indians and mestizos in the Cochabamba valleys in the eighteenth century, the yanaconas were stigmatized as the lowest-ranked laborers, who occupied inferior positions of servitude and subordination to a landlord and who passed their position on to their children (see chapter 5).

As long as the yanaconas were among the flotsam and jetsam of the conquest—the uprooted vagabonds of a land torn by strife and violence—they could be dismissed as "misfits" who had slipped between the cracks of encomienda and repartimiento. But as their ranks swelled and as the colonial state began to tighten control over the movement and labor of native Andeans, they could no longer be ignored. When Toledo traveled to Chuquisaca in late 1572, he was apprised of the magnitude of yanaconaje in Charcas, and he was confronted with an agressive group of chacareros who wanted royal sanction to tie the yanaconas down. Toledo felt that two concerns were at issue. First, the yanaconas were an untapped resource, as far as the state was concerned, and Toledo wanted them to be taxed. Second, since yanaconas dwelled outside state jurisdiction, on isolated rural estates, and were often witness to the corrupt behavior of their masters, they were in need of the sacraments and moral teachings of the church. Hence, the viceroy enacted, in 1574, a series of ordinances that was to govern relations between landlord and yanacona on the chácaras throughout Alto Perú.[75]

Among other provisions, the ordinances called for a priest on every rural estate, the religious instruction of Indian boys, a prohibition against intoxicating beverages among yanaconas, and the protection of Indian women from abusive behavior by unmarried landlords. The ordinances also established a set of mutual obligations between landlords and peasants. Landlords had to allocate land to each yanacona family for its subsistence needs, and they were to provide a plow and draft animals during planting season and grant the peasants time in which to cultivate their family plots. They were obligated to supply a piece of rough woolen cloth to their yanaconas each year, to care for the sick and infirm, and to grant one day of rest each week (except during planting and harvest). In return, the yanaconas were to work daily between dawn and sunset for the benefit of the landlord and at his behest.

Legally, the yanaconas were free, but in the context of colonial-

75 "Ordenanzas acerca de los indios yanaconas de la provincia de Charcas, como han de ser doctrinados y el tributo que han de pagar," in Levillier, ed., *Gobernantes del Perú*, 8: 241-256.

ism, their "freedoms" merely camouflaged the bonds that impeded their movement and crushed their will. Thus, yanaconas could not be legally sold along with rural estates, but at the same time they were declared to be perpetual tenants and were forbidden to own land. Yanaconas had rights to subsistence lands on the estate, but they could not abandon the property of their lord, nor could they sell their labor to others, except for ten days each year—enough time to earn their tribute dues. They were permitted to transport their master's grains to Potosí and to sell small surpluses of their own crops in the marketplace there, but they could not otherwise engage in commerce. Essentially, yanaconas were to be kept on the rural estates, sealed off from the market (and from corrupt European influences) and isolated from other rural laborers on nearby chácaras.[76] The intrusion of the state into the private, rural domain circumscribed landlord-peasant interaction and dictated the interaction of yanaconas with the wider world as well.

Toledo's attention to the rights and obligations of yanaconas arose out of more than his presumed moral responsibilities. In an encounter with Potosí mineowners and authorities in 1572, Toledo discovered an incipient but growing competition between the mining industry and the agrarian estates for Andean labor. As will be discussed in chapter 3, this conflict became the leitmotif of seventeenth-century politics in Alto Perú. But already under Toledo, the Potosí mineowners considered the chacareros of Chuquisaca and Cochabamba to be their economic rivals. They wanted the yanaconas returned to their ayllus and villages, where the Indians would again be subject to the mita.[77] The Spanish landholders, on the other hand, believed that such a measure would doom many chácaras to extinction. Thus, Toledo had to mediate between these rival factions and strike a balance between the dominant extractive mode of exploitation (upon which the mita rested) and the emerging, still subordinate private mode of exploitation. In geopolitical terms, the conflict pitted the western, highland mining interests against the eastern, lowland agrarian interests.

Toledo's bias was toward the mining interests. It was he who was assembling the machinery with which to force Andean communities in the highlands to subsidize the Potosí mines. But he was too wise an administrator to take a one-sided stand. Returning the yanaconas to their original communities (or transplanting them to new royal villages) would enlarge the pool of draft labor, but only at great

76 Levillier, ed., *Gobernantes del Perú*, esp. ordinance 11, 8: 251-252.

77 Barnadas, *Charcas*, 296ff.

cost to the colony. The chácaras had to survive simply because they produced much of the food sustaining the mining towns. Thus, he based his policies on the complementarity between mining and agriculture in Alto Perú. In spite of their opposition, the mineowners needed the chacareros. On the other hand, Toledo agreed that the private agrarian sector had to be kept subordinate to the export interests at Potosí. Above all, the leakage of Indians from their official communities to Spanish estates had to be halted. In the 1574 ordinances, Toledo granted legal status to all yanaconas who had lived on Spanish estates for four years or longer. They could not be evicted, nor could they abandon their landlords. More recent migrants were given the choice of staying or returning to their homelands. But the ordinances also forbade landlords to recruit new yanaconas to their farms and ranches. Thus, the size of the native labor force in commercial agriculture in Alto Perú was fixed (except for changes that might take place through natural growth). Chacareros would have to rely on sources of rural labor that were not subject to the mita—African slaves and contract or day workers.[78]

In the valleys and serranías of Cochabamba, the ordinances limiting yanaconaje probably had little impact on the quest for permanent, servile labor on Spanish lands. The chacareros there continued to press Indian migrants into peonage by whatever means available. In these efforts, they were opposed not by the mining aristocracy but by the caciques of Cochabamba's five pueblos reales. The chacareros' aggressive pursuit of Andean laborers threatened the caciques' already precarious hold over their peasantries. For beyond the maize fields lay Spanish territory and the seeming "freedom" from state and community obligations. Neither distance, nor mountain, nor climate was there to separate the villages from the chácaras, where an alternative way of life awaited. Thus, a bitter struggle erupted between chacareros and caciques over the legitimacy of yanaconas on private lands.

In 1598, the caciques of the five pueblos reales petitioned the audiencia of La Plata for an inspection of the province.[79] Their aim was to ferret out the chacareros who had "usurped" Indians from their

---

78 Levillier, ed., *Gobernantes del Perú*, 8: 247-249 and 253-254. In 1600, the audiencia of La Plata sought to legalize the status of yanacona only for those Andeans who had lived on Spanish estates for a minimum of ten years as opposed to the previously stipulated four-year period. Had this become policy, many fewer rural yanaconas would have enjoyed legal protection. Levillier, ed., *Audiencia de Charcas*, 3: 411-447, esp. 418-427.

79 "Los indios de Cochabamba sobre el pago de jornales," ANB, EC no. 15 (1598).

villages. The caciques said that, in times past, many Indians would spend a season on Spanish lands, often tending the herds of Spanish landlords. Presumably, such labor was one means by which communities earned money to pay their tribute. But many such Indians did not return to their villages, and their Spanish employers meanwhile refused to remit the accumulated wages to cover their tribute dues. To the caciques, the usurped shepherds were "lost" tributaries, whose dues then had to be covered by the rest of the village, and they demanded that a head count of them be taken. A census was commissioned by the oidores, and it was revealing. Sipesipe had lost 30 tributaries from Anansaya and 51 from Urinsaya to nearby Spanish estates. There were 22 tributaries missing from El Paso and about 29 from Tiquipaya. Many of these Indians had been absent for fifteen or more years. The caciques calculated that the missing tributaries had accumulated debts amounting to the worth of a "standard" ten-mule train loaded with maize and silver coin (*peara de mulas*). Such debts were an obstacle to those Indians who wished to reintegrate themselves into village life. Some of the usurped peasants may originally have sought protection from tribute burdens. Against state prohibitions and the objections of their own caciques, they had lived on Spanish lands until their status of jornalero or *indio usurpado* had been forgotten and they were indistinguishable from yanaconas. Their new status was apparently even becoming hereditary. The landowner Diego Pérez de Orellana had usurped an Indian herder, identified as Rodrigo in the special census. Rodrigo, a member of the Guaillanco ayllu of Sipesipe, had died on the chácara, leaving his children to become shepherds in his place and to serve the master in his house. Without the caciques' intervention, the children would have inherited, de facto, the servile status of yanacona.[80]

The audiencia's position was sympathetic to the caciques' pleas. It ordered the royal inspector to calculate the sum of Spanish debts owed to the five villages and to reduce all the usurped Indians they could identify to those communities. How effectively these orders were implemented is a matter of speculation. But as we shall see in chapter 3, such meliorating gestures did not stem the tide in any case. Ironically, Toledo's reforms, which were supposed to stabilize

---

80 Ibid. (Sipesipe census). The loss of several dozen tributaries to haciendas was not numerically significant, in terms of the percentage of the pueblos' tributary populations registered in the Toledan census of 1573 (see table 2). Rather, the point is that this struggle over usurped Indians from El Paso, Tiquipaya, and Sipesipe presaged a deepening conflict between village and hacienda over land and labor in the Valle Bajo.

the distribution of the Andean population between the royal villages and the private sector, threw open the floodgates of Andean migration in the seventeenth century.

In the struggle over land and labor in the eastern valleys, the chacareros had seized the advantage over the caciques by the end of the sixteenth century. Thereafter, the caciques were ever more on the defensive, engaged in a struggle for survival against the forces of attrition that gnawed away at the edges of communal life. Even under the encomienda, the caciques of the maize valleys had found themselves under siege by powerful and aggressive Aymara lords seeking to recover mitmaq lands. In that interethnic struggle, many of the valley chiefs fell back on their precarious alliances with local encomenderos to defend their territorial jurisdiction over lowland resources. They did not command the power, respect, or solidarity of the ethnically fragmented groups under their wing that they needed to confront the highland hereditary chiefs. Nor, on the other hand, could they count upon the centralizing colonial state to buttress their authority and protect their communities from outside incursions. Toledo was ambivalent toward the Indian communities of Cochabamba, and the caciques were increasingly vulnerable to a new threat—the private agrarian enterprise. While they were mounting their defenses against the chacareros, the Toledan state was erecting the apparatus of extraction. The valley dwellers would not be exempt from forced mine work at Potosí, after all.

Potosí cast yet broader shadows across the valley landscape. In the 1580s and 1590s, the mercantile power of the mining town stimulated commercial agriculture in the valleys and turned small-scale chacareros into wholesale cereal exporters. The short-term success of Toledo's mining reforms and the ensuing "silver rush" turned Potosí into a legendary boom town of some 100,000 people around the turn of the century. The dizzying pace of production fanned the fires of inflation, with rapid price increases even for the staples of life.[81] The city suffered from a chronic shortage of maize and wheat, and prices fluctuated wildly from year to year.[82] These conditions created

81 Levillier, ed., *Audiencia de Charcas*, 2:332, and Assadourian, "Producción de la mercancía dinero," 282ff.

82 The cabildo of Potosí was concerned about stabilizing commodity prices of imports, particularly food crops, and its records during the 1580s and 1590s are full of references to price fluctuations and the need for stricter regulation: ANB, Biblioteca Nacional de Bolivia, "Libros de acuerdos del cabildo de Potosí," vols. 5–8. See esp. the discussions about food shortages and price increases during the drought years of 1590 and 1591, when the price of maize rose by more than 50

a climate for mercantile and speculative investment in overland trade. Even such bulky products as wheat and maize could be transported profitably. Potosí drew cereal in abundant quantities and from distant regions across the broken landscape. In 1603, pack trains brought in sacks of wheat flour whose estimated worth surpassed one million pesos. Another one million pesos worth of maize flour entered the city that year (destined, no doubt, for fermentation into chicha).[83] Potosí's greatest commercial power rested not with exotic luxury goods from Europe, but with its capacity to attract the staples of life, hauled on the backs of men and beasts, from vertical niches scattered across a vast mountainous interior.[84] Under other circumstances, European and Andean grains could not have burst out of the circuits of a regional market network.

In this situation, the early commercial enterprises in Potosí rapidly turned into trading partnerships and speculative ventures and led to annual treks to the mines, where huge quantities of wheat and maize fetched prices that were often four times higher than local ones.[85] Cochabamba was emerging as one of the principal sources of grain for the mining town. In 1605, Bishop Reginaldo de Lizárraga reported that the valleys produced enough grain to feed Potosí and several minor mining towns besides. Some thirty years later, Váz-

percent, and that of wheat by more than 33 percent, over "normal" price ranges: ibid., vol. 6 (1591-1593), f. 70v. On the mercantilist role of the cabildo, see John Preston Moore, *The Cabildo in Peru under the Hapsburgs: A Study in the Origins and Powers of the Town Council in the Viceroyalty of Peru, 1530-1700* (Durham, N.C.: Duke University Press, 1954), 160-175, and Frederick B. Pike, "Aspects of Cabildo Economic Regulation in Spanish America under the Hapsburgs," *Inter-American Economic Affairs* 13 (1960): 67-86.

83 "Descripción de la villa y minas," 380.

84 Assadourian, "Producción de la mercancía dinero," and his "Integración y desintegración regional en el espacio colonial: Un enfoque histórico," in Assadourian, *Sistema de la economía colonial*, 109-134 (see also related articles in that book); Gwendoline Ballantine Cobb, "Supply and Transportation for the Potosí Mines, 1545-1640," *Hispanic American Historical Review* 29 (1949): 25-45; and Brooke Larson, "Merchants and Economic Activity in Sixteenth-Century Potosí" (Master's thesis, Columbia University, 1972).

85 ANB, Biblioteca Nacional de Bolivia, "Libros de acuerdos del cabildo de Potosí," vol. 5 (1585-1590), f. 309v. In the late sixteenth and early seventeenth centuries, various schemes were advanced in the cabildo to undermine the power of middlemen and grain speculators, whose activities even further inflated the prices of foodstuffs at Potosí: BNB, AP, Tomo 5 (1585-1590), f. 313; Tomo 6 (1591-1593), f. 44; Tomo 8 (1596-1599), ff. 5-12.

quez de Espinosa was equally impressed.[86] Perhaps they exaggerated, but it is worth noting that the archbishopric of La Plata counted on the Cochabamba province for its greatest source of tithe revenue around the beginning of the seventeenth century (see table A-1). It had become a major cereal bowl of Alto Perú.

During the process, the chacareros established their hegemony in the regional economy. By 1630, a landed aristocracy was in place. But it was neither autarkic nor immune to changes in the wider political economy of colonialism. Having triumphed over the contentious caciques in the region, Cochabamba's landlords would once more confront the mining elite, which resented their seeming control of Andean rural laborers.

---

86 Reginaldo de Lizárraga, *Descripción breve de toda la tierra del Perú, Tucumán, Río de la Plata, y Chile* (1609) (Madrid: Atlas, 1968), 74-75, and Vázquez de Espinosa, *Compendio y descripción*, 410.

CHAPTER THREE

Declining State Power and the Struggle over Labor

On Monday mornings, the mitayos gathered at the base of Huayna Potosí (the hill for which the town was named) to receive work assignments for the week; and on one of those Mondays early in 1617, the recently arrived corregidor of Potosí inspected the assemblage. Armed with official lists of the sixteen newly formed "companies" of mitayos (each usually consisting of the members of a single ethnic or community group), the corregidor checked over the contingents to see whether the required one-third of the companies had reported for mine work. The corregidor's inventory confirmed the alarming report that had been issued five years earlier by Viceroy Juan de Mendoza y Luna: the mita was shrinking. From a corpus of 13,500 mitayos in Toledo's day, the registries now showed only 10,460. Still worse, the corregidor discovered that only about half the men who were subject to the mita had come to Potosí at all. The remaining mitayos now appeared only on paper, as *indios de plata*—i.e., those who had commuted their service by monetary payments (*rezagos*).[1] These payments were made to the owners of mills and mines who were entitled to allotments of mitayos, and they were supposed to cover the expenses of hiring free wageworkers. But there was much contemporary dispute over this practice.[2] The concern continued as the magnitude of commutation grew in

1 "De la mita de Potosí y reducciones del reino," cited and discussed in Thierry Saignes, "Notes on the Regional Contribution to the Mita in Potosí in the Early Seventeenth Century," *Bulletin of Latin American Research* 4 (1985): 65-76. The document is also discussed in Zavala, *Servicio personal*, 2: 67-70. Its author was probably Rafael Ortiz de Sotomayor, the corregidor of Potosí in the second decade of the seventeenth century.

2 Jeffrey A. Cole, "An Abolitionism Born of Frustration: The Conde de Lemos and the Potosí Mita, 1667-1673," *Hispanic American Historical Review* 63 (1983): 313-314; and Zavala, *Servicio personal*, 2: 118-119, 143-147, 150, and 175.

later years, reaching annual levels of as much as 600,000 pesos in the 1660s.[3]

Reports issued during the second decade of the seventeenth century revealed how extensively Andean peoples engaged in mercantile activities of all kinds in order to purchase exemption from the dreaded mita. Particularly in the southern half of the "obligated provinces," numerous indios de plata commercialized charcoal, lumber, ceramics, and food crops to accumulate the necessary cash. Others bought their way out by working temporarily for wages in mining enterprises at Potosí and elsewhere, where they had somewhat more control over the conditions and terms of exchange.[4]

However, commercial activities were not the only method used by Andean peoples to avoid the mita. Many of them simply abandoned their official villages and dispersed among smaller hamlets in the region.[5] In 1610, for example, a company of Jesuits called attention to a group of Carangas communities on the shores of Lake Poopó that had become mere shells of the towns they once were.[6] The depopulation of these villages, as of many others, was the result both of the spread of European diseases and the flight of the villages' inhabitants. This turn of events signaled the deterioration of the institution of forced mine labor itself and the declining ability of the state and its ethnic collaborators to mobilize mitayos. The Toledan scheme to rationalize extraction, even while preserving communal access to resources, had set migratory streams in motion all across the Peruvian landscape.

Effects of Andean Flight

Flight and migration were more radical strategies of resistance than market participation. Although the latter entailed European means,

3 Manuel A. Fuentes, ed., *Memorias de los virreyes que han gobernado el Perú durante el tiempo del colonaje español,* 4 vols. (Lima: Felipe Bailly, 1859), 3: 175; Cole, "Abolitionism," 310-311; and Nicolás Sánchez-Albornoz, *Indios y tributos en el Alto Perú* (Lima: Instituto de Estudios Peruanos, 1978), 71.

4 Saignes, "Ayllus." Sánchez-Albornoz (*Indios y tributos,* 108) notes the irony of the fact that so many Indians migrated to Potosí to work in the mines as mingas, in order to earn enough money to buy their exemption from the mita.

5 Nicolás Sánchez-Albornoz, "Mita, migración, y pueblos: Variaciones en el espacio y en el tiempo—Alto Perú, 1573-1692," *Historia boliviana* no. 3 (1983): 40.

6 "Sobre la mita de Potosí y reducción del reino: Los padres de la Compañía del Colegio de Potosí," March 31, 1610, in Vargas Ugarte, ed., *Pareceres jurídicos,* 116-131; also cited and summarized in Zavala, *Servicio personal,* 2: 45-48.

the end result was not necessarily adverse to indigenous norms. After all, the peasant family that engaged in long-distance trade and paid its commutation fees was essentially buying back its right to continue to participate in the labor and ceremonial life of its kin group and community. It represented one less family that the silver mines would claim. But the residents who fled were not only abandoning their ancient lands and huacas, relinquishing their kinship ties, and forsaking their complex of rights and responsibilities to the group; they were also throwing the burden of their mita turn onto the rest of the community. It was the entire community, and ultimately the cacique, which carried responsibility for the mita. Cash payments might make up for shortfalls for a season or two, but an increase in the rezagos also meant greater pressures on caciques and kin groups to find the money, or else to recover their human resources. Thus, in the wake of the Andean "economic refugees" there followed a dogged group of caciques, hilacatas, collectors (*cobradores*), and sometimes Spanish judges. They pursued the migrants across provincial boundaries, into distant lands, cities, and mining camps, in hopes of redeeming the debts owed to the community and the state. Even in the late seventeenth century, caciques were still tracking down errant kinsmen to demand their outstanding dues.[7] But they often ran up against the resistance of host Indian communities, local corregidores, or hacendados willing to shield their workers from the claims arising out of previous affiliations.

The flight of Andeans, however, did not always lead to alienation from their ayllus. The recent work of Saignes cautions us against oversimplified views of the migrants who appeared on tribute registries as "foreigners" (*forasteros*), "tenants" (*agregados*), or yanaconas.[8] Many forasteros—migrants to Indian communities or Spanish estates, mining towns, or cities who had neither rights to land nor obligations to the colonial state—maintained the kinship links and the rights and responsibilities they had had in the villages from which they had come. They could reaffirm their relationship and loyalty to their distant kin group by paying tribute dues or in symbolic ways that were not recorded and so are not easily traced today. Indeed, the very question of ethnic identity was an elusive one that defied the colonial schemes of categorization. Astute colonial au-

7 Ibid., 37, and Sánchez-Albornoz, *Indios y tributos*, 92ff.

8 Saignes, "Ayllus" "Políticas étnicas," and "De la filiation à la résidence." See also the recent work of Ann Zulawski, "Labor and Migration in Seventeenth-Century Alto Perú" (Ph.D. diss., Columbia University, 1985).

thorities like Polo de Ondegardo had distinguished between llactas runas—temporary migrants, who retained strong links to their original ayllu (see chapter 1)—on the one hand, and forasteros or *yanaconas del rey*—"rootless Indians," who had ruptured all ties to their ethnic group—on the other.[9] But by the middle of the seventeenth century, such nuances were a fiscal nuisance. Authorities wanted to be able to classify every Andean in a clear-cut category for purposes of more orderly taxation.[10] The migrants themselves by then had less ability to maintain ethnic associations over politically divided distances. Nevertheless, some forasteros still hoped to return home and reintegrate themselves into their kin groups. Illustrative is the case of Diego Paredes, a forastero in the village of Tiquipaya, whose grandfather had come from the town of Arapa, in the province of Azangaro, in the late sixteenth century. In the 1650s, Paredes found himself designated a forastero and working on a chácara "as if he were a yanacona." Through the royal protector of Indians, Paredes petitioned for the right to return to his original village "to pay tax and serve the mita," and his petition was granted in January 1658.[11] Forastero in the fiscal records, yanacona in his host community, Paredes managed, in effect, to establish a "subjective status" as a llacta runa.

The very fact that Diego Paredes had to petition for permission to leave his adopted community suggests that migratory and settlement patterns were less fluid than before. For if once it was difficult for migrants to break social and ideological ties to their original community, it was now increasingly hard to remain socially isolated in the new one. A host of new obligations and subsistence needs bound the migrants to their host communities. Departure remained an option for forasteros and yanaconas, but there were obstacles, especially as the native population continued to decline and competition for labor sharpened in the seventeenth century. Furthermore, the fiscal system hardened, making forasteros increasingly liable for tribute, at least in theory. If they were to escape paying double taxes, the migrants had to sever ties to their original ayllus and forsake their rights to communal resources. The Toledan system of colonial ex-

9 Polo de Ondegardo, "Relación de los fundamentos," 158, cited and discussed in Nicolás Sánchez-Albornoz, "Migracion rural en los Andes: Sipesipe (Cochabamba), 1645," *Revista de historia económica* 1 (1983): 31.

10 Sánchez-Albornoz, "Mita," and Sánchez-Albornoz, *Indios y tributos*, chap. 2.

11 "Petición del Diego Paredes, indio de Tiquipaya, 1594-1659," AHMC, Leg. 1046 (uncatalogued and erroneously dated 1804).

ploitation militated against the flight of Andean peasants, but once Indians had broken out of the cultural orbit of their ayllus, it was in the interest of the state to reroot them in their host communities or on haciendas, in order to register them as forasteros (and potential tributaries).

A detailed study of one pueblo real in Cochabamba affords a glimpse of the impact of Andean migrants. Sánchez-Albornoz has analyzed a census taken in 1645 of Sipesipe, which was situated at the western edge of the Valle Bajo, where the Incas' royal herds once grazed.[12] In the preceding fifty or sixty years, Sipesipe's population of tributaries—i.e., the total number of adult males—had shrunk from 815 to 160. The magnitude of its population loss was even greater if the numbers of mitayos and *ausentes* (those who had fled the community temporarily or permanently) are considered. Most of the mitayos came from two ayllus of Anansaya, and thus their loss was borne unevenly within the community. So, too, most of the 33 ausentes came from a small sector of the community: the plateros (originally from Ica on the Pacific coast), the ayllu Guaillanco of Anansaya, and the moiety Urinsaya.[13] On the other hand, like many other Andean villages in the fertile maize valleys of the kichwa zone, Sipesipe had absorbed a substantial migrant population, which mitigated the effects of its population loss. Sipesipe had 145 forasteros, a number not much smaller than that of its *originarios* (native tributaries). The total population of Sipesipe, including women and children, was 648 originarios and 551 forasteros. Birthrates were so low, however, that neither group physically reproduced itself. The stabilization of Sipesipe's population thus depended upon a steady in-migration of Andeans who chose to stay and assimilate themselves. The 1645 census showed that the forasteros had come from villages scattered across the Collao, to the west and north of Lake Titicaca; from the provinces of Sicasica, Pacajes, Omasuyos, and others near La Paz; and from southern Charcas. Most of them, however, had come from the nearby town of Toledo, in the province of Paria, which still had mitmaq clusters in certain localities in Cochabamba (including Capinota).[14]

Some of the migrants to Sipesipe may have maintained their ties of kinship to their native villages, but most seemed to be in the proc-

12 Sánchez-Albornoz, "Migración rural."

13 Ibid., 21.

14 Ibid., 19, 23, 25-27.

ess of assimilation. One indication is the extent to which they inter-married. At least 41 percent of the forastero population whose origi-nal communities were identified had married exogenously. Many of the men from the lake region had married women from villages in the Collao and apparently had migrated to the Cochabamba valley thereafter. But many other marriages coupled people from different regions; in almost one-third of the cases, they united forasteros with originarios of Sipesipe.[15] These marriage patterns intensified the eth-nic amalgamation that had been going on since the creation of en-comiendas from the vestiges of mitmaq and Incaic settlements. The continuing inflow of first-generation forasteros may have regener-ated ethnic strains within the village, but the frequency of ethnic intermarriage suggests that most migrants adjusted to the new cir-cumstances and attached themselves to their adopted village. Never-theless, the permanent forastero population composed a stratum of peasants subordinate to the originarios. The migrants, composing al-most half of Sipesipe's population in 1645, not only diluted the com-munity's original ethnic mix but also created a cleavage in village society which deepened in the eighteenth century (see chapter 4).

Sipesipe was not unusual in the proportion of forasteros in its pop-ulation. In the middle of the seventeenth century, contemporary au-thorities were beginning to suspect that migration was destroying the system that Toledo had established almost a century earlier. In-deed, a group of azogueros at Potosí issued a dire prediction that the silver industry would collapse if the mita were not revitalized.[16] To do so would mean that the colonial authorities would have to curb migration and population dispersion. In the early 1680s, the Duque de la Palata, the then viceroy of Peru, was ordered to undertake the first comprehensive census of Andean communities since the Tole-dan inspections, in preparation for a new labor repartimiento.[17] Fur-thermore, the ambitious viceroy launched a project to enumerate the Indian population in all eighty-three Peruvian corregimientos, not

15 Ibid., 28ff.

16 Jeffrey Cole, "Viceregal Persistence versus Indian Mobility: The Impact of the Duque de la Palata's Reform Program on Alto Perú, 1681-1692," *Latin American Research Review* 19 (1984): 40.

17 On Palata, see Fuentes, *Memorias de los virreyes*, 2: 244-264; Rubén Vargas Ugarte, *Historia del Perú*, 5 vols. (Lima: Librería Stadium–Imprenta López, 1956), 2: 389-394; Sánchez-Albornoz, *Indios y tributos*, chap. 3; Margaret Cra-han, "The Administration of Don Melchor de Rocafull, Duque de la Palata, Viceroy of Peru, 1681-1689," *Américas* 27 (1971): 389-412.

simply in the southern *provincias obligadas,* and at the same time to have the corregidores (in collaboration with local priests and caciques) register the forasteros living outside their native domain. Palata's intentions were, among other things, to redistribute the burden of tribute and mita among the originario and forastero population, close the loopholes in the system, and extend the mita to formerly exempt corregimientos.[18]

The census project ran into formidable obstacles, and it took five years to complete. Ironically, it precipitated a new wave of migration among Andeans fearful of being subjected to tribute and the mita. The viceroy himself died before any of his reforms could be implemented. But the census did reveal the magnitude of population decline and dispersion that had taken place. It found, for example, that the Indian population had declined by almost 50 percent since 1573.[19] Ten corregimientos in central and southern Alto Perú had lost 57 percent of their originario population between 1573 and 1683; in Cochabamba, the originario population had declined by more than 75 percent. The overall number of tributaries had fallen from 34,621 to 14,858 during that period.[20] However, as in Sipesipe, the decline of originarios in Alto Perú was offset by the rise in the number of Andeans who had resettled in "foreign" places. The census counted 12,138 of these forasteros: adult male Indians and their families living apart from their kin units in the central and southern provinces of Alto Perú—45 percent of all tributaries.

The magnitude of *forasteraje* in the southern Andes was confirmed by another census in 1754. By then, forasteros composed more than half the tributary population in both the northern bishopric of La Paz and the southern bishopric of Chuquisaca (see table 4).[21] Within each area, the distribution of forasteros was extremely

18 Cole, "Viceregal Persistence," 41-42 and 44; Sánchez-Albornoz, "Mita." Palata initiated a number of other reforms, including a reduction in the ratio of work weeks to rest weeks for mitayos from 1:3 to 1:1 and a standardization of wages.

19 Cole, "Viceregal Persistence," 43, and Sánchez-Albornoz, *Indios y tributos,* 30.

20 Sánchez-Albornoz, *Indios y tributos,* 29-30.

21 This census was partially compiled from earlier estimates and is somewhat unreliable. See Sánchez-Albornoz, *Indios y tributos,* 52; Karen Spalding, "The Colonial Indian," *Latin American Research Review* 7 (1972): 71, n. 47; and Jürgen Golte, *Repartos y rebeliones: Túpac Amarú y la contradicciones del sistema colonial* (Lima: Instituto de Estudios Andinos, 1980), 47.

Table 4. Originario and Forastero Populations, by Bishopric, 1754

Bishopric	Number of:		Total	Percentage of Forasteros
	Originarios	*Forasteros*		
Chuquisaca	11,589	15,359	26,948	57
Mizque	3,182	506	3,688	14
La Paz	10,550	13,644	24,194	56
Cuzco	20,711	12,053	32,764	37
Arequipa	3,083	667	3,750	18
Huamanga	8,587	1,933	10,520	18
Lima	17,720	5,371	23,091	23
Trujillo	12,788	5,387	18,175	30
Total	88,210	54,920	143,130	38

Source: Sánchez-Albornoz, *Indios y tributos*, 52.

uneven (see figure 5). On the puna, forasteros were clustered in the mining towns, particularly Potosí and Oruro. Even after a prolonged period of economic decline, these towns were still attracting migrants, vagabonds, seasonal workers (who often stayed on), and itinerant traders. Beyond them lay bleak lands where few forasteros settled. The villages scattered across the high steppes of Porco counted as migrants a little more than one-third of their Andean population; Chayanta's forasteros composed only 29 percent of the Indian population; and in Carangas, they constituted only 15 percent.[22] Highland forasteros were predominantly urban dwellers.

In the eastern kichwa tiers, rural forasteros were found in large numbers in Indian villages and on Spanish agricultural estates. They composed more than half the tributary population in the well-populated valleys and slopes along the eastern frontier, from the province of Larecaja in the north to Tarija and Chichas in the south. Some of these provinces were originally outside the boundaries of the provincias obligadas; from Toledan times, they had attracted economic refugees from the highlands. Other valleys, such as those in Chulumani and Cochabamba, drew migrants to commercial agrarian enterprises which offered shelter from tax burdens, at least until Viceroy Palata and his successors instituted "reforms." Migrants also gravi-

22 Golte, *Repartos y rebeliones*, 55. For a discussion of the regional distribution of forasteros throughout Peru, see ibid., 58 and 60. For an analysis of the relationship between the spatial distribution of forasteros and the patterns of social protest in 1780-1781, see Oscar Cornblit, "Society and Mass Rebellion in Eighteenth-Century Peru and Bolivia," in R. Carr, ed., *St. Antony's Papers*, no. 22 (Oxford: Oxford University Press, 1970), 9-44.

Figure 5 Forastero Concentrations in Alto Perú, 1754
Source: Adapted from Golte, *Repartos y rebeliones*, map 5.
Note: Shaded provinces are those in which 80 percent or more of the tributary population was classified as forastero.

tated toward the villages that suffered sharp demographic declines. The intensive maize agriculture in such valley communities as Sipesipe and Tiquipaya required (and could support) substantial numbers of settlers to replace their originarios who had fled and, even more so, the victims of the epidemics in the second and third decades of the eighteenth century.

Of all the eastern provinces of Alto Perú, Cochabamba developed the most extreme imbalance between native and forastero populations. Even by 1683, more than nine out of ten married male Indians were listed as forasteros (table 5). The competition for Indian labor between the Indian villages and the haciendas in the Toledan era had been resolved in favor of the latter: more than two-thirds of the province's tributaries were living in Spanish towns or haciendas. Furthermore, within the Indian villages, forasteros outnumbered native in-

Table 5. Residence and Classification of Tributary Population of Cochabamba, 1683 and 1786

Residence and Classification	1683		1786	
	Number	*Percentage*	*Number*	*Percentage*
Total tributary population	6,735	100	10,698	100
Spanish towns and haciendas	4,556	68	7,828	73
Pueblos reales	2,179	32	2,870	27
Originarios	411	6	433	4
Forasteros	1,768	26	2,437	23
All forasteros[a]	6,324	94	10,265	96

Sources: AGN, Sala 13, Padrones, 18.1.1, Leg. 41; 18.1.3, Leg. 43; 18.2.1, Leg. 46; 18.2.2, Leg. 47; and 18.2.3, Leg. 48.
[a] Forasteros in pueblos reales + all tributaries in towns and haciendas.

habitants by approximately four to one. One hundred years late, another census found still greater demographic imbalances in the region. Nearly three-quarters of the tributary population of the region resided in the Spanish towns and haciendas; and in the Indian villages, originarios were outnumbered by forasteros by almost six to one, and they constituted a mere 4 percent of the total tributary population.

These statistics demonstrate that, as colonial authorities had suspected, Cochabamba had become the preeminent province of forasteraje. Its Indian demographic profile was the result of the breakdown of the Toledan model of indirect rule. To a greater extent than in other provinces, rural migrants had been removed from the orbit of their communities. The pattern of ethnic identification in the region was decaying. Some valley Indians still maintained symbolic and material links to their original highland ayllus, but to an increasing degree they were differentiated according to their economic and social position in the local native hierarchy and by their fiscal status, rather than by their ancestral ethnic roots. Outside the peasant villages, sociocultural boundaries were even more blurred. As the forasteros assimilated themselves into the lower ranks of Spanish society, the sociocultural distance between "indio forastero" and "mestizo" (or "cholo") was diminished, and as reforms in the tribute and mita systems advanced, those boundaries were increasingly crossed. In the southern Andean world, then, Cochabamba was the most troublesome province for colonial authorities who were trying to resurrect the extractive institutions that had crumbled under the impact of Andean flight and resistance.

What Was To Be Done?

Almost from the outset, colonial authorities had tried to chart the crosscurrents of Andean migration. Particularly after the Toledan reforms impelled more of the native peoples to abandon their ayllus and communities, the motivations, destinations, and routes of Andean migrants occupied the thoughts and reports of Spanish officials. Viceroy Montesclaros, who in 1615 was the first to assess the magnitude of mita commutation and absenteeism, speculated about the movements of the cimarrones. He feared that many Indians vanished into the uncharted lands stretching into the jungle, where they were swallowed up by nature. Other migrants, he believed, melted into Spanish towns and mining camps, seeking work that conferred exemption from tribute and mita service. But the viceroy doubted that most Andeans, even those laboring in the mines, assimilated themselves successfully into the urban sector. Sooner or later, the migrants sought protection in rural settings: on the "estancias [ranches] and haciendas of Spaniards and rich Indians of other districts . . . where they eventually [acquire] the status of yanacona and free themselves of the mita." He estimated that, already in his day, about 25,000 yanaconas inhabited rural properties throughout Alto Perú.[23]

Later in the century, the Duque de la Palata, as part of his effort to revitalize the mita, identified three main destinations of the migrating Indians: Spanish cities and towns, the northern "free provinces" and eastern fringe areas outside the orbit of the mita, and Spanish and creole haciendas. He did not think that many Indians headed for Andean villages, except perhaps in the free provinces. Instead, they seemed to move into Spanish colonial society or into distant lands that had traditionally beckoned southern Andeans struggling to escape mita service and pursuing caciques. Palata focused especially on the Spanish hacendados who offered shelter to Indians from tribute and the mita. The hacendados were not the only ones to blame for the exodus of highland Andeans; like his contemporaries, Palata believed that the root of the forastero problem grew deep in the subsoil of village life, where Indians were abused by caciques, corregidores, and priests alike. But the problem of population dispersion, in the viceroy's view, was compounded by the greediness of hacendados who used property ownership to entice Indians into submission.

---

23 Zavala, *Servicio personal*, 2: 52, summarizing "Relación que el Marqués de Montesclaros, virrey del Perú, deja a su sucesor . . ."

Sometimes through false promises and coercive means, the hacendados captured a docile labor force and protected it behind barriers that even royal authority could not easily penetrate.[24]

Throughout the seventeenth century, the apologists for and beneficiaries of compulsory Andean labor at Potosí were haunted by the specter of powerful landlords draining highland Indian communities of potential mitayos. Times had changed since the halcyon days of Potosí's second silver boom, when the chacareros of Cochabamba had forged commercial alliances with merchants and mineowners at Potosí and all groups had capitalized on the export boom. As Andean migration and population decline grew worse over the course of the seventeenth century, particularly in its later decades, the azogueros of Potosí and the landlords of the eastern valleys increasingly looked upon each other as competitors for Indian labor. Their opposition intensified in the 1680s, as Palata moved to impose tribute on the forasteros. Hacendados throughout Alto Perú gave voice to their protests and discontent about the viceroy's reforms.[25]

A century had passed since Toledo had launched his agrarian policy in an effort to mediate the rivalry between Potosí's mineowners and the landlords of the eastern kichwa zone. But neither Toledo nor the Council of the Indies (with its ordinances of 1609) could prevent the redistribution of Indians between Indian communities and private agrarian estates. Nor were they able to establish parameters within which private enterprise might stabilize and thereby maintain the equilibrium achieved by the Toledan state between private and extractive modes of exploitation (see chapter 2). Nor was state power of any use in coping with high mortality rates among the subject population. The only viable political strategy, then, was to censure the perpetrators of abuse within the Indian community and to

---

24 Fuentes, *Memorias de los virreyes*, 2: 244ff.; Sánchez-Albornoz, *Indios y tributos*, 88-89; and Zavala, *Servicio personal*, 2: 186-187. Cf. the similar observations by a Lima oidor in 1644: "Some Indians . . . have fled to provinces so distant that they are never heard from again. They . . . are hidden and detained on the chácaras, ranches, [and] obrajes [textile workshops] . . . of owners, who are so powerful that neither corregidores nor mita captains can wrench [them] free" (quoted in Sánchez-Albornoz, *Indios y tributos*, 112, n. 37; my translation). On Andean migration to Spanish haciendas in the Cuzco region, see Magnus Mörner, *Perfil de la sociedad rural del Cuzco a fines de la colonia* (Lina: Universidad del Pacífico, 1978), 46-55. For a fascinating comparison with migration patterns and consequences among the Mayans, see Nancy Farriss, *Mayan Society under Colonial Rule* (Princeton: Princeton University Press, 1984), chap. 7.

25 Cole, "Viceregal Persistence," 48.

somehow contain the power of the labor-hungry hacendados. But how?

The most urgent issue in the seventeenth century was the deterioration of the mita. Long before Palata mounted his ambitious projects, Potosí's mining elite, audiencia magistrates, authorities in Spain and Peru, and clerics engaged in countless debates over how to ensure an abundant, cheap labor force for Potosí's silver mines. Various schemes were contrived to enhance the power of the state to recruit mitayos or to supplant the mita with the colonization of Potosí's hinterlands by Indians who would work "voluntarily" in the silver mines.[26] The most militant mineowners demanded no less than a second reducción, on the scale of the first (Toledan) reducción. They urged Viceroy Montesclaros to forcefully repopulate the official Indian villages with yanaconas and forasteros. Once the reservoir of compulsory laborers was restocked and mita obligations distributed more evenly, they argued, Indians would not have to be recruited so often nor driven so hard.[27]

However concerned Montesclaros was about the mita's decline, he was unwilling to mandate the resettlement of all forasteros inhabiting hacienda lands without taking into consideration the labor requirements of those agrarian enterprises. He intended to relocate only Indians on Spanish properties who were not performing "vital tasks" for the benefit of the kingdom. Like his predecessors, Montesclaros wanted to repopulate the Indian communities, but he refused to expel all recent migrants to the valleys. Instead, he proposed that barriers be erected to stop the flow of migrants between prov-

---

26 In 1610, the company of Jesuits at Potosí proposed a plan for colonizing the city's hinterlands with 25,000 Indians. They would be settled in the abandoned towns of Puna, Chaqui, and Yura, where they would engage in agriculture and also work for wages in the mines. The clerics believed that many Indians longed to escape the abuses they suffered in their own villages, and this scheme would both free them from the tyranny of their caciques and enable them to work in the mines without having to endure the hardships of the mita journey and the long absence from their villages, while at the same time providing a stable Indian labor force for the mines. Such a project would of course have required coordination and enforcement by the colonial state. It was never carried out. See Zavala, *Servicio personal*, 2: 45ff. The debates and regulations concerning mine labor run through all three volumes of that work. See also Arzáns y Orsúa y Vela, *Historia de la villa imperial*, and Cole, *Potosí Mita*.

27 "Parecer en materia de si conviene que los indios de la mita . . . asistan en ella y su comarca, o vengan de sus tierras como se ha fecho [sic] hasta aquí" (Apr. 1, 1610), report of a special commission of oidores of La Plata, cited and summarized in Zavala, *Servicio personal*, 2: 48-50.

inces. The obligated provinces would become quasi principalities, cordoned off from one another by border guards, sentinels, and toll gates. Corregidores would monitor the movement of Indians and expel vagabonds and migrants caught inside their territorial jurisdiction.[28]

This policy had a European derivation in medieval statutes banning overland travel and enforcing compulsory residence. Indeed, a few decades earlier, the English parliament under the Tudors had issued a series of ordinances forbidding vagrancy and vagabondage, a problem that had mushroomed out of control under the impact of the enclosure movement. But however difficult it may have been to enforce in the gently rolling English countryside, a statute limiting geographic mobility in the mountainous interior of Peru was pure folly. Even had the state equipped itself with militia, guards, and spiked gates at every crossroad, Andeans had countless ways of eluding the authorities in the rugged landscape that they knew so well.

As the quality of ore continued to deteriorate in the 1620s and 1630s, Potosí's mineowners demanded more action from the colonial state. Once again, they called for a second reducción. In 1634, the outspoken *procurador* (attorney) of Potosí, Sebastián de Sandoval y Guzmán, urged the crown to sacrifice the interests of the landowners for the benefit of silver mining and the entire kingdom. His tactical approach to the agrarian question was rather unique. He acknowledged the risks in and obstacles to a second reducción, and he admitted that it would provoke the wrath of chacareros and ranchers who saw their workers rounded up by colonial authorities and driven off to their original communities. Spaniards might even refuse to obey the royal orders. Some opponents of the plan had argued, too, that such a drastic measure might impoverish the Andean kingdom in the long run, leaving fertile lands lying fallow and herds untended. But the procurador proceeded to refute the objections to his proposal. In particular, he dismissed the warning that a second reducción would doom commercial agriculture. Hacendados, he suggested, could purchase African slaves to replace the Indians they lost. If there was still a shortage of labor, village Indians might then be or-

---

28 For further discussion of Montesclaros's schemes and policies with respect to the mita, see Zavala, *Servicio personal*, 2: 51-53. A contemporary of Montesclaros proposed that the state go one step further and issue internal passports to itinerant Indians—anticipating a device of social control that was to become common in Africa under European rule in the late nineteenth century.

dered to serve periodically in an agricultural mita (reminiscent perhaps of the Incaic mit'a of Cochabamba).[29]

Sandoval y Guzmán went so far as to challenge the very legitimacy of land ownership by Spaniards. He questioned the rights of landowners to acquire, by the payment of fees (*composiciones*), titles to parcels of vacant land that had belonged to Indian communities at the time of the Toledan reducción. He was especially outraged by an ordinance issued in 1631 that had permitted a new wave of land acquisitions. Thus, ironically, his interest in rejuvenating the mita by recolonizing highland Indian villages led him to a defense of communal Indian landholding interests. He questioned the definition of "vacant land" and the propriety of a royal order alienating parcels of community land simply because they lay fallow. He urged the crown to annul the sale of all village land to Spanish hacendados, even if it meant paying them indemnity from the royal treasury or treasuries of the communities whose land had been taken. In short, the salvation of the mita and hence of the silver industry of Potosí required, in his view, a two-pronged attack on the private agrarian sector: the expulsion of recent Andean immigrants from the haciendas and the return of community lands acquired by composiciones. Such a proposal posed a formidable threat to the hacendados.

But while imperial interests obviously had a stake in silver mining, the colonial authorities were not mere creatures of the mining elite. Even Toledo, who used state power to force Andean communities to subsidize Potosí's industry, ultimately tried to arbitrate between the private agrarian sector and the institutions that served the interests of the miners (see chapter 2). Nor was the audiencia of La Plata entirely in favor of mining interests when they conflicted with those of valley landlords. In 1611, the audiencia issued a defense of chacareros, arguing that Indians fled to the eastern valleys to escape the unbearable conditions in the mines.[30] Furthermore, viceroys and jurists knew full well that the azogueros themselves often collected cash payments in lieu of mitayos and pocketed the income rather than earmarking it for the wages of mingas. Such arrangements contributed to the decline in mining production and therefore in royal

---

29 Sebastián de Sandoval y Guzmán, "Pretenciones de la villa imperial de Potosí," cited in Cole, "Viceregal Persistence," 51, and Zavala, *Servicio personal*, 2: 98-103.

30 Saignes, "Polítícas étnicas," 11. The following year, the audiencia warned that to eject migrants in a second reducción "would destroy the chácaras and evaporate food supplies." Ibid.

revenue.[31] Calls for a second reducción, then, were met with skepticism and reluctance on the part of the viceregal authorities. Even in the 1650s, when the Council of the Indies did order a new repartimiento, its ambivalence toward the mining elite was reflected in its rejection of requests to reduce the price of mercury and the royal share of silver.[32]

The larger problem, however, was structural: even if the colonial state had thrown its full support behind the mining sector, its capacity to rebuild the earlier model of exploitation had been greatly reduced. Historians have written extensively about the colonial bureaucracy that had grown increasingly slack, ineffectual, and distant from imperial and even viceregal centers of power.[33] Steps by the Hapsburg rulers after 1678 to commercialize key colonial offices, such as systematically auctioning the post of corregidor, further removed power from viceregal authority. The post of corregidor was the highest provincial office in the viceroyalty, but it was subordinate to the viceregal and audiencia authority. However, the commodification of the post gave rise to a group of provincial bureaucrats whose authority and conduct were virtually unchecked. The diffusion of power among provincial authorities undercut the ability of the viceroy to intervene in local affairs or to mediate between conflicting interest groups. In comparison to Toledan times, the higher echelons of authority in Peru in the late seventeenth century seemed to be going into political retreat. The problem of the Hapsburgs' political lethargy was compounded, in the Andean area, by the geopolitical remoteness of Alto Perú.

The azogueros of Potosí could no longer count on an interventionist state to shore up the Toledan system. In 1670, Viceroy Conde de Lemos proposed that the mita be abolished. The proposal aroused

31 "Varios apuntes sobre asignación de indios . . . ," ANB, Minas, no. 1898 (Manuscritos Rück 575, Tomo 14), f. 67; Cole, "Abolitionism," 332.

32 Cole, "Abolitionism," 313-315.

33 See, for example, John Lynch, *Spain under the Hapsburgs: Spain and America, 1598-1700*, 2 vols. (New York: Oxford University Press, 1969), vol. 2; John Parry, *The Sale of Public Office in the Spanish Indies under the Hapsburgs* (Berkeley and Los Angeles: University of California Press, 1953); John L. Phelan, "Authority and Flexibility in the Spanish Imperial Bureaucracy," *Administrative Science Quarterly* 5 (1960): 47-65; John TePaske, "La crisis del siglo XVIII en el virreinato del Perú," in B. García Martínez, ed., *Historia y sociedad en el mundo de habla española* (Mexico City: Colegio de México, 1970), 263-280; and Guillermo Lohmann Villena, *El corregidor de Indios en el Perú bajo los Austrias* (Madrid: Ediciones Cultural Hispánica, 1957).

the azogueros' bitter opposition, and it was never put into effect.[34] Although Palata finally succeeded in matriculating forasteros, his plans to tax them and impose mita obligations came to naught. His successor, Viceroy Conde de la Monclova, rolled back the mita and tribute reforms, freeing the forasteros from tributary exactions for the time being. A more pointed example of the inconsistency of vice-regal policy could hardly be found. Where Palata was determined to take almost any step to introduce the mita into the northern and eastern fringe provinces, Monclova had little sympathy for the miners' dependence upon the state to force Andeans to work. Monclova never quite embraced abolitionism, but he managed to undo the work of his predecessor and to crush the hopes of Potosí's mineowners.[35]

Little wonder, then, that an azoguero living at the beginning of the eighteenth century might feel removed from and even disdainful of viceregal authority. Despite all the debate that had raged over the agrarian question, and despite all their demands for a new reducción, the mineowners never managed to wrest Andean migrants from the grip of the hacendados.

Toward the Subjection of the Forasteros

Between the decades of the 1680s and the 1730s, Potosí's mining industry experienced a deep recession, owing partly to the deteriorating quality of the ore and partly to the declining silver prices on the world market. Mineowners complained about the metals being extracted from the Cerro Rico: "Where before a load of metal weighing 50 quintales [hundredweights] yielded between 200 and 400 pesos corrientes, today [in 1734] it earns only 100 or 150 pesos, and it costs 100 pesos to extract, grind, refine, and cast that load of metal."[36] Moreover, the ore had to be mined from greater depths, with all the attendant problems of flooding, labor exhaustion, and cave-ins, and, to make matters worse, mercury shipments from Huancavelica were erratic. For a while, the crown diverted the flow of Spanish mercury from New Spain to Potosí. But as Potosí's industry deteriorated further, the crown cut off the supply of mercury from Spain, leaving Potosí's mills dependent upon Huancavelica's quicksilver.

34 See the detailed account in Cole, "Abolitionism."

35 Sánchez-Albornoz, *Indios y tributos*, chap. 3, and Cole, "Viceregal Persistence," 48-50.

36 Quoted in Zavala, *Servicio personal*, 3: 34.

Potosí's troubles translated directly into dwindling royal income. From a peak of 27,184,785 pesos during the first decade of the seventeenth century, net income from Potosí declined steadily and reached a low of 10,543,949 pesos in the last decade.[37] Taxes collected at Potosí were sent to Lima, where a portion was set aside to cover colonial government costs; the rest was sent on to Spain. Between 1651 and 1700, Potosí transferred 170,000,000 pesos to Lima. But the magnitude of the transfer was declining, gradually at first and then sharply. By 1770, the flow of surplus revenue had dried up altogether.[38] And as Lima's income dropped, so too did Spain's. During the second half of the seventeenth century, Peru sent 16,000,000 pesos to Seville, less than one-quarter of what it had remitted to Spain in the preceding half-century. That decline did not reflect simply the collapse at Potosí. A larger share of revenue was being kept in the colony to cover the growing cost of the bureaucracy and, especially, of military defense.[39] In addition, the *peruleros* (contraband traders from São Paulo) and other contrabandists siphoned off silver through illegal channels of trade.

The fiscal and mining problems of the Andean kingdom occurred at a time when England's agriculture and industries (textiles, shipping, and coal), as well as its domestic market, were expanding rapidly. England had also emerged the stronger military and diplomatic power following the War of the Spanish Succession (1700-1713). British contraband in the Western Hemisphere was getting out of control just when the Bourbon dynasty ascended to the Spanish throne. The Bourbons eventually were to introduce various schemes, based upon mercantilist thinking, to close the gap between the thriving economies of northern Europe and those of Spain's more backward regions (see chapter 8). But in the early eighteenth century, they still pinned their hopes on mineral exports and the flow of bullion from the New World. Furthermore, tribute revenues and income from the sale of offices were also deemed crucial. The crown's wish was to continue selling corregimientos, while still entrusting the corregidores with the task of raising more tribute monies for the royal treasury. How-

37 TePaske, "Fiscal Structure," 86, and Bakewell, "Registered Silver Production."

38 TePaske, "Fiscal Structure," esp. 77.

39 Lynch, *Spain under the Hapsburgs*, 2: 219-224; Herbert Klein and John J. TePaske, "The Seventeenth-Century Crisis in the Spanish Empire: Myth or Reality?" *Past and Present*, no. 90 (1981): 116-135; Javier Tord Nicolini, "Sociedad colonial y fiscalidad," *Apuntes* 4 (1977): 3-28.

ever preposterous that proposition might have seemed, it meant that officials in the Peruvian viceroyalty had to grapple once more with the vexing problem of the forasteros and, ultimately, with the agrarian question.

Viceroys and other royal authorities trying to generate more tribute income in Peru at that time faced formidable odds. Since Palata's day, the rural Andean world had undergone wrenching change. In the midst of the mining depression, epidemics of bubonic plague, influenza, and measles ravaged the land in 1719 and 1720, and again in the early 1730s. The indigenous population, which had been slowly declining during the seventeenth century, dropped precipitously in the early decades of the eighteenth, reducing Peru's Andean population to a quarter of its size at the time of the European intrusion.[40] The demographic curve turned gently upward in about 1740, but during the preceding decades, the human landscape was marred by epidemic, economic paralysis, and peasant penury.[41]

It was precisely the conjuncture of demographic disaster and mining recession that prompted Viceroy Marqués de Castelfuerte, who ruled from 1724 until 1736, to organize a new census count and an inspection of all the provinces. The rationale for the census count was to readjust tribute quotas in the wake of the epidemics, which would presumably be to the advantage of the tributaries. But Castelfuerte had another, more ominous motive. He believed many villages were "taking advantage" of the recent calamities to reduce their tax payments. His inspectors were therefore ordered to determine the true magnitude of population decline. Furthermore, they were to expose any corregidores, curates, and caciques who were pocketing tribute monies. Although Castelfuerte believed tribute embezzlement to be widespread, he wanted particularly to inspect those provinces where population decline seemed most dramatic and where he believed political malfeasance to be most blatant.

By these criteria, the province of Cochabamba provoked the viceroy's interest. Castelfuerte suspected foul play among the provincial authorities. He stated flatly that "the cause of the unfortunate decline [of tribute revenues] is embezzlement. Local authorities use the pretext of epidemic to hide Indians and exploit them in their own

40 Sánchez-Albornoz, *Indios y tributos,* 34; Noble David Cook, "La población indígena en el Perú colonial," *Anuario de Instituto de Investigaciones Históricas,* no. 8 (1965): 73-105.

41 A vivid description of social conditions in those years is found in a 1724 report by P. Manuel de Toledo y Leiva, rector of Jesuits in Huancavelica, in Vargas Ugarte, ed., *Pareceres jurídicos,* 168-183.

obrajes [textile workshops] and on their ranches and haciendas."[42] Behind the accusation lay a deep-seated distrust of private agrarian interests (which were beginning to emerge even within the matrix of village society). Once more, Cochabamba appeared as a region of recalcitrant landowners conniving to defraud the state of its tribute. Castelfuerte believed not only that tributaries were undercounted, but also that many Indians in the province were "passing" as mestizos—i.e., as people with one European parent, who were officially exempted from paying tribute. In his view, most people of mixed ancestry should be paying tribute, and he referred to them generically as *cholos*, who, as people with one European grandparent, were *not* exempted from paying tribute. Indeed, he protested that if cholos were exempt, Cochabamba "would be without tributaries."[43]

The viceroy's observations about the cholos reveal the ambiguity of sociocultural statuses in the eastern valleys and the extent to which the caste system had eroded. It suited the viceroy's purposes, of course, to attribute the apparent rapid growth of Cochabamba's mestizo population to the efforts of Andean peoples to evade royal tribute collectors. Castelfuerte believed that the "alleged mestizos" of Cochabamba were simply Indians and cholos who had exchanged their indigenous cultural garb for western clothing and identity. To his mind, the most permeable fiscal and racial boundary was that which separated cholos from mestizos. How could passage across this boundary be prevented in a region where ethnic and racial differentiation had long been blurred?

The extent to which *mestizaje* in Cochabamba was a phenomenon of transcultural movement is still a matter of conjecture. Future work with local parish records may reveal, for example, the magnitude of ethnic intermarriage in the region in the early eighteenth century. Meanwhile, there is only impressionistic evidence. We know that formal and informal unions had been taking place between Europeans and Andeans since early colonial times, and this has sometimes been given as the explanation for the size of the mestizo populations.[44] However, it is surely no accident that the region's

---

42 "Castelfuerte sobre la revisita a Cochabamba" (1731), AGI, Charcas, Leg. 343. On similar accusations levied against other corregidores in Alto Perú, see Arzáns de Orsúa y Vela, *Historia de la villa imperial*, 3: 192, 227-228, 260-261, and 271-272.

43 Castelfuerte to the crown, Apr. 29, 1731, AGI, Charcas, Leg. 343.

44 See, e.g., Humberto Guzmán Arze, *La realidad social de Cochabamba* (Cochabamba: Amigos del Libro, 1972), 36-37, and Guzmán, *Cochabamba*.

mestizo population seemed to increase most at those times when the colonial authorities were making renewed efforts to collect tribute from forasteros.[45] Beginning with Palata's regime and periodically thereafter, the status of forastero would lose its favorable position, and the only way its occupants could avoid tribute obligations was to slip into the category of mestizo.

The relative ease of passing as mestizo cautions against employing this term to define a social group, whether in terms of a common racial identity or a shared function, role, or position in the class structure. Like "forastero" and (to a certain degree) "originario," "mestizo" was fundamentally a fiscal category: one that defined an interstitial group that was different from "Indian" (the latter including "cholo") and that was therefore exempted from the rights and obligations assigned to Indians by the colonial state. The ambiguous and arbitrary status of mestizo in Cochabamba was reflected in later documents in which colonial authorities tried to describe or define exactly who was a mestizo. In the first regional census (1788) in which mestizos were separately counted, they were found to be 31 percent of Cochabamba's population (see table 13). The intendant Francisco de Viedma, under whose administration the census was conducted, listed the typical occupations of Cochabamba's mestizos: artisans, weavers of *tocuyos* (rough, unbleached cotton cloth), petty traders, and poor laborers in the central valleys. Other contemporary observers said that mestizos were also peasants who "leased land from the propertied and offered their labor in return."[46] Trial records from the same period show mestizos who were tenants (*arrenderos*) joining with Indian tenants, their neighbors, to denounce the abuses of a tyrannical landlord.[47] Tribute collectors even had difficulty separating mestizos from forastero tributaries. As one mestizo peasant so poignantly put it, "We [arrenderos] all live under the same wretched conditions."[48]

Whatever the problems of determining status, Castelfuerte was determined to systematize the collection of tribute. Specifically, he wanted to finally carry out Palata's plan to subject the forasteros

45 Sánchez-Albornoz, *Indios y tributos,* 169.

46 "Don Francisco de Hervoso y Figueroa, Obispo de Santa Cruz, sobre piezas sueltas de Santa Cruz" (1790), AGI, Charcas, Leg. 410, f. 8v.

47 "Exp. del yndígena Esteban Pablo contra su patrón Manuel Almarás en la hacienda Caporaya" (1795), AHMC, Leg. 1273.

48 "Real provisión sobre no ser yanaconas los indios de hacienda de Carasa" (1747), ANB, EC no. 6396.

to the payment of tribute. He also added a provision for the redistribution of some communal land to forasteros, creating thereby the new fiscal category of *forastero con tierra* (forastero with land), which carried with it an obligation to serve in the mita, as well as to pay tribute. According to Sánchez-Albornoz, this step was effective in bringing most forasteros into the tribute system.[49] Thus, the decade of the 1730s marked the end of the tax-exempt category of landless Indians. The new tax structure officially closed the agrarian loophole through which so many Andean migrants had sought relief from the pressures of village life. However, Castelfuerte's reforms were not enforced for another half-century, until after the Indian rebellions of 1781 and the reorganization of the colonial bureaucracy (see chapter 8).

Castelfuerte's reforms still required resolution of the question of the definition of the tribute-exempt category of mestizo. Again, the ambiguity rested with the cholos—those who could claim only one-quarter European ancestry. Castelfuerte's agents and inspectors were ordered not to give people of mixed ancestries the benefit of any doubt: if mestizo status could not be positively proven by parish records or by other means, the individual in question was to be assigned the status of forastero. In his single-minded pursuit of increased revenues, the viceroy was determined to unmask the "alleged mestizos" of Cochabamba and make that province an example of the new, stringent state policy toward tribute evaders.

To execute his reforms, Castelfuerte commissioned a royal inspection of the Cochabamba province. The visitador, Manuel Venero de Vera, arrived in Challacollo, on the western highland boundary of the province, in November 1730. His mandate was to expose tax frauds, particularly the underregistration of tributaries and the embezzlement of tribute monies. Many peasants feared that the inspector would register and assess them as forasteros unless they produced clear proof of mixed ancestry. Almost as soon as Venero de Vera registered new tributaries in the pueblos of Challacolla and Sicaya, rumors raced through the region to the effect that the inspector had "reduced" many mestizos to forasteros. Downriver from the towns under inspection, an angry crowd gathered in the central plaza of Capinota, one of the region's pueblos reales. Many of the protesters were mestizos, but they were joined by Andeans and by a few

---

49 Sánchez-Albornoz, *Indios y tributos*, 166, and Sánchez-Albornoz, *Population of Latin America*, 93.

Spanish patrons. The crowd soon turned into a violent mob that rampaged through the village and surrounding areas.[50]

Perhaps the crowd might have been contained had the royal inspector restricted himself to identifying the embezzlers of tribute funds and bringing order to the process of collection, and had he acted more prudently in the registration of forasteros. But Venero went in aggressive pursuit of people on the margins of the quasi-racial categories. The situation was exacerbated by rumors that the corregidor was bribing Venero's aides and assistants so that they would overlook irregularities in the tribute registries. Thus, the tributaries would have to pay their dues, while the corrupt officials would go unpunished. Nor did the inspector improve his standing with the local population when he ordered the militia to crush the rebellion at Capinota. Venero's intransigence and blunders turned a local crowd action into a regional tax rebellion.

As the month of November drew to a close in 1730, crowds of peasants, artisans, and laborers collected in the towns of Quillacollo and Cochabamba. The few sympathetic creoles who had stood with the protesters earlier that month now withheld their support because of their fear of what might happen. The picture sketched in official reports of what did happen is indeed an ugly one of mob action, in which two hundred insurgents killed the alcalde (mayor) of Cochabamba and fifteen vecinos and then pillaged the towns, stealing and committing "unspeakable atrocities." Although the viceroy and the king admitted that the inept inspector had made mistakes, they characterized the uprisings as race wars between the cholos and mestizos and the white vecinos, who had always lived in fear of mestizo violence and hatred.[51] The mestizo rebel leader, Alejo Calatayud, had tried to legitimate his actions by claiming loyalty to the king and calling for "death to bad government" (a slogan that would echo throughout the southern Andes almost fifty years later). He and his comrades paid with their lives: they were strangled in the central

50 Most of the official documents pertaining to the 1730 tax rebellion in Cochabamba are in the AGI, Charcas, Leg. 343 and 344. For a detailed study of the rebellion, based primarily upon this documentation, see Patricia C. Hutchins, "Rebellion and the Census of Cochabamba, 1730-1732" (Ph.D. diss., Ohio State University, 1974).

51 "Real cédula a la audiencia de La Plata sobre la sublevación de mestizos de Cochabamba con motivo del empadronamiento de los indios," (1732), RAH, ML 9/1758, tomo 103. See also Scarlett O'Phelan Godoy, *Rebellion and Revolts in Eighteenth-Century Peru and Upper Peru* (Cologne: Bohlau, 1985), 74-80.

plaza and their dismembered bodies were strewn along the road as a gruesome warning to the restless plebe.

Yet the colonial authorities did not really believe that this barbaric punishment would serve to "discipline the masses." The viceroy recalled Venero and suspended the census count. He sent another inspector to the province a year later, but the registration of "alleged mestizos" as forasteros was ended. Instead, the tribute dues of forasteros were fixed at six pesos two reales—one of the highest forastero tribute rates in Alto Perú.[52] But from 1731 on, the authorities regarded the "mestizo province" of Cochabamba as a land of restless, refractory people who might turn seditious at any moment. Even the hacendados who had once willingly sheltered Andean migrants from tribute obligations and helped them pass into the ranks of cholos and mestizos, now watched warily over this "dangerous class." Cochabamba's peasantry and artisans had vividly demonstrated the limits of state power.

New Conditions and New Conflicts

In about 1740, a confluence of economic and demographic trends pushed the viceroyalty out of recession, and over the next sixty years, the Andean colonial economy experienced an uneven recovery. The Andean population also began to grow. Kubler's study of tribute records had indicated a vigorous rate of growth, but more recent studies have cast doubt on the reliability of his sources, and the weight of the evidence now is that there was a modest expansion of the Andean population during the second half of the eighteenth century, with considerable regional variation. As we shall see later, Potosí's population did not share in this growth.[53]

---

52 The total amounts of tribute owed by a community were adjusted from time to time in accordance with changes in the number of adult males. One such change took place in 1738, under Viceroy Villa García: AGN, Sala 13, 18.2.1 (1785).

53 George Kubler, *The Indian Caste of Peru, 1795-1940: A Population Study Based upon Tax Records and Census Reports* (Washington, D.C.: Smithsonian Institution, 1952); Sánchez-Albornoz, *Population of Latin America*, 110-111, and Sánchez-Albornoz, *Indios y tributos*, 34; Herbert Klein, "Peasant Response to the Market and the Land Question in the 18th and 19th Centuries," *Nova Americana*, no. 5 (1982): 103-134; Mörner, *Perfil de la sociedad rural*, chap. 1. For Cochabamba, see tables A-2 and A-3. On Potosí, see María del Pilar Chao, "La población de Potosí en 1779," *Anuario del Instituto de Investigaciones Históricas*, no. 8 (1965): 171-180.

This period was also marked by a gradual increase in agricultural production, particularly in subsistence crops. The analysis by Tandeter and Wachtel of tithes levied on grain grown on private lands (indigenous grains grown on communal lands were not subject to the tithe) in the archbishopric of Charcas shows that, after a sharp cyclical drop in the 1720s, there was a clear increase, beginning in the late 1730s and lasting until the early years of the nineteenth century, although it was not until after 1760 that agricultural production and tithe revenue reached the levels of the late seventeenth century (figure 6).[54] By the same token, however, the prices of agricultural products fell.[55] If Potosí's commodity market mirrored price trends in the

Figure 6   Value of Tithes in the Archbishopric of Charcas (La Plata), 1670-1820
Source: Enrique Tandeter and Nathan Wachtel, *Precios y producción agraria: Potosí y Charcas en el siglo XVIII* (Buenos Aires: Estudios CEDES, 1984), 72. Reproduced by permission.

54 This study—Enrique Tandeter and Nathan Wachtel, *Precios y producción agraria: Potosí y Charcas en el siglo XVIII* (Buenos Aires: Estudios CEDES, 1984)—is the first to chart prices for all of Alto Perú over the course of a century. However, several earlier studies examined agricultural production and price trends in different areas; see esp. Ruggiero Romano, "Movimiento de los precios y desarrollo económico: El caso de Sudamérica en el siglo XVIII," *Desarrollo económico* 1-2 (1963): 31-43; and Marcello Carmagnani, "La producción agropecuaria chilena: Aspectos cuantitativos (1680-1830)," *Cahiers des Amériques latines* no. 3 (1969): 3-21.

55 Romano, "Movimiento de los precios." Because of this price drop, which Tandeter and Wachtel confirmed in their work, tithes and agricultural output were inversely correlated. Thus, in order to infer the trend of agricultural production from tithe revenues, Tandeter and Wachtel charted the secular movement of tithes (*diezmos*) deflated by the annual index of agricultural prices as

rest of Alto Perú, then the general recovery and growth in agrarian production had a deflationary effect on prices, in contrast to the inflationary effect of Potosí's boom in early colonial days. This situation had great significance for the internal evolution of Cochabamba's agrarian class structure in the latter half of the eighteenth century (see chapter 5 and 6).

Beyond the fertile lands of Alto Perú, recovery was also manifest in the silver mines, both new and old. The expanding economies of Europe required increasing supplies of monetary metals to lubricate the trade with Asia, Africa, and the Americas. Repercussions were felt throughout Latin America, as prospectors staked out gold fields in Minas Gerais, struck rich silver deposits in Guanajuato, and revamped the interior works of older mines. As part of this change, the output of Potosí's mines, after many decades of decline, began to rise.[56] The growth in silver output was sustained, with some pauses and hesitations, until the Independence Wars broke out.

But the magnitude of the upturn in Potosí's production must have disappointed contemporaries who hoped for a bonanza on the scale and intensity of the second silver cycle of Toledo's day. The pace of expansion was much slower than it had been in the late sixteenth century (figure 7). Silver production doubled between 1740 and 1780, whereas during the peak decades of 1580 and 1590, it had more than trebled. In absolute terms as well, Potosí's recovery was only partial. Silver output rose only to the level achieved in the middle of the seventeenth century. During the decade of the 1790s, when the average annual output was higher than at any other time in the eighteenth century, the mint stamped three and one-half million pesos, far less than the seven million pesos minted by Potosí in a decade two hundred years earlier.[57] Thus, neither in scale of production of its mines nor in the size of its population did Potosí recover its former importance. Under the new stimulus of the world market,

---

well as by the index of moving averages of those prices, as registered in contemporary account books at Potosí. (However, the values shown in figure 6 are the actual, not the adjusted, values.) For a discussion of tithes as an indirect indicator of agricultural production in Cochabamba, see Brooke Larson, "Rural Rhythms of Class Conflict in Eighteenth-Century Cochabamba," *Hispanic American Historical Review* 60 (1980): 407-430.

56 Brading and Cross, "Colonial Silver Mining," 569; Enrique Tandeter, "La rente comme rapport de production et comme rapport de distribution: Le cas de l'industrie minière de Potosí, 1750-1826" (3rd Cycle Doctorate, Ecole des Hautes Etudes en Sciences Sociales, Paris, 1980), chap. 2.

57 Brading and Cross, "Colonial Silver Mining," 573 and 578.

Figure 7   Estimated Total Peruvian and Potosí Silver Production, 1560-1800
Source: David Brading and Harry Cross, "Colonial Silver Mining: Mexico and
Peru," *Hispanic American Historical Review* 52(1972): 569; Reproduced by
permission.

mines were being opened everywhere. Where once the Cerro Rico
and surrounding mines of Porco (the province in which Potosí was
located) produced 70 percent of all Peruvian silver, in 1774 they
yielded only about 40 percent.[58] Furthermore, the crown seemed
rather indifferent to the fate of the Potosí mines. While it still
granted privileges to the azogueros and to the exploiters of the Potosí
mines in general, it increasingly pinned its hopes on the silver mines
of Mexico, which were proving to be far more competitive on the
world market.[59]

58 Major rivals were the new mines of Cerro de Pasco in Peru's central sierras.
See John Fisher, *Minas y mineros en el Peru, 1776-1824* (Lima: Instituto de Estudios Peruanos, 1977), 34ff.

59 Enrique Tandeter, "Forced and Free Labor in Late Colonial Potosí," *Past and
Present*, no. 93 (1981): 99-100; Arzáns de Orsúa y Vela, *Historia de la villa impe-
rial*, 3: 10ff. On Mexican silver mining in the eighteenth century, see David
Brading, *Miners and Merchants in Bourbon Mexico, 1763-1810* (Cambridge:
Cambridge University Press, 1971), 152.

In contrast to the Toledan era, no centralizing colonial state engineered Peru's economic growth in the mid-eighteenth century. Indeed, the resources and patrimony of the colonial state had diminished, as had its corresponding power to control a civil and religious clientele. Of course, the Bourbons continued to discuss plans to revamp the tribute system and enforce the institution of mita. But after the blunders of Castelfuerte, most viceroys gave up their grand designs for tribute reform and instituted, instead, piecemeal changes on the local level. Until the 1780s, the overall orientation of the state was a rentier one: it was content to sell offices to corregidores and allow power and perquisites to these provincial authorities in return for a steady, secure income. The crown's revenue from the sale of five-year terms of office increased, as corregidores themselves were able to realize a higher return on their investment in office. In the early 1750s, the crown further enhanced the value of corregimientos, and its own income, by granting corregidores the right to distribute a fixed volume of commodities to the Indians under their jurisdiction. This measure allowed the state to tax the value of the legal *repartimiento de mercancías*, giving the state yet another benefit from the system. But even before the crown institutionalized the repartimiento de mercancías, it had been inclined to tolerate the widespread practice among corregidores, for this nefarious activity provided the economic underpinnings of the commodification of the highest provincial post. There would be little incentive for a creole or peninsular to invest funds in the office if such lucrative activity were not available. Thus, the crown was inclined to turn its back on the shady dealings of the provincial officeholders, until measures of control became absolutely necessary.

The combination of decentralized rule and growing opportunity for mercantile gain created more room for extralegal enterprise as well. On paper, Spanish law continued to be, as Coatsworth has described it in Mexico, "full of restrictions, prohibitions and regulatory provisions governing labor relations, property rights, water allocation, permissible crops, minimum wages, tax obligations, and religious duties."[60] Nevertheless, in practice, the upper echelons of government in the Andes were remote and ineffectual. The locus of power was local or regional, and no "visible hand" of imperial power controlled the scope or direction of economic change. Private agrarian enterprises revived and flourished in the fertile valleys of coastal

60 John Coatsworth, "The Limits of State Absolutism: The State in Eighteenth-Century Mexico," in Spalding, ed., *Essays*, 35.

Peru, in the tropical eastern yungas, and in pockets along the south-eastern frontier of Chuquisaca and Santa Cruz.[61] Obrajes, *chorrillos* (small, primitive textile workshops), and later tocuyo looms began to hum with activity, in spite of royal prohibitions and increased competition from European contrabandists. But more than the growth of small, productive enterprises across the Andes, this period of royal remoteness gave free rein to commercial ventures. Increasingly over the course of the eighteenth century, until the outbreak of rebellion in 1781, corregidores forged economic alliances with Lima's merchant elite and harnessed merchant capital to political power.

The interlocking interests of coastal merchants and corregidores were recognized by some contemporaries. In 1749, Jorge Juan and Antonio de Ulloa exposed the inner workings of the compulsory market, driven by the capital of merchants and the coercive tactics of corregidores.[62] Corregidores counted on Limeño merchants to contribute to the cost of office and to supply commodities. In return, the merchant-sponsor received a share of the profits.[63] This union of merchant capitalism and political force, which the crown legitimized in 1754, produced a vast compulsory market in commodities sold at artificially high prices to Andean peasants. Regional authori-

---

61 Historians are still charting the contours of commercial agriculture in eighteenth-century Peru and Alto Perú. Early studies tended to emphasize the stagnation of agriculture and trade; see, for example, Guillermo Céspedes del Castillo, "Lima y Buenos Aires: Repercusiones económicas y políticas de la creación del virreinato de La Plata," *Anuario de estudios americanos* 3 (1946): 667-874; and Oscar Febres Villarroel, "La crisis agrícola en el Perú en el último tercio del siglo XVIII," *Revista histórica* 27 (1964): 102-199. More recently, several historians have studied dynamic regional economies, where haciendas specialized in marketable crops for export to Potosí and other distant cities; see, for example, Nicolas Cushner, *Lords of the Land: Sugar, Wine, and Jesuit Estates of Coastal Peru (1600-1767)* (Albany: State University of New York Press, 1980). On the growth and labor needs of coca plantations in the yungas east of La Paz, see Herbert Klein, "Hacienda and Free Community in Eighteenth-Century Alto Perú," *Journal of Latin American Studies* 7 (1975): 193-220.

62 Jorge Juan y Santacilia and Antonio de Ulloa, *Noticias secretas de América* (Buenos Aires: Mar Océano, 1953). An English-language edition is available: *Discourse and Political Reflections on the Kingdoms of Peru*, ed. and trans. John J. TePaske and Besse A. Clement (Norman: University of Oklahoma Press, 1978).

63 Ibid. See also A. Moreno Cebrián, *El corregidor de indios y la economía peruana en el siglo XVIII* (Madrid: Instituto Gonzalo Fernández de Oviedo, 1977); Javier Tord Nicolini, "El corregidor de indios del Perú: Comercio y tributos," *Historia y cultura* (Lima), no. 8 (1974): 173-214.

ties and their agents forced Andean villagers to "accept" mules imported from the ranches of Tucumán, bales of cloth imported from Quito, baskets of yungas coca, brandy processed in coastal vineyards, and European textiles and trinkets. The pressure to pay off debts and to capitalize on political officeholding within a five-year period impelled the corregidores to use political means for mercantile ends. Their entrepreneurial behavior led to a diffusion of the marketplace from its loci in cities, towns, ports, mining camps, and transit crossroads to peasant villages in remote areas. The marketplace came, unbidden, to the Andean community. In the process, the merchant houses of Lima discovered an inland market so vast and lucrative as to help compensate for the end of their monopoly over transatlantic trade.[64]

Potosí's recovery in the middle decades of the eighteenth century mirrored the spontaneous development of informal enterprises that undermined the monopolistic control of azogueros. In production and commerce, small-scale, informal enterprises mushroomed in the mining towns, as mineworkers, too, took advantage of the rising demand for silver. Unlike the highly capitalized mercantile enterprises of the corregidores and their merchant collaborators, the mineworkers' production of silver was atomized among many small, illicit operations. In the eyes of Potosí's mining elite, the economic recovery was a mixed blessing, because it stimulated "internal competition" from an aggressive group of free mineworkers (mingas) who scavenged discarded ore from the slag heaps and, as before, stole chunks of ore from the interior veins.[65] The threat lay not only in their numbers, but in the degree to which they were able to exert control over both mineral extraction and refining.

The *kajchas* or "silver thieves" of Potosí organized themselves into work gangs led by skilled pickmen.[66] During the thirty-six hours

64 Spalding, *Huarochirí*, 202-203.

65 Enrique Tandeter, "La producción como actividad popular: 'Ladrones de minas' en Potosí," *Nova Americana* no. 4 (1981): 43-65; Tandeter, "Rente comme rapport de production," chap. 3, esp. 188-212. (All citations to chap. 3 of this work refer to a Spanish version, entitled "Mita, minga, y kajcha," kindly provided by the author.)

66 On the basis of contemporary estimates, Tandeter ("Mita, minga, y kajcha," 134) suggests that the number of kajchas fluctuated between about 2,000 and 4,000 between 1759 and 1782, the number being higher at the beginning of that period than at the end. On the problem of their control of the industry, see "Relación que hace don Manuel Amat . . .," cited and summarized in Zavala, *Servicio personal*, 3: 64; and Tandeter, "Producción como actividad popular."

or so on Saturday and Sunday when mining operations were required to cease, the kajchas entered the mines to recover chunks of ore they had concealed during the preceding week of legal labor or to cut and smuggle out fresh ore. The ore was brought to small-scale refiners, *trapicheros*, who processed it in mule-driven mills, more primitive affairs than the great water-powered mills of the azogueros. The refined silver was sold to the Banco de Rescates, following its establishment in 1752. Thus, even though *kajcheo* was illegal, the royal bank received the stolen ore, which in the late 1750s probably represented about 30 percent of all silver traded at Potosí.[67] Indeed, despite warnings from Potosí's corregidor, who saw a danger in allowing gangs of mineworkers to flout the law, higher royal authorities implicitly tolerated the practice, presumably because of the additional silver that it brought into commerce.[68]

In spite of the increase in world silver prices, therefore, the mining elite of Potosí feared a deterioration in its economic position. The state was unable or unwilling to put an end to the kajchas' activities, nor would it put in place the machinery to draft more mitayos, in order to raise their number above the 2,919 who worked at Potosí in 1754.[69] The mining elite dealt with this situation in one of two ways: by leasing their operations to others, or by squeezing more surplus value out of the mitayos under their control.[70] The latter was accomplished by shifting from wage work to piecework and then increasing the piecework requirement. A mitayo in the 1750s was required to haul five "sets" (*pallas*), each set equivalent to fifteen loads, during a period of five days or nights of work. Ten years later, each set was made the equivalent of thirty loads.[71] The only way a mitayo could cope with this increased demand was to mobilize auxiliary workers, among his kin or as temporary wage laborers, to carry some of the load. In other words, the mineowners shifted a portion of labor costs to the mitayo himself. Further, mitayos gave up their authorized rest weeks to work almost continually through their year at Potosí. Finally, as their sixteenth-century forebears had done, the

---

67 Tandeter, "Mita, minga, y kajcha," 136, and Tandeter, "Producción como actividad popular," 51-52.

68 Tandeter, "Mita, minga, y kajcha," 137-139, and "Producción como actividad popular," 56-57.

69 Tandeter, "Forced and Free Labor," 103.

70 Tandeter, "Producción como actividad popular," 45.

71 Tandeter, "Mita, minga, y kajcha," 84, and Tandeter, "Forced and Free Labor," 107.

mitayos depended upon assistance from members of their own families and their native communities. The harsher work regime mandated some kind of collective strategy at Potosí, both in the fulfillment of work quotas and in the daily struggle for subsistence.

From the mineowners' point of view, the forced speed-up of silver production made the difference between the success or failure of their enterprises. In 1790, the mitayos' average weekly wage was two reales less than that of the mingas, yet they had to deliver one-third more ore than the free laborers.[72] With a static labor supply at Potosí and an old technology, there was no way to increase silver output except by altering relations of production and bearing down harder on some workers. Tandeter contends that it was "the manipulation of [the work] quota which enabled the mines of Potosí to double their production between the 1740s and the 1790s."[73] When the mita was abolished after independence, the increased labor costs involved in shifting entirely to free wageworkers swallowed up the margin of profit and rendered the mines noncompetitive. Thus, the mita made possible the survival of the industry, but for those who were caught in its claws, it was a brutal existence.

During these decades of "slow, painful growth" at Potosí,[74] the political economy of colonialism developed its own momentum and moved in directions that did not always serve royal interests. After the long period of royal retreat, the colonial state in the Andes no longer possessed the internal cohesion, political program, or bureaucratic apparatus to contain or channel the currents of socioeconomic change. In theory, the state was still a direct, autonomous claimant on the resources of Andean communities, but in reality, the corregidores manipulated tribute collection for their own private gain. Tribute embezzlement reached scandalous proportions in the 1750s.[75] In theory, again, the state continued to protect the corporate

72 Tandeter, "Forced and Free Labor," 134; Francisco de Paula Sanz to Antonio Valdés, June 30, 1790, cited and summarized in Zavala, *Servicio personal*, 3: 75-76. For a description (and denunciation) of the quota system by Cochabamba's intendant, see Viedma, *Descripción geográfica*, 179.

73 Tandeter, "Producción como actividad popular," 107.

74 Enrique Tandeter, "Rent As a Relation of Production and As a Relation of Distribution in Late Colonial Potosí" (paper presented at the Eighth National Meeting of the Latin American Studies Association, Pittsburgh, April 5-7, 1979), 10.

75 In one case in the mid-1750s, corregidores and caciques in the Cuzco area siphoned off more than 50 percent of tribute dues: Tord Nicolini, "Corregidor de indios del Perú," 199. For more general discussions of corregidores and corrup-

integrity of Indian villages, but in fact, the corregidores engaged with impunity in all kinds of extortionist practices. On paper, the state was also still committed to coordinating the flow of forced migrants to Potosí, yet the mita continued to wither, particularly as work conditions worsened at Potosí and as more and more corregidores impeded the movement of mitayos. In short, the political apparatus of Peru in the mid-eighteenth century was in shambles: it neither ensured the functioning of the extractive institutions (tribute and mita) nor did it protect the subsistence economies that underpinned those institutions. And finally, the state did not have the leverage or authority to arbitrate effectively among conflicting colonial interest groups.

In the southern Andes, the crisis of political authority was manifest in the open antagonism between Potosí's mining elite and the corregidores, who had come to wield considerable power over the Indians under their jurisdiction. Although the mining elite itself stood on shaky moral ground, its members protested against the abuses perpetrated by the corregidores on the Andean peasants. The corregidores, however, were emboldened by royal tolerance and, after 1754, by the crown's sanction of their coercive mercantile activities. Increasingly, the corregidores crossed the threshold of "tolerable" or "acceptable" levels of extortion and began to threaten the interests of the mineowners themselves. They underregistered or hid tributaries, thus removing them from the mita labor pool.[76] They converted village Indians to permanent laborers on their haciendas and in their textile workshops.[77] The behavior of the corregidores provoked new

tion in an earlier period, see Lohmann Villena, *Corregidor de indios*, and Sánchez-Albornoz, *Indios y tributos*, chap. 3, esp. 95-99 and app. 2.

76 In the 1740s, for example, the corregidor of Cochabamba was accused of hiding many Indians from the royal tax collectors and defrauding the crown: AGI, Charcas, Leg. 367 (1746). The royal authorities in Huancavelica heard complaints about corregidores whose commercial activities were interfering with the mita; see the 1748 report of the governor, cited and summarized in Zavala, *Servicio personal*, 3: 39. On the case of a corrupt corregidor of Porco who was impeding the flow of tribute and mitayos, see Arzáns de Orsúa y Vela, *Historia de la villa imperial*, 3: 192, 227-228, 260-261, 271-272. The most important chronicle of the tactics of the corregidores is still Juan y Santacilia and Ulloa, *Noticias secretas*. Clerics were not immune from similar accusations; the azogueros declared that they were exploiting Indians and obstructing the flow of mitayos: "Exp. relativo a la averiguación de las entradas y gastos q. tienen los curatos de la provincia de Cochabamba" (1760-1761), ANB, Mano de obra, no. 788.

77 See, for example, the report of Castelfuerte in AGI, Charcas, Leg. 343, April 21, 1731.

waves of Andean migration.[78] In the 1770s, Viceroy Manuel Amat warned that corregidores were overburdening Indians with unwanted merchandise and driving them to desert their villages (see below).

The crown's attitude toward this set of issues was ambivalent. On the one hand, the crown recognized that the actions of the corregidores were adverse to its fiscal interests. On the other hand, it needed the considerable revenue from the *alcabala*, the "sales tax" on the value of a legalized repartimiento de mercancías.[79] Furthermore, the crown was unwilling to abandon the internal colonial market to the free play of market forces. Contemporary observers, even ones as astute as Juan and Ulloa, believed that Indians were by nature indolent and that they needed "pressuring" if they were to purchase the kinds and amounts of goods that the corregidores distributed. The alternative would be economic atrophy and decline. Wrapped in this philosophical cloak, the crown stood behind the corregidores and in 1754, as already noted, granted them the right to distribute a stipulated volume of goods at fixed prices to the people of their district.[80] Thus, the ambivalence of the crown was resolved in favor of a mercantile-political alliance, at least for the time being.

78 The corregidor of Cochabamba was also accused of driving Indians out of their villages and causing an increase in the number of ausentes: AGI, Charcas, Leg. 367, 1746. In 1753, of the 130 mitayos that Cochabamba's villages were supposed to dispatch, only 59 actually set off for Potosí: ANB, Manuscritos Rück, no. 131, ff. 107-110. Migration and absenteeism were not the results only of the commercial practices of the corregidores or their oppression of local populations; the periodic epidemics were also a factor. So also was the old problem of the *indios rescatados*, who purchased exemption from the mita by paying fees of 80 or 100 pesos to their caciques. The caciques would then hire forasteros or their own servants to serve on the mita for a fraction of the exemption fee. However, the hired forasteros often fled, thus aggravating the problem of drafting mitayos: "Avios sobre . . . el mejor régimen, establecimiento, y gobierno de la real mita . . ." (1762), ANB, Minas, no. 789.

79 Even Viceroy Amat, who perceived the danger of unregulated corregidor activities, noted that the taxes on the repartimiento de mercancías benefited the crown, but he was under no illusion that the taxes set limits on the volume or value of forcibly distributed merchandise: Manuel de Amat y Juniente, *Memoria de gobierno*, ed. Vicente Rodríguez Casado and Florentino Pérez Embid (Seville: Escuela de Estudios Hispanoamericanos, 1947), 189. The magnitude of this source of royal revenue is worth noting. In 1751, when the tax rate was 4 percent, the total value of alcabalas on the repartimientos in the viceroyalty was 217,160 pesos: John Fisher, *Government and Society in Colonial Peru: The Intendant System, 1784-1814* (London: Athlone, 1970), 14-15.

80 On the legalization of the repartimiento de mercancías, see Golte, *Repartos y*

To the mining elite, the corregidor, always a political rival, now appeared as an economic rival as well, in the competition for scarce Indian labor. The problem was an old one: since the early seventeenth century, the mita had not functioned at full capacity (see chapter 2). Potosí's mineowners historically had issued reclamations, registered protests, and demanded action to shore up the Toledan system. But conditions had now changed, and new protagonists had emerged in the struggle over Andean peasant labor. The mineowners' traditional enemies, the hacendados of the eastern valleys, had faded from the arena. As the private agrarian sector became entrenched and the state showed itself incapable of constraining Andean migration toward the eastern valleys and towns, or unwilling to do so, the scope and terms of the conflict began to shift as well. By the mid-eighteenth century, the debate was not fundamentally over the proper balance between two modes of exploitation (private and extractive) and the distribution of Indian laborers between them, and few azogueros demanded a "second reducción" or the massive expulsion of Indians from valley haciendas to highland villages, where they could be tapped for tribute and mita. At issue, rather, was the conduct of the colonial authorities who were responsible for collecting tribute and dispatching mitayos. After years of royal neglect and the accumulation of power in the hands of provincial and local bureaucrats, the corregidores and their collaboratos menaced mining interests. The eighteenth-century variant of the agrarian question, then, was the issue of the power of the local authorities who reached inside the Andean communities, exploited peasants for personal gain, and blocked the outflow of draft labor to the mines. When the invigorated Bourbon state finally took tribute and mining interests to heart again, in the 1780s and 1790s, it shifted attention to the alarming state of affairs within the Andean community. By then, the crown had abolished the post of corregidor, but, as we shall see in chapter 8, the social legacies of mercantile exploitation survived rebellion and the dismantling of the corregimientos.

Political Unrest in the Valleys

The crisis of colonial rule that gripped the viceroyalty in the mid-eighteenth century was played out, on a small scale, in the Cochabamba region. Tensions mounted in the region, as the burden of the

rebeliones, 84-85. The royal tariff of 1754 is published in ibid., 87 and 98-100, and in Moreno Cebrián, *Corregidor de indios*.

repartimiento de mercancías grew heavier. Peasants who inhabited communal lands were increasingly vulnerable to the corregidor's economic power. A group of Indians from the community of Tapacarí confronted the corregidor of Cochabamba in court. The suit unfolded in the late 1740s and early 1750s, the beginning of a thirty-year period during which Indians throughout Alto Perú waged judicial struggles against the authority of corregidores and their mercantile practices. The litigation initiated by the Tapacarí Indians illuminated the larger struggle over Andean peasant labor that fractured and weakened the colonial bureaucracy in this period.

Under the terms of the royal decree of 1754, the repartimiento de mercancías in Cochabamba amounted to 186,675 pesos in a five-year period during the 1770s—2,000 mules (25 pesos each), 4,000 *varas* of cloth from Quito (some at 7 pesos, some at 7 pesos 4 reales), 20,000 varas of rustic clothing (1 peso), 30 quintales of iron for plows (100 pesos), 10 *pearas* of coca (9 pesos per basket), and imported clothing of various sorts (total of 50,000 pesos).[81] In absolute terms, this was a larger value of commodities than was absorbed by any other province,[82] but since Cochabamba's population was also relatively large—about 26,500 Andeans lived in the province in 1754—the per capita value, about 7 pesos, was comparable to that in other provinces.[83] Of course, these figures do not include the value of goods forcibly distributed outside the legal limits.

The data indicate how involved the corregidor was in long-distance trade in colonial commodities. About 73 percent of the repartos were products from Andean workshops, estancias, plantations, and mines. The mules were probably supplied by the ranches of Salta and Tucumán in the south, while the *bayetas* (coarse woolen cloth) came from obrajes in the province of La Paz and the highlands to the north, closer to Cuzco.[84] The corregidor procured the finer "quiteño"

81 AGN, Sala 13, 18.1.5, Leg. 45. A *vara* was a measure of length approximately equal to thirty-three inches; a *peara* was a measure regarded as what could be carried by ten mules.

82 Spalding, *Huarochirí*, 202-205.

83 Golte, *Repartos y rebeliones*, 104-105. The value of the legal allotment of repartos in Cochabamba province represented about 3 percent of the total value of legal merchandise distributed by all the corregidores of Alto Perú.

84 In a discussion of the origin of the repartos in Peru, Golte (*Repartos y rebeliones*, chap. 3) argues that the forced participation of Andean peasants in trade stimulated an increase in the production of articles of consumption throughout the viceroyalty. The origin of repartos distributed in Cochabamba can be sur-

cottons from Lima merchants. The connection to coastal merchants was also important, since the corregidor had license to distribute 50,000 pesos worth of imported textiles. In allotting repartos for forced distribution, the corregidor didn't necessarily discriminate between subsistence products and luxury goods; Andean victims of the repartimiento often found themselves indebted to the corregidor for snuff boxes, combs, or buckles, along with the mules and baskets of coca they were compelled to "purchase."

Before the repartimientos were legalized, the corregidores had sought their "clients" in the pueblos reales, which were directly subordinate to the provincial colonial hierarchy. Deprived of even the tenuous protection of a landlord, whose self-interest lay in shielding his tenant-laborers from outside claimants, the village Indians were exposed to the corrupt, coercive practices of local authorities. Furthermore, the corregidor, by co-optation, pressure, or imposition of an outsider, used members of the native hierarchy as intermediaries in the distribution of commodities among peasant households. Finally, the repartimiento de mercancías required, for their effective functioning, that the corregidores intervene in the political affairs of the Andean villages, and that they establish a network of collaborators to facilitate the flow of commodities and enforce the debt obligations of Indian consumers.

The logic of compulsory exchange and the dependence of the corregidores upon Indian collaborators produced contradictory effects in the Andean villages. On the one hand, the behavior of the corregidores threatened the political autonomy of village life and infringed upon local traditions, and so provoked moral indignation among the Indians. Yet on the other hand, the villagers could not present a united front against the corregidores, for their moral outrage had to be directed not only toward them but also toward the native collaborators. Caciques were turned against each other, and the internal divisions in the Andean communities were sharpened. Sometimes, the expressions of moral indignation precipitated upheaval within a community, destroying any semblance of solidarity (see chapter 4).

For the present, it is sufficient to note the growing political unrest in the valleys during the time when the repartimiento de mercancías flourished. Long before the outbreak of the rebellions of 1781, the Indians of Tapacarí sought retribution from the audiencia for their

mised from the alcabala records that were systematically kept in the last two decades of the eighteenth century; for a detailed discussion, see Brooke Larson, "Economic Decline and Social Change in an Agrarian Hinterland: Cochabamba in the Late Colonial Period" (Ph.D. diss., Columbia University, 1978), 232–240.

suffering under the rule of Cochabamba's corregidor, Bartolomé Fiorilo Pérez. Some time during the 1740s, about 75 Tapacareños journeyed to La Plata, where they testified against the abuses perpetrated by the corregidor and his collaborators, both creole and native.[85] Although witnesses accused different individuals, their basic objection was to the use of force that penetrated to the heart of the community and reduced them to debtors. The mercantile-political alliance in the village exposed them to economic shocks from which they could not shield themselves. A seventy-year-old man accused Gerónimo de los Ríos, the corregidor's lieutenant, of distributing "with all the rigor and force of authority" brandy, iron, mules, rustic cloth, maize, sheep, and baskets of coca.[86] A bilingual though illiterate mestizo spoke out against the same lieutenant and against the cacique Pedro Condori, who had sold him grains and a mule for sixteen pesos on a six-month credit term; when he defaulted on his debt, the man was thrown into prison.[87] Another witness confessed to serving as an agent of the corregidor, out of fear of imprisonment. A group of forasteros testified that the corregidor had forced them to accept 100 varas of bayeta, at one peso each.[88]

The forced purchases were not all that the Tapacarí Indians were suffering from. They protested an "artisans' tax" that was levied on weavers even when they had no wool to spin or weave. They complained about the alcabalas imposed on the Indians of the ayllu Guaico, turning a sales tax into a head tax of four pesos. In effect, they were paying double tribute—to the king and to the local authorities.[89] The repartimiento de mercancías, then, was only the most prominent mechanism of extraction employed by the corregidores.

To the Indians of Tapacarí, the audiencia of La Plata seemed to offer the only means of protecting themselves against the corregidor's excesses. The viceregal authorities had lost their power to

85 "Juicio en grado de apelación sobre los capítulos que se lee a don Juan Guillermo Liro de Córdova, por el indio Blas Condori, sobre las tierras en el pueblo de Tapacarí," ANB, EC no. 46 (1753), f. 136 (hereafter cited as "Juicio de Liro de Córdova contra Condori"). Some of the litigation is also in "Exp. sobre los capítulos puestos a d. Bartolomé de Fiorilo," AGI, Charcas, Leg. 367 (1752-1756) (hereafter cited as "Exp. sobre . . . Fiorilo").

86 "Exp. sobre . . . Fiorilo," ff. 199-200.

87 Ibid. f. 205.

88 Ibid. f. 210.

89 Ibid. ff. 209-210.

shield, and so the Indians appealed to the judicial authorities as a last resort, invoking the norms guaranteeing communal autonomy and subsistence security in return for complying with state exactions. But once the repartimientos were legalized, the struggle could no longer be waged on moral grounds. The issue of an unjust use of force then became irrelevant. Instead, the Andeans began to base their pleas on the difficulty of meeting their obligations to outside authorities under such harsh conditions. Increasingly, it was coming down to a choice between redeeming debts to the corregidor, on the one hand, and paying tribute and serving the mita, on the other. The magistrates heard Indians threaten to join the thousands of others who had, over the years, cast loose from their villages and thrown off their yoke to the colonial state.[90] More than ever, the corregidor loomed as a menace to the social order of Alto Perú.

In the 1740s, when the Tapacarí Indians testified before the audiencia of La Plata, the magistrates were already antagonistic toward the rapacious corregidores of Alto Perú. Corregidor Fiorilo fit the stereotype well, and he soon found himself on the defensive against charges of fraud and corruption. Specifically, he was accused of charging excessive prices for repartos and of embezzling tribute payments. He requested that the audiencia order a royal inspection of the province. This was done, and, as he hoped, the royal inspector absolved the corregidor of malfeasance. But the Tapacarí Indians rejected the inspector's report. They complained that the vecino who was in charge of investigating whether the corregidor had underregistered tributaries had not conducted his own census count but had simply solicited lists of resident Indians from local hacendados. A lawyer pointed out on behalf of the Tapacareños that landlords chronically underregistered their forastero tenants. The oidores eventually indicted Fiorilo on two counts: hiding tributaries and overcharging Indians for repartos.[91]

This action provoked opposition far from the scene of the crime and the court. In Lima, the case against Fiorilo seemed to represent the mountain court's offensive against corregidores and their mercantile pursuits, in which Lima's merchant aristocracy was heavily involved. The merchants believed that the audiencia of La Plata, in-

90 "Exp. que tiene recurso de los indios de pueblos de Tapacarí, Mojosa, Yaco, y Cavari en Cochabamba y La Paz sobre derechos parroquiales . . .," ANB, EC no. 31. (1761). See also Golte, *Repartos y rebeliones*, 128-139, and Zavala, *Servicio personal*, 3: 51-65.

91 "Exp. sobre . . . Fiorilo," Cuadernos 3 and 7.

clined to favor the mining interests in the area, was turning into a forum in which Indians and other aggrieved people could make their protests, and they demanded that the Lima court, which had superior judicial authority, stem the tide that threatened the alliance of mercantile and political interests embodied in the figure of the corregidor.

Fiorilo himself appealed his case to the Lima court. The oidores of La Plata were slow in responding, and the viceroy accused them of deliberately stalling the judicial review process by failing to remit the proper papers to Lima. But in the end, Fiorilo was exonerated. In 1753, the Council of the Indies endorsed the decision to acquit the corregidor. However, although the council seemed to stand squarely behind the coastal mercantile and political elites of the viceroyalty, that is not all there was to its deliberations. One member of the council praised Fiorilo for his stern rule of the Cochabamba province. The corregidor, he said, may have indulged in corrupt activities at the expense of the royal exchequer, but he imposed ten years of "peace and order" on that volatile land.[92] Only about twenty years had passed, after all, since the bloody rebellion of Calatayud and the mestizos of Cochabamba, and the members of the council presumably had that in mind.

Nevertheless, the council failed to realize how dangerous the state of Andean affairs was becoming. The audiencia of La Plata was almost powerless, and the legitimacy of relations between the colonial state and the village peasants had been destroyed. In Cochabamba, where most Indians lived outside the village structure, the inflated power and the commercial activities of the corregidor were affecting peasants and the urban poor everywhere, not merely in the pueblos reales. In the 1760s and 1770s, voices of discontent were heard in new corners of the province, outside the Andean communities. In 1773, for example, Andean peasants who lived on haciendas in the parish of Yani, in the *partido* (district) of Ayopaya, brought a protest before the oidores of La Plata. They were supported by the testimony of a creole mayor who had served as an intermediary in the repartimiento and found himself a victim of debt because, even with threats and force, he was unable to distribute all the merchandise consigned to his district.[93] Five years later, the city council of Cochabamba rose up against its corregidor and denounced the practice of

92 Ibid., Cuaderno 3.

93 "Testimonio del expediente de teniente de Ayopaya contra el corregidor de Cochabamba," ANB, EC no. 139 (1773).

forcefully distributing goods in the province. The repartimiento must be abolished, the council members argued, because of "all the misery it causes all classes of people . . . threatening them with violence to accept an excessive quantity of goods they do not need; demanding payment before their credit term is over; and obligating others to serve against their own will as debt collectors for the corregidor."[94]

Toward the end of his administration (1761-1776), Viceroy Manuel Amat y Juniente issued a sober warning: "If the present situation continues, the kingdom will fall into ruin, the Indians will vanish . . ., lands will lie fallow, . . . and the mines . . . will be deserted. . . . no peace will reign if [corregidores] continue to persecute Indians."[95] And indeed, violent insurrection did break out throughout the southern Andes in 1780 and 1781, jolting the imperial bureaucracy out of its lethargy. It was only then that the Peruvian viceroy suppressed the repartimiento de mercancías, on the grounds of "the injuries and wrongs which they cause the Indians, whose complaints have flooded the tribunals."[96]

But the measure came too late to prevent a wave of violence from engulfing the land. From Cuzco to Jujuy, peoples of Andean and mixed ancestries joined the rebel guerrillas of Túpac Amarú, in the north, and Túpac Catari, in the south. Almost everywhere, the principal target of attack was the corregidor, the most despised symbol of corruption and exploitation. The uprisings destroyed the bureaucratic apparatus that had permitted the crown to retreat behind the unbridled greed of the corregidores and forsake its obligations to Andean communities.

Against this backdrop of political unrest and ultimately open rebellion, Andean peasants saw their communities threatened. In some villages, they managed to confront the forces of change with a measure of unity and solidarity. But in others, two centuries of colonialism had created disparate and irreconcilably hostile groups. The political tensions of the age magnified the internal class and ethnic divisions. In the Cochabamba valleys, at least, the conjuncture of political and economic forces in the middle and later decades of the eighteenth century could not but disrupt the web of village life.

94 AGN, Sala 9, Interior, 30.1.6, Leg. 4, Exp. 13 (1778).

95 "Relación que hace don Manuel Amat," quoted in Zavala, *Servicio personal*, 3: 61.

96 The quotation is from a proclamation by Viceroy Jauregui in December 1780, as quoted in J. Fisher, *Government and Society in Colonial Peru*, 21.

CHAPTER FOUR

Andean
Village Society

Through the lenses of sixteenth-century documents, the historian can view an uneven, contradictory process of change in the southern Andes—a process in which Andean peoples accommodated and adjusted to some European elements and melded others with Andean traditions to ensure the social reproduction of their culture and communities. The insightful observations of Polo de Ondegardo and Hernando de Santillán, not to mention the native chroniclers, were richly textured with ethnographic detail that revealed keen sensitivity to the norms and customs of the autochthonous groups.[1] They interpreted the values and traditions of Andean societies to the European world and, in the process, documented the resilience and resourcefulness of those societies in the face of the powerful, destructive forces unleased by the arrival of the Europeans. The dialectic of native resistance through adaptation and change is also revealed in early colonial litigation and sometimes even in notarial records chronicling the prosaic or heroic activities of Andean peoples coping with the burdens imposed by the new colonial order. As we saw in chapter 1, such records may show the ways Indians imposed the logic of their own society on the Europeans by manipulating colonial law and concepts of justice to preserve or regain mitmaq colonies in

1 Polo de Ondegardo, "Relación de los fundamentos" and "Informe . . . al Lic. Briviesca de Muñatones"; Hernando de Santillán, "Relación del origen, descendencia, política, y gobierno de los Incas . . ." (1563-1564), in *Collección de libros y documentos referentes a la historia del Perú*, Vol. 9, ser. 2 (Lima: San Martí, 1927), 536a. The most important published indigenous source for seventeenth-century Peru is Poma de Ayala, *Primer nueva corónica*. On the conquest period, see Diego de Castro Titu Cusi Yupanqui, *Relación de la conquista del Perú* (Lima: Biblioteca Universitaria, 1570; 1975), and Frank Salomon, "Chronicles of the Impossible: Notes on Three Peruvian Indigenous Historians," in Rolena Adorno, ed., *From Oral to Written Expression: Native Andean Chronicles of the Early Colonial Period* (Syracuse: Syracuse University Press, 1982), 9–39.

distant maize or coca valleys, for example, or by accumulating capital to purchase land titles as another means of retaining their access to multiple ecological zones. Contemporary narrative reports and the recorded transactions and petitions of Indians in the sixteenth century paint a vivid picture of two societies in collision and demonstrate that Andean peoples were not immediately or absolutely crushed by the weight of colonial rule. Rather, they adapted, often in subtle ways, to the new circumstances in order to preserve small spaces for their traditional practices and beliefs.[2]

The ethnographic detail of sixteenth-century documents is often absent in those of the eighteenth century. In the earlier period, for example, different ethnic strands in the Andean social fabric would be identified, but eighteenth-century bureaucrats rarely bothered to differentiate the Carangas from the Caracaras or the Charcas. Cultural differences among the Andean peoples faded into the background as colonial authorities homogenized Andean peoples into a single category of "Indian," or else differentiated among them according to the territorial-administrative grid that their predecessors had established. The consolidation of a colonial regime, with ideological roots deeply embedded in an ethos of cultural and racial superiority, relegated indigenous cultural distinctions and rivalries to the margins of consciousness and life in this exploitative and conflictual social order. After the frontiers had closed and the intruders had effectively subordinated the indigenous peoples, the Spanish agents of empire no longer felt it necessary to deal with them as near equals or to exploit traditional native enmities. And with the imposition of Spanish hegemony, the opportunities for the Andean peoples to collaborate with the intruders or to manipulate colonial practices to advance their own tribal or ethnic interests against rival Andean groups gradually disappeared.

Thus, the relative absence of European references to indigenous ethnic diversity in the eighteenth century bespeaks the lack of importance that colonial authorities attached to cultural differences among Indians, rather than any process of fusion of various ethnic elements into one mass of "Indians." Indeed, some Andean groups retained their cultural integrity and identity into the late twentieth century.[3] Moreover, colonial civil authorities could afford to ignore

2 See the discussion of the dialectics of tradition and acculturation, resistance and accommodation, in Wachtel, *Vision of the Vanquished*, 140-168, 188-200.

3 See the rich ethnographic literature on contemporary Andean societies in the southern Andes, particularly O. Harris, "Kinship and the Vertical Economy" and

the meaning of culture for Andean peoples only as long as they did not threaten the social order. In periods of unrest, native rebels jolted colonial rulers out of their indifference and ignorance into sharp awareness of native consciousness and respect for the power of cultural identity. At such times, the rulers found that native Andean leaders could effectively manipulate cultural symbols and identities to inspire solidarity or to provide ideological justifications for insurgency. If Spanish authorities were to prevent the frequent Indian revolts from spreading, they had to anticipate the cohesive or divisive cultural forces at work in the heart of Andean rural society. However, in normal times, when natives passively expressed their resistance to colonial rule in daily actions or rituals that are largely hidden from historians, most high-level administrators were only dimly aware of the complexities of ethnic cultures or the beliefs and rituals that infused meaning into agricultural work and other ordinary activities.

In the same way, eighteenth-century European observers failed to appreciate the significance of hierarchy in Indian societies, perceiving it primarily in terms of European standards of status, function, or wealth. The dominant image was that of villages inhabited by homogeneous groups of barefoot peasants living perilously close to the margin of subsistence and ruled or governed by a privileged group of caciques. To European eyes, Andean societies were internally stratified either according to a native's relationship to the state or outside administrator (e.g. as tributary, mitayo, or cultural broker) or according to his access to local resources. The sensitive Spanish observers of the sixteenth century, who recognized the ideology and practice of reciprocity and redistribution that both governed and mitigated the relations of hierarchy and subordination among members of the same ethnic group had few counterparts in the eighteenth century. Moreover, the eighteenth-century records of the censuses (*padrones*) carried out by the colonial authorities concentrate their attention on the village unit, neglecting Andean self-definitions of kinship and community at either the subvillage or the transvillage level. Ayllus, mitmaq strands, and other native forms of affiliation do not readily appear in these census reports. After two centuries of colonial rule, ethnic and kinship affiliations were certainly harder to trace, but colonial authorities were not assiduously looking for them, either. As the Bourbons tightened and centralized state authority over In-

"Labor and Produce," and Platt, "Espejos y maiz" and "Role of the Andean Ayllu."

dian communities in the aftermath of the 1781 rebellions and tried
to reverse the trend toward population dispersion and migration
among the Indians, they were intent upon resurrecting the old Toledan model of the village. The search for more tributaries prompted
royal authorities to redivide Andean settlements into discrete clusters of households. As Toledo had done two hundred years before (see
chapter 2), Bourbon administrators in the late eighteenth century
transmuted Andean concepts of space and association into Spanish
territorial and administrative units although they continued to rec-
ognize native moieties, because these were useful subvillage units of
governance and tribute collection. In many census records, villages
were further divided into spatial and administrative subcategories,
which sometimes overlapped with indigenous definitions of communal groups. In the cabecera village of Tapacarí, for example, census records grouped people into *anexos* (which vaguely corresponded
to ayllus) and *estancias* (spatial clusters of peasant households).

The padrones, then, provide a kind of three-dimensional view of
village society: a hierarchy of territorial and administrative units;
clusters of originarios and forasteros; and a society atomized into individuals and households, whose fiscal status was determined by
sex, age, and ascriptive status in the community of residence. Obviously, they are rich sources for the historian, but their administrative purpose of pinning down tributaries and holding in check the
number of tax evaders and ausentes skewed the vision of most colonial observers in the late eighteenth century. Few among them
caught sight of vestigial forms of vertical archipelagos or understood
the contradictory forces that governed social relations among peasant households, extended kin groups, or moieties. For deeper com-
prehension of the texture of village society and the content of social
relations, the historian must rely on judicial records that give voice
to Andeans' expressions of protest, denunciation, or denial and that
reveal, in moments of crisis, the moral sinews that held their societies together.

Even phrased in European or administrative terms, however, the
Andean village remains a useful analytic construct through which to
study the intersection of colonial forces of change and the actions
and consciousness of Andean peoples responding to broader historical patterns. A principal unit of social control under colonial rule,
the village was always a sensitive pressure point of the often contradictory forces of political economy to which Andean peasants responded, by acquiescence, transformation, or resistance. The village
is also a point of departure for studying the ways in which Andean
peoples initiated change and altered colonial society, sometimes im-

posing their own dictates or limits on the power of the colonial state or market when it threatened to violate their own material and cultural integrity.

And yet, while they might draw upon their cultural heritage, ethnic identity, and communal tradition to mitigate or defy the pressures of alien institutions, village Indians were more exposed to imperial policies and naked force than were those Indians who inhabited hacienda lands and whose relation to the outside world was mediated by a landlord. Village Indians had greater scope and authority in structuring the social and technical arrangements within their society to ensure subsistence to its members and to meet their obligations to the state, but they also carried many more burdens of obligations to claimants both outside and inside their community than did most peasants living on estates. Theoretically, village Indians who collectively shared the rights and responsibilities bestowed by community membership drew upon a wellspring of tradition and ideology that placed a premium on self-sufficiency and subsistence, reciprocity and community. These ideals set parameters of economic and social justice, which the Toledan state originally preserved in modified form. In the late colonial era, Andean peoples still invoked the traditional normative order to censure deviant behavior within their own societies and to challenge the legitimacy of authorities both inside and outside their communities. The extent to which those norms actually governed social relations among factions and individuals within village society, however, is only beginning to be explored in the historical literature.[4]

The Pueblos Reales in Flux

Probably more than most other Andean communities in the eighteenth century, Cochabamba's pueblos reales were marginalized, weak, and "contaminated" by outside economic and ideological in-

4 On social relations in village society during the latter half of the colonial period, see Spalding, *Huarochirí* and her earlier work, *De indio a campesino: Cambios en la estructura del Perú colonial* (Lima: Instituto de Estudios Peruanos, 1974); Stern, "Struggle for Solidarity" and "The Age of Andean Insurrection, 1742-1782: A Reappraisal" (paper presented at the Social Science Research Council/University of Wisconsin Conference on Resistance and Rebellion in the Andean World, 18th-20th centuries, Madison, Wis., Apr. 26-28, 1984); Sánchez-Albornoz, *Indios y Tributos*; Brooke Larson, "Caciques, Class Structure, and the Colonial State," *Nova Americana*, no. 2 (1978): 197-235; Rasnake, "Kurahkunah," chap. 3; and Daniel Santamaría, "La propiedad de la tierra y la condición social del indio en el Alto Perú, 1780-1810," *Desarrollo económico*, no. 66 (1977): 253-271.

fluences. The five villages (Tapacarí, Capinota, Sipesipe, El Paso, and Tiquipaya) were not equally decayed or factionalized, but in comparison to communities elsewhere in Alto Perú, which had preserved their ethnic identity, collective strength, and group self-sufficiency, they were in a sorry state. The historical roots of their malaise went back to the time of the conquest and the Toledan reforms, when royal villages were created, almost arbitrarily, out of an amalgam of ethnic splinter groups, both autochthonous and mitmaq (see chapters 1 and 2). In many cases, chieftains were named for their association with the Incas, not because they were the "natural" leaders of a particular ethnic polity. Such community cohesion and solidarity as existed were forged by the imperatives of the colonial situation. Leadership in the valleys was imposed from above and was dependent upon the support of encomenderos and, later, the colonial state. But even the sanction of community status by the Toledan state was not sufficient to protect the five pueblos from the advance of private landowning and the seepage of tributaries to the chácaras. Already internally fragmented in the late sixteenth century, the villages were increasingly confronted by European colonists who extended their control over the fertile lands, competed for access to water, and pressed against the frail boundaries of the Indian communities. By the early seventeenth century, private estates had gained the edge over the Indian communities in the competition for land and labor. By the end of the first decade of the nineteenth century, the five villages contained less than 25 percent of the "Indians" recorded in the tribute census (table 6). To be "Indian" in this region was, for the most part, to live under the domination of a landlord, side by side with peasants, traders, and artisans of mixed ancestry and ambiguous cultural origins.

⁀ The villages of Cochabamba were subject to another outside force

Table 6. Tributary Population of Cochabamba, 1683-1808

	1683	1737	1786	1793	1808
Total Tributary population	6,735	5,484ᵃ	10,773	8,854	11,718
Tributary population of the pueblos reales	2,179	1,918	2,864	2,935	2,859
Percentage of total in pueblos reales	32	35	27	33	24

Sources: See table A-1.

ᵃ Does not include tributary population of the district of Ayopaya.

during the colonial period: the influx of forasteros. As pointed out in chapter 3, the pueblos assimilated a large proportion of forasteros. Even by the time of Palata's census, the forastero population constituted about 80 percent of their inhabitants. Conversely, in four of the five censuses taken between 1683 and 1808, originarios and their families composed less than one-quarter of the villages' population (table 7). The social consequences of Andean immigration for the patterns of landholding and social relationships in those villages cannot be determined from the padrones alone, but it is likely that forasteros remained in their host villages for longer than a generation, at least during the second half of the colonial period. Most forasteros (or their forebears) originated in a distant, "foreign" village. While there may have been some "crossovers" between the categories of forastero and orginario, as Platt found for the villages of Chayanta, the preponderance of forasteros in the Cochabamba pueblos has to be explained primarily by in-migration and settlement.[5] In a material way, then, the forastero influx peopled the valley pueblos in the face of sharp population decline. But in so doing, they further fragmented the ethnic makeup of village society. While the villages may have assimilated forasteros through religious sodalities (cofradías) religious rituals, communal obligations, and intermarriage in the early period,[6] by the eighteenth century they were so "bottom heavy" with forasteros that there was but a small core group to perform that function. We may speculate then, that forasteros increasingly were "outsiders" in their host villages. The padrones of the eighteenth century assumed that forasteros had no landholding rights, or the attendant communal responsibilities, in their villages. They did have access to community resources through such economic relationships as paying rent or dues in return for usufruct rights or perhaps through the patronage of a cacique. But in neither case did they enjoy communal membership or share in the community's obligations to the state. Even after forasteros were converted to tributaries, they still found insulation from certain onerous burdens. But as a group of outsiders, they were subordinate to and dependent on the

5 Platt, *Estado boliviano y ayllu andino*, chap. 2. A major difference between Chayanta and Cochabamba, however, was the relatively small proportion of forasteros in the former. In 1754, the percentages of forasteros in Cochabamba and Chayanta were 83 percent and 29 percent, respectively: Golte, *Repartos y rebeliones*, 55.

6 Saignes, "Políticas étnicas," p. 13.

Table 7. Originario Population of the Villages of Cochabamba, 1683-1808

	1683		1737		1786		1793		1808	
Village	Number	Percentage of Total Population	Number	Percentage of Total Population	Number	Percentage of Total Population	Number	Percentage of Total Population	Number	Percentage of Total Population
Tapacarí	75	12.8	165	28.0	150	10.2	200	13.6	202	12.9
Sipesipe	65	16.8	68	25.0	68	17.0	156	37.1	133	36.1
El Paso	113	26.4	56	26.3	38	22.3	108	45.8	99	49.0
Tiquipaya	77	22.4	161	70.0	90	23.5	143	33.0	143	34.4
Capinota	81	19.3	187	30.4	87	19.2	83[a]	—	79	26.0
Total	411	18.9	637	33.2	433	15.1	690	23.7	656	23.0

Sources: AGN, Sala 13, Padrones, 18.1.1, Leg. 41; 18.1.5, Leg. 45; 18.2.2, Leg. 47; 18.2.5, Leg. 50; and 3.4.4, Leg. 54.
[a] Census report not available; this figure is the average of the figures for 1786 and 1808.

native authorities in their host villages. Forasteros, for the most part, inhabited the poorer and less secure niches of village society.

Another index of the villages' weak defense against outside forces was the impoverishment of their communal property. None of the Indian villages possessed a capital stock—valued in money—sufficient to guarantee a minimum income to community members in times of crop failure or to underwrite their tribute dues. It is true that the peasants of Capinota and Tapacarí retained access to high-altitude pastures and arable fields, as well as to warm, moist acreage suitable for maize cultivation, which afforded the kind of social insurance against drought, flood, frost, and blight upon which Andean peoples traditionally had depended. But colonial authorities measured the economic stability of villages in terms of the monetary value of their communal holdings and, particularly, the liquid capital in their treasuries. Periodically, colonial officials expressed concern about the decapitalized condition of the Indian communities and devised schemes to restock the villages' larders. They blamed the pauperization of village Indians not on the colonial system itself, but on corrupt corregidores, caciques, or landowners who drained the villages of their cash reserves.

In the 1770s, when colonial authorities were attempting to increase tribute-producing revenues, they spoke out once more against the burden on village treasuries. They admonished landowning families who still owed money to village Indians and ordered them to pay their debts. Many creole landowners in Peru had inherited mortgages that originally drew upon the treasuries of Andean villages and were subsequently swollen by unpaid interest at the rate of 5 percent per year. A royal inventory in 1776 showed a total of 120,000 pesos of such debts still outstanding; a single hacienda, one of several named Queroquero, owed 5,430 pesos to the village of Sipesipe—most of it interest that had not been paid for 181 years (see table A-4). Twenty years later, Francisco de Viedma was still complaining about these debts. He calculated that Indians had claims against hacendados for 202,365 pesos in principal and 579,044 pesos in interest. In his own intendancy, the five pueblos had liquid assets amounting to only 2,142 pesos; yet the village of Tapacarí alone was owed interest in the amount of 150,000 pesos.[7]

At the same time, the Indian villages of Cochabamba supported a

---

7 "Correspondencia con los gobernadores e intendentes de Cochabamba y La Paz" (July 24, 1797) AGI, Charcas (Ramo Secular), Leg. 436; and Viedma, *Descripción geográfica*, 183-187.

heavier tax burden than many other communities of the altiplano. The reason was that royal tax collectors in the late eighteenth century set the tribute rates of originarios according to the assessed market value and productivity of village lands. In Cochabamba's maize valleys, as well as in other eastern lowland regions, the originario landholders paid high tribute dues for usufruct rights to superior acreage.[8] The originarios of Capinota, who occupied what was considered to be some of the richest territory in the region, were assessed at 10 pesos 1.5 reales, and the rates for the originarios of the other villages were not much lower (see table 8). The originarios in the region had the option of delivering a portion of their dues in maize, but they probably did not exercise it very often, since the value of the crop was arbitrarily fixed at 12.5 reales per fanega—a value that was probably always lower than its market price. Whether they paid entirely in cash or partially in kind, the village Indians of the maize valleys paid about twice the annual tax that highland village Indians were assessed. The originarios of Pacajes, for example, paid only 5 pesos each in tribute, and the Indians of Chayanta, 4 pesos 7 reales. Even the landless forasteros of Cochabamba's maize valleys paid a higher rate (6 pesos 2 reales) than the landholding inhabitants of highland villages.[9]

The Indian villages of Cochabamba were not all equally impoverished or vulnerable to outside commercial forces. Sipesipe, El Paso, and Tiquipaya appeared to be in the worst state of decay (see table 9). El Paso, once the rich and prized encomienda of Polo de Ondegardo, was almost extinct by the late eighteenth century. A mere 38 originarios inhabited the village in 1786, compared to the 684 tributaries registered by Toledo in 1573, although this population loss had been partly mitigated by the entry of forasteros, who numbered 192 by then. But mestizos and creoles outnumbered Indians of both categories in the village. During his inspection of El Paso in the 1780s, Francisco de Viedma described the village as a ghost town, abandoned by Indians who feared the mita or who never returned from the mines.[10] Viedma commissioned a royal inventory of village lands that were not being cultivated by village peasants and ordered them to be leased on five-year terms. The rent proceeds were to go to the

8 "Informe de la contaduría de retasa sobre la revisita del partido de Santa Cruz" (Feb. 25, 1793), RAH, ML, 9/1733, Tomo 78.

9 AGN, Sala 9, Justicia, 31.3.4, Leg. 7, Exp. 91 (1778), and AGN, Sala 13, Padrones, 17.6.1, 17.10.2, and 18.2.1, Leg. 46 (1786-1787).

10 Viedma, *Descripción geográfica*, 67-68 and 180.

Table 8. Annual Tribute Dues in Pueblos Reales, Census of 1785-1787

	Originarios			Forasteros		
Pueblo Real	Monetary Tribute per Originario	Total Monetary Tribute	Maize (fanegas)	Monetary Tribute per Forastero	Total Monetary Tribute	Total for Pueblo Real[a]
Tapacarí	9/2	1,400	76	6/2	10,137	11,628
Sipesipe	9/7.5	617	50	6/2	2,081	2,757
El Paso	9/7.5	351	22	6/2	1,200	1,578
Tiquipaya	9/5	794	62	6/2	950	2,817
Capinota	10/1.5	—	—	6/2	—	3,167

Sources: AGN, Sala 13, Padrones, 18.2.1, Leg. 46; 18.2.2, Leg. 47; 18.2.3, Leg. 48.

Note: Monetary tribute per originario or forastero is given in pesos corrientes and reales; amount of total tribute is given in pesos corrientes.

[a] Including value of maize at officially fixed price of 12.5 reales per fanega. Total tribute payments given in primary source differ from calculated sums of tribute dues (including maize) for each pueblo.

Table 9. Tributary Population of the Five Pueblos Reales of Cochabamba,
1573 and 1786

Pueblo Real	1573 Total	1786 Total	Originarios	Forasteros
Tapacarí	1,173	1,465	150	1,315
Sipesipe	819	401	68	333
El Paso	684	230	38	192
Tiquipaya	504	402	90	312
Capinota	419	366	87	279

Sources: "Tasa de la visita general de Francisco de Toledo," AGI, Contaduría, Leg. 1786;
AGN, Sala 13, Padrones, 18.2.1, Leg. 46; 18.2.2, Leg. 47; 18.2.3, Leg. 48.

royal treasury. El Paso, along with its neighboring villages, Sipesipe
and Tiquipaya, apparently had large tracts of such "excess lands" (*so-
brantes de comunidad*).[11] Neither land shortage nor population den-
sity seemed to be an important factor in the exodus of originarios
from El Paso.

El Paso was flanked on the southwest by Sipesipe, the ancient
royal pastures and maize fields of the Incas and the fertile headlands
of the valley, and by Tiquipaya on the east. As in El Paso, clusters of
peasants cultivated irrigated lands in both those villages. The population was racially mixed, with natives composing 56 percent of the
inhabitants of Sipesipe and 40 percent of Tiquipaya's population in
the 1780s.[12] Among the native population, forasteros greatly outnumbered originarios in all three of these villages (table 9). Their influx into Tiquipaya brought the tributary population in 1786 to
about 80 percent of the size of the tributary labor force in 1573. Sipesipe's tributary population, on the other hand, was still only half
what it had been two centuries earlier.

The three villages had enjoyed little political or cultural insularity
during the colonial period. Occupying some of the richest irrigated
land in the entire region, they were a choice target of non-Andeans.
Before the end of the seventeenth century, they had lost portions of
their territory to colonial encroachers, who leased or squatted on
parcels of land. Sipesipe had lost 27 percent of its tributary population to private landholders. Some of those peasants may have lived
outside the boundaries of the pueblo, on estate land, while they continued to pay tribute dues to their community, but many others

11 "Informe del Augustín Antesana sobre las tierras de Sacpaya (pueblo de Capinota)" (Dec. 24, 1821), AHMC, Leg. 1068.

12 Viedma, *Descripción geográfica* 66–68.

probably were absorbed by Spanish landholders who leased or expropriated village lands along with their peasant inhabitants (mostly
forasteros). Tiquipaya, too, had lost some of its maize lands and almost 20 percent of its resident Indian population to Spanish landholders.[13] The villages also were invaded by creole and mestizo traders, landholders, pack drivers, and artisans. In 1788, Tiquipaya was
inhabited by more non-Andeans than by natives, and almost half of
the total populations of Sipesipe and El Paso consisted of outsiders.[14]
The incursion of outsiders probably intensified even further toward
the end of the colonial era. In the Quillacollo parish, contiguous to
the valley pueblos, the number of private landholding units increased from the sixteen listed in the 1786 census to thirty-three in
the 1804 census.[15] By land reclamation and the advance of arable
land, and by the internal division of Spanish-held property units,
pressure on the pueblos became ever greater. Trial records from this
period are replete with challenges and counterchallenges over land
and, particularly, water rights. Typical was the struggle of Tiquipaya
to prevent the wealthy and powerful hacendado and merchant family, Boado y Quiroga, from siphoning off precious water flowing
down from the mountains. Boado y Quiroga controlled fields situated upland from the village and was able to divert the stream to his
own lands. The Indians claimed they had rights to the *mita de agua*
for ten days and nights each month during the growing season, rights
which they contended had been ratified by the colonial court in
1647.[16] But even under the invigorated Bourbon state, following the
1781 rebellions, the villages could not count on the state's protection against the forces of attrition (see chapter 8). Situated in the
heartland of the maize valleys, densely populated with peasants,
smallholders, and hacendados, the three pueblos reales could do little to shield themselves.

West and southwest of the Valle Bajo, where the valleys narrowed
and followed the flow of the rivers cutting their way through the
mountains, lay Capinota and Tapacarí (see figure 1). Less is known
about Capinota than about any of the other pueblos of Cochabamba.

13 AGN, Sala 13, Padrones, 18.1.1, Leg. 41, and 18.1.3, Leg. 43.

14 Viedma, *Descripción geográfica*, 66-68.

15 Sánchez-Albornoz, *Indios y tributos*, 178.

16 Land transactions, stock holdings, and other fragments of information about
the Boada y Quiroga family's wealth are found in local notarial books of the second half of the eighteenth century. See also, "Los caciques de Tiquipaya sobre la
mita de agua . . ." ANB, EC no. 46 (1793).

Geographically separated from the central valleys by a small mountain range, the village was somewhat protected from the advance of Spanish landholding that was occurring there. Yet it was not an isolated village. Its fertile lands flanked the Arque River, which carved a trade corridor through the mountains. The village served as a way station for travelers and traders en route to Chuquisaca and Potosí, and it was the point of departure for the caravan of pack animals and mitayo families that left the province each year for the mines. Sheltered by the mountains, watered by the river, the valley of Capinota was one of the most fertile corners of the region. Its peasants cultivated high-quality grain and alfalfa in the alluvial soil and tended fruit orchards. The rivers powered local mills, owned by creoles, where Indians ground their corn. In years of abundant harvest, Capinota peasants probably marketed a portion of their crop in the market town of Arque, the next town up the river toward the western puna. Capinota's excellent agricultural conditions and the town's location attracted many settlers. More than one thousand people, variously labeled as Spaniards, cholos, and mulattoes, lived among the village's 2,400 Indians in 1788.[17] Some of those people were transient pack drivers, who stationed themselves in the town of Capinota while they waited for business. Others owned mills in the area or leased parcels of village land. Two large Spanish haciendas occupied land inside the village territory and supported 220 forasteros (table 10). Consequently, the peasants of Capinota sometimes were forced to fight to protect their rights to the mita de agua and their herds and pastures. In 1788, Juan José Paniagua, one of the wealthier landowners in the province, claimed title to certain Indian lands on the

Table 10. Indian Population of the Village of Capinota, 1787

	Moiety of Anansaya	Moiety of Urinsaya	Total
Originarios	156	218	374
Forasteros with land	45	16	61
Total landed tributaries	201	234	435
Forasteros without land			1,446
On estancias (n = 28)			1,044[a]
On haciendas (n = 2)			220
In villages (n = 2)			182

Source: AGN, Sala 13, Padrones, 18.2.3, Leg. 48, ff. 606-607.
[a] Including 112 forasteros at the ranch and mill of Sicaya.

17 Viedma, *Descripción geográfica*, 67-68.

ground that they had not previously been cultivated—a tactic frequently employed by local hacendados and one that was similar to the justification being used in North America around the same time.[18] Paniagua had cleared a hillside field for the planting of maize and had built a reservoir and canals to irrigate the field. The Indians accused him of seizing their animals that were grazing in the vicinity.[19]

While hacendados were testing the borders of village autonomy and territory, highland caciques challenged the authority of the caciques of Capinota in a land dispute that had its origins in early colonial times. The subparish of Arque, San Cristóbal de Sicaya, was inhabited by a small group of Carangas mitimaes who were associated through kin ties to their nuclear village of Toledo, located in the highland province of Paria. This was probably the strongest surviving ethnic network in the Cochabamba province that still bound lowlanders to their highland kin groups, administrative boundaries notwithstanding. These mitimaes, numbering only 112 persons in 1787, still possessed rich lands, herds, and grain mills in the "hacienda Sicaya," as it was listed in the padron.[20] The caciques of Capinota apparently accepted their presence as forasteros in the subparish, but in the 1780s the highland caciques claimed jurisdiction over them and argued that they should have originario status, since the mitimaes' land rights had originally been granted by the highland caciques. If this claim were upheld, the highland caciques would then be entitled to the revenue from the mitimaes. On the other hand, it was in the interest of the caciques of Capinota to apply European standards of village membership: they considered the mitimaes to be immigrants—forasteros who had settled on village land that rightfully belonged to their own people of Capinota and who therefore owed taxes as forasteros to the village of Capinota. Classification of the mitimaes of Sicaya as forasteros of Capinota meant a heavier tribute burden on them, for although forasteros usually paid tribute at a lower rate, in this case the forasteros of Cochabamba were considered to have access (through the payment of rent) to such high-quality acreage that they were assessed at a higher rate than

18 On land claims in North America based on a European interpretation of "vacant" lands, see Robert F. Berkhofer, *The White Man's Indian* (New York: Knopf, 1978), 119ff.

19 "Exp. por el indio pral. José Tastara contra Juan José Paniagua por daños . . . que le hace en sus sementeras, con sus ganados," AHMC, Leg. 999 (1788).

20 AGN, Sala 13, Padrones, 18.2.2, Leg. 47 (1787).

most originarios in Alto Perú. As mitimaes of the highland village of Toledo, the Sicaya Indians would owe the crown five pesos annually, but as forasteros in the fertile river valley, they paid the standard forastero rate of six pesos two reales. It is hardly surprising, therefore, that a royal inspector resolved the dispute in favor of Capinota's caciques.[21] In doing so, he obliterated one of the region's last vestiges of vertical landholding articulated through kinship ties.

Capinota was divided into moieties (parcialidades): an upper division, Anansaya, and a lower division, Urinsaya. These groups were administered separately by their own caciques, who were responsible for delivering tribute and dispatching mitayos. Urinsaya was the larger of the two, but the originario population of both these parcialidades did not amount to more than 20 percent of Capinota's Indian households (see table 10). The originarios has access to lands on various tiers of the vertical landscape within the village territory, though their holdings were concentrated on the alluvial plain that fanned out from the river banks. Forasteros, on the other hand, were dispersed among the hillsides, where they cultivated maize, wheat, and potatoes in drier soil and tended their herds. They lived and worked in the units listed in the padrón as estancias, which did not seem to be subordinated to caciques of either moiety.

The pattern of settlement was quite different in the village of Tapacarí.[22] The town of that name was located at the confluence of two rivers, which irrigated nearby lands, nibbled away at the hillsides, carved passageways through the cordillera, and flooded their banks for three months each year during the rainy season, isolating the town from the central valleys. The territory of Tapacarí was vast, stretching across some 4,733 *fanegadas* of mostly unirrigated land at altitudes ranging from 8,200 to 14,800 feet. (A fanegada was the area of land that could be sown with a fanega of seed.) Few non-Indians inhabited the village, but forasteros outnumbered originarios even more than in the other pueblos reales of the province (see table 9). The parcialidad of Anansaya was larger than that of Urinsaya. Outside the immediate environs of the pueblo of San Augustín de Tapacarí, members of Anansaya were distributed among forty estancias, those of Urinsaya among only twenty estancias (see table 11). According to Sánchez-Albornoz, on only three of these estancias did members of the two parcialidades mingle with each other. By and

21 "Exp. sobre que se cobre el tributo de indios forasteros en Arque (pueblo de Capinota)," AHMC, Leg. 1256 (1786).

22 Sánchez-Albornoz, *Indios y tributos*, 173-176.

Figure 8   The Pueblo Real of Tapacarí

large, the members of Anansaya lived in Tapacarí proper and in the anexos and estancias of its hinterlands (Tallija, Guaico, Chicmuri, and Tirata). The originarios and forasteros of Urinsaya also cultivated lands near the town of Tapacarí, but many forasteros of Urinsaya inhabited remote estancias of Muclli or occupied land on haciendas in the Spanish parishes of Calliri and Ramada, two islands of white settlement to the east of the community. The dispersion of forasteros among the numerous estancias shows how far settlement conditions had deviated from the original Toledan model of the nucleated village.

Still more striking is the degree of integration of originario and forastero families. Forasteros lived in all the estancias, outnumbering originarios there by nearly nine to one, but there was at least one originario family in almost every estancia as well. A detailed census of the anexo of Tallija illustrates the pattern (see table 12). In each of the seven estancias there were between one and three originario households, along with an average of thirty forastero families.

This pattern of distribution of forasteros and originarios among Tapacarí's estancias and anexos raises important questions about the relations of production and exchange in the village. Sánchez-Albornoz speculates about a hierarchical relationship between originarios (who perhaps served as overseers) and forasteros.[23] If that was the case, how deep was the social divide between these groups? Were

23 Ibid., 175.

Table 11. Places of Settlement of the Tributaries of Village of Tapacarí, 1786

Parish	Parcialidad of Anansaya				Parcialidad of Urinsaya			
	Settled Places	All Tributaries	Originarios	Forasteros	Settled Places	All Tributaries	Originarios	Forasteros
Tapacarí								
San Augustín	1	9	0	9	1	8	2	6
Estancias	40	411	53	358	20	137	29	108
Tallija								
Anexo	1	54	3	51	—	—	—	—
Estancias	7	119	7	112	—	—	—	—
Guaico								
Anexo	1	14	1	13	1	39	6	33
Estancias	16	233	18	215	—	—	—	—
Chicmuri								
Anexo	1	25	1	24	1	18	0	18
Estancias	3	44	2	42	4	25	3	22
Tirata								
Anexo	1	30	5	25	—	—	—	—
Estancias	6	83	5	78	—	—	—	—
Itapaya								
Anexo	1	48	9	39	1	37	5	32
Estancias	3	9	0	9	2	21	0	21
Muclli								
Anexo	—	—	—	—	1	19	0	19
Estancias	—	—	—	—	4	61	0	61
Ramada								
Haciendas	—	—	—	—	5	21	1	20
Calliri								
Haciendas	—	—	—	—	16	307	0	307
Number of tributaries in anexos[a]		180	19	161		121	13	108
Number of tributaries in estancias		899	85	814		244	32	212
Number of tributaries in haciendas		0	0	0		328	1	327
Total number of tributaries		1,079	104	975		693	46	647

Source: Adapted from Sánchez-Albornoz, *Indios y tributos*, 174. (Differences between the figures in this table and those in other tables on related subjects are due to differences in the primary sources used.)
[a] Including the town of San Augustín.

Table 12. Distribution of the Population of Anexo of Tallija, 1798

Location	Adult Males			Adult Females			Minors	
	Tributaries	Reservados[a]	Ausentes	Married	Unmarried	Widowed	Adolescent Boys	Others
Village								
Originarios	3	0	0	2	1	0	1	4
Forasteros	69	13	2	69	27	29	15	140
Estancias								
Yarbicoya								
Originarios	3	0	0	3	3	0	0	3
Forasteros	13	3	1	11	5	3	0	31
Antagacua								
Originarios	3	0	0	3	0	0	0	6
Forasteros	34	6	4	31	7	8	8	58
Challoma								
Originarios	2	0	0	3	0	0	0	1
Forasteros	12	3	0	12	3	1	3	17
Casilliri y Caramarca								
Originarios	1	1	0	2	1	0	0	3
Forasteros	11	1	0	11	3	1	4	17
Guaylla								
Originarios	1	0	0	1	1	0	0	3
Forasteros	3	0	0	3	0	1	1	8
Challa Abajo								
Originarios	3	0	0	3	0	0	0	8
Forasteros	34	9	3	32	2	3	8	51
Challe del Medio								
Originarios	3	0	0	3	0	0	2	5
Forasteros	36	7	3	33	7	7	8	68
Total	231	43	13	222	60	53	50	423
Originarios	19	1	0	20	6	0	3	33
Forasteros	212	42	13	202	54	53	47	390

Source: AGN, Sala 13, Padrones, 18.3.2, Leg. 52 (1798).
[a] Elderly or disabled (exempt from tribute).

forasteros an underclass of landless and dependent peasants? Or did tributary status have little bearing on the social relations of production and the conditions of life in the village? Did class relations and social differentiation perhaps cut through the village social hierarchy in different ways?

Obviously, the static picture of village society provided by the padrones reveals very little about these relations or about the normative order that legitimated them. But judicial records containing the testimony of Andean peasants and village authorities open perspectives on the internal tensions, alignments, and conditions of life and work in the villages. As we saw in chapter 3, Tapacarí around midcentury was caught in the throes of a bitter struggle between two cacique families. That feud began to intensify under the rule of the corregidor Fiorilo Pérez, who threw his support behind one of the rival caciques and meddled in internal village affairs. Moreover, Fiorilo and his collaborators imposed repartos on Tapacarí peasant households and aroused the resentment of Tapacareños by intensifying the economic pressures on them. On the surface, the judicial records chronicle the peasants' protest against their common enemy, the corregidor, but they also reveal the deeper crosscurrents and conflicts in Tapacarí society, where caciques fought each other to preserve their authority and legitimacy and where peasants resisted the burdens they bore at the expense of their own well-being.

A Cacique Rivalry

Beginning in the 1740s and lasting for twenty years or more, a bitter rivalry raged between two cacique families in the village of Tapacarí. The protagonists were on the one hand, Pedro Condori, a cacique of Urinsaya, and his son Blas; and, on the other, Juan Guillermo Liro de Córdova, son and heir of a former cacique of Anansaya who had been stripped of his authority by the corregidor Fiorilo.[24] The central issue in the dispute was the control of village lands. Pedro Condori and Liro de Córdova accused each other of expropriating communal lands, whose fruits were supposed to meet the subsistence needs of village peasants in times of need or tribute deficits and to supply mitayo caravans. The privatization of these lands was a violation of

---

24 "Juicio de Liro de Córdova contra Condori." Other sources pertaining to this feud are in AGI, Charcas, Legs. 367 and 525. Information about the Liro de Córdova family and its holdings and political status in Tapacarí is found in wills and property transactions in local notarial records, cited in note 65. See also AGN, Sala 9, Tribunales, 37.3.6, Leg. 9, Exp. 164.

Andean principles (sanctioned by the colonial state) governing their management, use, and redistribution, and it was held to be corroding the moral economy of Tapacarí. Perhaps more important, a cacique trying to win the sympathy and support of the magistrates in the court of La Plata knew the land issue mattered to the colonial authorities. As pointed out in chapter 3, there was at this time growing concern that caciques and corregidores were carving haciendas out of community land and tying Indians down, hiding them from tax collectors and obstructing the flow of mitayos to Potosí. The feuding caciques were aware of this issue.

In one of the court cases that marked the dispute, Pedro Condori described the rich pastures and bountiful crops of Tapacarí. He listed thirty-three wheat fields, seven patches of white and dark maize scattered across the *quebradas* (ravines) and hinterlands and in the puna, eight parcels of quinoa land, fourteen fields of potatoes, and two "chacras" of ocas. He estimated that the community harvested more than 1,400 fanegas of wheat in an average year and 2,000 fanegas in a good season. So endowed, the peasants of Tapacarí should have been able to meet their tribute obligations without strain. And yet, Condori said, Tapacarí tributaries were always in arrears.[25]

The problem, he argued, lay in the way the community's productive resources were distributed. He charged that the Liro de Córdova family had cornered most of the reserve land, and to prove his accusation, he presented an inventory of the "excessive amount" of land in Liro de Córdova's possession: the hacienda Aparumiri, comprising irrigated and dry lands on the outskirts of Tapacarí; the hacienda and chacra of Amaru; the chacra of Tirata, located in the highlands of Tapacarí (listed in a later padron as an anexo); the estancia Escalera, with fields of barley, quinoa, and ocas; and the estancia Quenuasunturu.[26] Condori accused Liro de Córdova of "ruining their generation" of Indians and threatening the community's economic integrity by parceling out its lands to his followers and minions—all of them outsiders, whom Condori described as follows:

> They are only newly arrived forasteros, but because they are his partisans and part of his faction, they enjoy and possess many parcels of land and privileges which they readily abuse, so that

25 "Juicio de Liro de Córdova contra Condori," ff. 6 and 19.

26 Ibid., ff. 19-20; AGN, Sala 13, Padrones, 18.2.2, Leg. 47 (1787). The estancia Escalera is listed in the 1787 census under the anexo of Guiaco; the estancia Quenuasunturu is not listed in that census at all.

you could almost call them hacendados, for they sow 30 to 40 fanegas of wheat seed and they leave other lands fallow, and these people have many other Indian tenants who work for them in exchange for land rights.[27]

In later testimony, Blas Condori admitted that the Condori family also possessed "a parcel of irrigated and dry land and a second plot of potato land in the [Tapacarí] estancia of Guari." He justified these holdings on two grounds: that he had made capital investments in them (presumably to improve them and enhance their value), and that they were payments for his service in the mita twice during his life, once as a mitayo and once as a captain.[28] Thus, we have a curiously twisted argument from this cacique: while he defended the community's right to preserve its communal resources and denounced Liro de Córdova for privatizing "reserve lands," Condori himself considered land to be a commodity whose value could be increased through capital investment. And he claimed his ownership rights on contradictory grounds: his individual entrepreneurial activities and his "service to the collectivity."

Liro de Córdova responded both by defending himself and by making countercharges against Pedro Condori. Some parcels of land ("one in the river valley and pasture land in the puna") he declared he had purchased with cash. He admitted that some of his properties were located within the boundaries of the pueblo real, but said that they were "modest holdings" whose yields benefited the entire community. On the other hand, he spoke of Condori's "great number of chacras" (he listed six estancias) and said they were illegally held because "he neither pays tax nor covers the expenses of the community." What more could the magistrates expect, Liro de Córdova asked, from an Indian who possessed the title of cacique not through inheritance but through appointment by a corrupt corregidor?[29]

Thus, Liro de Córdova did not deny that both he and Condori held community lands in their personal domain, but he insisted that he had rightfully inherited those lands, that he was the poorer of the

---

27 "Y siendo yndios foranos adbenedizos solo por ser parciales y de facción suya gosando y poseen cantidad de tierras y unos provilegios que se abusan de manera que se pueden llamar hazendados pues siembran 30 y 40 fanegas de trigo y para otras tantas dejan para hacer barbechos y estos tienen muchos yndios arrimados a quienes les dan tierras por su trabajo" "Juicio de Liro de Córdova contra Condori," f.4.

28 Ibid., ff. 4-5.

29 Ibid., f. 35.

two rivals, and that his succession to the cacicazgo had not bestowed a patrimony in crops or other forms of community wealth. On the contrary, he had managed the cultivation of his lands using his own seeds and remunerating the labor of Indians.

> When I entered the government they gave me none of the crops that amounted to more than 900 fanegas of wheat, besides potatoes and oca, which are planted in abundance; all those products were collected by Blas Condori . . . , and I did not receive even a grain of seed. I sowed fields with my own seeds, paying for the communal labor of the Indians, as is customary, at one real per day's work.[30]

Liro de Córdova also assured the court that the fruits of his lands were used to satisfy community obligations: to cover tribute debts caused by death, absenteeism, and deprivation. They fed the village during the festivities (*hospicios*) when the corregidor visited Tapacarí, and they were stored for consumption by the mitayos who gathered for six or eight days in the town of San Augustín before setting off for Capinota and Potosí.[31]

In explaining why Tapacarí showed tribute deficits almost every year, Liro de Córdova stressed the sharp fluctuations in the wheat crop from year to year. "There is no doubt . . . that this year I planted 79 or 80 fanegas of wheat, but its yields vary . . . Even if it is a bumper crop and each fanega of seed bears 10 fanegas of fruit, we will only harvest 700 or 800 fanegas of wheat. We take out a fifth of this grain to dry in the granaries for next year's seed."[32] The village's tribute debts therefore could not be reliably paid with surplus crops. It was not a question of land expropriation, according to Liro de Córdova, but simply the fickle hand of Nature that determined how well Tapacarí could meet its obligations to the state.

Putting aside the verbal warfare between the caciques, there was a genuine issue of land concentration among the native elite in the village of Tapacarí. Condori made reference to wealthy Indians—he

---

30 "Quando yo entré al gobierno no se me dió parte en los frutos que esttaban existenttes que pasaron de nobicientos fanegas de trigo fuera de papas y ocas que son los efecttos que se siembran en mas abundancia y que toda dha porcion de efecttos se la cogió y recogió Blas Condori con su madrastra . . . de forma dhas. siembras las mandé hazer con mi propia semilla pagando a los indios su trabajo en lo que es costumbre a real por día." Ibid., f. 32.

31 Ibid., ff. 4-5.

32 Ibid.

called them "proto-hacendados"—who planted thirty or forty fane-gas of wheat seed on lands they individually controlled.[33] Perhaps his self-interest warped his view of land-tenure patterns, but the une-qual access to seeds and arable lands was confirmed many years later by an outsider. The intendant Francisco de Viedma, following a visit to the village in the mid-1780s, made the observation that "the lands that the originarios hold are unjustly and unreasonably distributed; some [originarios] do not hold the two *topos* of land stipulated by the royal statutes, while the caciques and principales have 50, 60, or more fanegadas of land"[34]

Viedma was referring to a native landed oligarchy which by virtue of its status and power, had access to abundant resources. Condori, and later Liro de Córdova, exposed illegitimate landowners other than native members of the political hierarchy. The caciques alluded to the mechanisms of land distribution whereby some forasteros were granted land in the village in return for favors or loyalty to their patron. As was mentioned earlier, forasteros theoretically had an im-personal, contractual relationship with other inhabitants of the vil-lage. They perhaps cultivated the same potato and wheat fields, but as rent-paying tenants, their relationship to nature was mediated through the market. In some cases, which are occasionally docu-mented in notarized wills and court records, forasteros gained land-holding privileges in their host villages through marriage to an en-dowed widow or to a young female member of a local ayllu or village.[35] But such prospects were unlikely under conditions where forasteros vastly outnumbered originarios. Marriage to originario women in Tapacarí (or in the other pueblos) probably did not propel many landless forasteros into positions of economic security or vil-lage membership in this period. Astute alliances with one or another cacique probably afforded a more open avenue for receiving land as-signments (*asignaciones*) in the village, particularly at times of in-tense rivalry and factionalism.

Behind the land question and the allusions to corrupt patronage lurked the issue of economic tyranny. Tapacarí's political fissure in the 1740s and 1750s revealed the accumulated grievances of its local people, and the accusing caciques were among the best chroniclers of the outrages inflicted (by their rival) on village peasants. Blas Con-

33 Ibid., f. 4.

34 Viedma, *Descripción geográfica*, 64.

35 See, for example, "Autos sobre el dro. a las tierras de Pultintiri (Tiquipaya)" AHMC, Leg. 1140 (1752).

dori charged that each person on the potato estancias of Lower Challa, Upper Challa, Antagua, Tallija, Apo, Muclli, and Guaylla was "obligated to cultivate 25 or 30 cargas of potatoes, which were later dried on the highest hillside and turned into chuño."[36] The pastoralists of the puna also paid rent (*yerbaje*) on the lands grazed by their llama herds. Those who owned mares, he claimed, had to pay ten or twelve reales a year, and all the peasants of the puna were required to purchase wheat harvested from Liro de Córdova's estates at fixed prices and on short-term credit. Condori said a group of hilacatas executed Liro de Córdova's orders and collected rent on his behalf.[37] The hilacatas to whom Condori referred may have been originario adult males assigned to live among the clusters of forasteros and to serve as sentinels and as nodes of social control in a network that bound the town of San Augustín de Tapacarí (center of the native hierarchy) to the remote estancias of the puna.

Yet even if this were so, it would hardly constitute the entire picture of Tapacarí's social hierarchy. The categories of originario and forastero were, of course, Spanish colonial constructs designed for fiscal and administrative purposes. However, as we have seen, some forasteros apparently managed to acquire land rights and employ tenants and sharecroppers, while Viedma observed many originario households living on the margin of subsistence. Thus, the status of originario alone did not determine a family's rights to seeds, lands, water, or herds or define its relations to the native hierarchy or to the resident forasteros. Many, perhaps most, members of the originario minority seemed to be impoverished, subordinated, and vulnerable to claimants both inside and outside the village.[38]

The rival caciques were uncharacteristically subdued on this point, but many originario witnesses decried their own inferior status and miserable living conditions. Widows claiming an authorized exemption from tribute and mita were particularly courageous in their denunciations of the caciques. One such widow, María Santuza, complained in 1758 that

> at present I am paying tribute because I refuse to leave my house to fulfill mita duties. I must give domestic service to that governor [Liro de Córdova] and other nobles of the pueblo. If I re-

36 "Exp. sobre . . . Fiorilo," f. 210.

37 "Juicio de Liro de Córdova contra Condori," ff. 34-35.

38 The intendant Viedma (*Descripción geográfica*, 173-174) later confirmed this impression, although he stressed the injustices that originarios suffered at the hand of religious authorities in the village.

fused to pay tribute they would seize my lands. To cultivate the reserve land of the community, I am obliged to lend six yoke of oxen, a plowshare, and laborers [*gañanes*] to plow, thresh, and gather the harvest. I never owed these obligations in the past, but now many widows and tributaries must pay them out of fear of the governors.[39]

She alluded to obligatory and coerced "rent" (in labor and kind) extracted from menfolk as well. Another widow told the magistrates that her husband had faithfully paid his tribute dues but still found himself obligated to render personal services to the cacique's lieutenant for one year. The woman claimed that her husband had helped to dig the irrigation ditches and construct the roof, walls, and patio of the lieutenant's hacienda in Tapacarí. After it was built, he spent the rest of the year as a domestic servant in the new estate. The widow said he had received no pay except for a daily ration of food.[40] Her words were echoed in the testimony by other originarios—men and women, cultivators and artisans, members of Anansaya and Urinsaya.

This record reveals a village torn apart by protracted factional disputes and sharply divided between an Indian minority wielding considerable economic power and a mass of peasants struggling for their livelihood. At first glance, it seems to contradict the impression left by the padrones that Tapacarí had withstood outside pressures more successfully than the smaller pueblos reales of the Valle Bajo. It is certainly true that the people of Tapacarí had managed to preserve their territory and shield themselves from an influx of non-Indians. Judged by this criterion, the village of Tapacarí had been able to reproduce its social system over two centuries of colonial rule. But the community had experienced profound internal transformations that had weakened its defenses against private accumulation and incipient class divisions in the interior of village society. Furthermore, the feud between cacique families had created a rift in Tapacarí that exacerbated social tensions and revealed the resentment that many peasants felt for members of both the native and the Spanish hierarchies. The peasants' testimony against the caciques and their clientele exposed a web of relations that bound them to their "overlords" through rent, obligatory loans of draft animals, domestic servitude,

39 "Juicio de Liro de Córdova contra Condori," ff. 22-23.

40 "Exp. sobre . . . Fiorilo," ff. 217v.-219.

and rotative field work on cacique-controlled lands.[41] Perhaps agrarian labor relations in the village still assumed reciprocal forms, but the social content had changed. Customary labor prestations had become *servicio personal* in the eyes of many peasants, and work on so-called community lands no longer guaranteed subsistence rights. When the cacique feud broke out, many peasants in Tapacarí took advantage of it to seek retribution in the colonial courts.

Class Relations and Colonial Legitimacies

The weak communal tradition and crisis of authority in Tapacarí left the village vulnerable to the divisive forces of class. Yet the advent of class differences and property ownership in Tapacarí did not entirely transform Andean social relations, based as they were on principles of kinship and reciprocity. The peasants managed to preserve some room for the reciprocal relations and collective work activities that knitted individuals and households into the traditional social fabric. Indians of the estancias probably maintained access to resources at different ecological tiers through reciprocal trading or labor arrangements with other estancias or with kinsmen. Work parties continued to be the norm on certain lands and at certain times in the agricultural cycle. The imperatives of subsistence agriculture and the need to pool risks and provide for insurance against crop failure ensured the survival of reciprocal labor relations, quite apart

41 There was, besides the caciques, another hierarchy, closely interwoven with the native one, that was an important source of tension in Tapacarí in the eighteenth century: the secular and regular clergy. San Augustín was the seat of an Augustinian monastery, and originario households were drafted, on a rotational basis, for a year of labor on the monastery's lands. Peasant families also subsidized the secular clergy. In an extensive list of grievances submitted to the court in 1796, Tapacarí Indians complained of the excessive labor services demanded by their parish priests whom they served as pack drivers, escorts, cooks, handymen, and field laborers. In addition, the petitioners challenged the custom of sponsoring religious festivities on the terms mandated by the priests. According to Indian testimony, the clerics appointed originario families each year to serve as patrons (*alfereces*) of one of the ten saints of the village. The annual cost per family of this patronage ranged between forty-seven pesos (in the subparish of Itapaya) and eighty-five pesos (in the village of San Augustín). Tapacareños complained that these parish dues "ruined even the more prosperous families." "Representación de los indios principales de Tapacarí . . . " (Sept. 26, 1796), RAH, ML 9/1675, tomo 20, f. 277. See also "Exp. que contiene recurso de los indios de Tapacarí sobre los derechos parroquiales . . . ," ANB, EC no. 31 (1761), and "Exp. sobre los abusos de los indios de Tapacarí . . . ," AGI, Charcas, Leg. 525 (1779).

from their ideological and ceremonial meanings. Modes of peasant livelihood called for some degree of collective decision-making about seed varieties, crop rotation, irrigation, and land and labor usage.[42] But these relationships are often not visible to historians; only in moments of stress or conflict do they sometimes come to light.

One such moment in the life of an Andean peasant household was the departure of a family for the mines of Potosí. When enrolled in the mita, a peasant family had to extricate itself from the multiple reciprocal relations that bound it to other households and had to entrust its meager resources to kinsmen who could be called upon in times of need. Such an arrangement might be phrased in Andean or commercial terms, but it rested on the principle of mutual aid. One example of such a caretaking arrangement comes from the village of Capinota in 1742. Called up for the mita, Ysidro Condo asked his son-in-law to safeguard his cattle, in return for which Condo would bring him maize, salt, and ají. This particular arrangement, tidy and even mercantile in form, eventually led to a lawsuit wherein Condo accused his relative of selling the cattle.[43] But what of the myriad other arrangements peasants made with their kinsmen, neighboring households, or ayllus, if they were to entrust their herds, lands, hut, and perhaps even children to others before they set off for the mines?

It is also conceivable that while the burdens of tribute and repartos turned peasants against members of the ethnic elite, they sometimes reinforced "horizontal" reciprocal or collective relationships. During the dispute between the two Tapacarí caciques which was discussed above, Pedro Condori accused Liro de Córdova of charging excessive ground rent to the potato cultivators of a highland estancia.[44] But that rent was paid by the entire estancia, not by individual peasant households. Among the rural forasteros of Tapacarí, such Andean forms of collectivity and reciprocity took root outside of traditional kinship and cultural contexts; there was no common ancestor-god, cultural heritage, or ethnic identity on which they could be grounded. They were born of a material and moral necessity to widen the range of subsistence options available.

But mutuality and reciprocity among peasants in the rural hinterlands of Tapacarí had little effect upon cacique rivalries or class

42 Halperin and Dow, *Peasant Livelihood*, esp. chaps. 2, 3, and 12.

43 "Testimonio del yndígena Ysidro Condo" (1742), AHMC, Leg. 1062.

44 "Juicio de Liro de Córdova contra Condori," ff. 4-5.

cleavages in the village. As we saw earlier, there was a privileged clique of natives who had accumulated wealth and entrenched themselves in the community as patrons of loyal factions, upon whose members they bestowed gifts of land and other resources. An incipient Indian landholding elite, certainly identifiable by Viedma's day, had distorted the traditional distribution of resources and violated the traditional normative order. Class tensions were already evident during the course of the feud between the caciques, who probably used the resources at their disposal to reinforce alliances with their clienteles. But by thus obtaining short-term economic and political gains, the caciques undermined their social standing in their own moieties. They could hardly pretend to serve as stewards of the community's norms and resources, mediators of disputes and conflicts, and overseers of the equitable distribution of lands and water, when they were clearly serving their own material and political interests. Their interstitial position in colonial society had always been a source of tension and contradiction. But once those contradictions were turned inward toward the collective well-being and undermined the self-sufficiency and subsistence autonomy of the peasants, reducing them to servicio personal or to supplicants of their own caciques, the village authorities had forsaken their moral stature. At a time when external pressures were growing and the corregidor was intervening more directly in village life, it was no longer possible for the caciques to balance colonial extraction against Andean legitimacy. In buttressing their own power and economic security through accumulation within the matrix of the community, they had sacrificed their integrity and authority. Once the feud was channeled through the courts and Tapacareños began to testify about conditions of life and work in the village, the caciques found themselves in the peculiar position of defending themselves to the magistrates of the audiencia. More than ever before, the caciques needed the support of the colonial rulers, when the greatest challenge to their position emanated from below—from the discontented, refractory peasantry.

But what was the criterion of a cacique's right to govern in the middle of the eighteenth century, in the opinion of the audiencia of La Plata? In conflicts between hereditary chiefs and those appointed by corregidores, who were seen as too ready to intervene in village life, the oidores were inclined to be on the side of tradition and noble lineage. Liro de Córdova did indeed attack Condori as an impostor, foisted on the community by Fiorilo. But the issue involved more than the question of inheritance versus appointment, for in villages throughout Alto Perú Indians were often appointed to serve as temporary chiefs (*caciques interinos* or *caciques gobernadores*) by colonial authorities, who took into consideration the quality of leadership and the comportment and usefulness of the appointees. Caciques had to carry out their duties within their villages, as well as meet their obligations to the state; they had to command their own people's respect and obedience, but they also had to ensure the delivery of tribute dues and mitayos. Furthermore, they were under increasing pressure to show that they would be able to make up any tribute deficits with their own personal wealth. Thus, Condori and Liro de Córdova had to both demonstrate their wealth to the magistrates and deny its origins in exploitative enterprises which violated the very Andean norms they were expected to respect and preserve.

Liro de Córdova, the deposed hereditary cacique, contended that he possessed the "finances necessary to guarantee the village's tribute."[45] The list of assets he presented was impressive: the hacienda Yllataco in Quillacollo and several houses nearby and in Tapacarí, and in the estancia Amaru; a quantity of silver plate; 50 oxen, 60 cows, 1,200 sheep, 70 horses, a mule train consisting of 10 animals, 8 mules equipped to transport wine, 15 burros, 8 riding mules, and 3 riding horses; and 360 fanegas of wheat and 40 fanegas of maize.[46] In addition, he named a half-dozen Indians who he said were willing to help him post bond for the tribute dues with the value of their own property or cash. Some of these bondsmen were principales of Tapacarí, but at least one, Bernardo Mamani, was an outsider, the brother of Sipesipe's cacique.[47] For his part, Condori warned the oidores about the insolvency of his rival's bondsmen and the sad little farm of 20 fanegadas of rocky, dry soil that Liro de Córdova called a hacienda. Condori declared that he would be able to cover tribute deficits through his own enterprise and his long-distance commercial ventures.[48]

The caciques' claims of prosperity and business acumen differed sharply from their uneasy, inconsistent testimony about their landholdings in the village. Neither one admitted that he controlled parcels of land in the village and charged rent in labor services. As we have seen, Condori said that estancia Indians paid Liro de Córdova

45 "Exp. sobre . . . Fiorilo."

46 Ibid., f. 55.

47 Ibid.

48 Ibid., ff. 66v.-73.

excessive rents, but Liro de Córdova said he enjoyed a benevolent relationship with the peasants who tilled his "reserve lands." How, he asked the magistrates, could he make Indians pay rent and forsake their right to pasture their herds and gather firewood on these lands? "The Indians may be poor, but they are aware of their legal obligations and would defy such [unjust] orders."[49] Nor did he force them to purchase wheat, he insisted, although he sold them wheat they needed to stock up for long journeys (presumably to Potosí). Liro de Córdova dismissed these charges with an economy of words. His use of the labor of Indians and their animals he explained in these words:

> In many other villages it is customary to oblige Indians to ride their mares to the wheat field and lend them for threshing the grain; the Indians must also help plant the seed and gather the ripened crop . . . ; but I never use my authority as governor to force people to work even when the crops are cultivated on community lands. My actions are infused with the spirit of Christianity . . . ; I solicit horses from village members and ask to borrow them. I also pay the Indian horse owners and give gifts . . . like jugs of aguardiente. And during the festivities on the day we thresh I give them abundant amounts of food and chicha.[50]

It is reasonable to assume that both Liro de Córdova and his traditional rival appreciated the symbolic importance of reciprocal gestures and generosity in their dealings with native laborers. Even when labor relations were essentially coerced and conflictual, the caciques probably supplied the food and drink to their workers that most hacendados customarily provided to their own peons at harvest time. But on an ideological level, Liro de Córdova tried to legitimate his authority in the eyes of the colonial magistrates by invoking Christian ideals as well as Andean norms of social behavior. His testimony projected the self-image of a native lord whose generosity took the specifically Andean form of gift-giving, supposedly part of an ongoing reciprocal relation with the village Indians, who then willingly contributed their horses and labor for the collective good. In presenting his case, Liro de Córdova obviously sought to narrow the social distance between himself and the peasants of Tapacarí and to camouflage the coercive nature of the labor that many Tapacareños testified to.

Throughout the trial, Condori and Liro de Córdova disputed each

---

49 "Juicio de Liro de Córdova contra Condori," ff. 4-5.

50 Ibid., f. 28v.

other's opinion about the capacity of Tapacarí's agricultural yields to cover tribute deficits. Condori claimed sufficient reserves existed; his rival denied it. Yet, as we have seen, both caciques declared themselves wealthy enough to personally make up any deficits. However, testimony by the caciques themselves and by originarios provide a very different picture of who bore the chronic burden of the village's tribute debts. Liro de Córdova stated that the caciques normally appointed thirteen originarios each year to collect tribute from each anexo in the parcialidades. These people, not the cacique, were responsible for covering the uncollected balance of the tribute quota. Liro de Córdova admitted that each of these "halacatas," as he called them, had accumulated debts for outstanding tribute dues, ranging from one hundred to three hundred pesos.[51] At other points in the trial, Pedro Condori similarly stated that the Indians whom he had appointed as tax collectors during the previous four years collectively owed him more than four thousand pesos.[52] Apparently, the practice of shifting the debt burden to these appointed collectors (*cobradores*) was common throughout the eighteenth century.[53] But the caciques, eager to prove to the magistrates their magnanimity, befitting Andean lords, assured them that they had seen to the prompt delivery of tribute dues, without imposing undue hardship on the debtors or the community. Condori told the judges that he raised tribute money by selling his own wheat in Arequipa and in the yungas of La Paz. He described his actions as personal sacrifices made to avoid selling community stocks or "confiscating the goods [of the cobradores] as I should have done" to meet the tribute payments.[54]

It is not known how often the caciques actually did cover tribute deficits out of their own assets. Condori's statement suggests that cobradores at least were at risk of losing their goods when there were deficits. The widow María Santuza told the oidores of her fear that her lands would be seized if tribute payments were not met (see

---

51 "Exp. sobre . . . Fiorilo," f. 64.

52 Ibid., passim, esp. ff. 64, 64v., and 66v.

53 Following the 1781 rebellions, provincial authorities often appointed caciques interinos to oversee tribute collection; their ability to cover tribute deficits was a necessary qualification for such an appointment. "Exp. sobre las elecciones de caciques interinos de Capinota," ANB, EC no. 72 (1796). On the economic hardships facing the cobradores, see AGN, Sala 9, Interior, 30.4.6, Leg. 30, Exp. 39 (1791), ff. 39-39v.

54 "Exp. sobre . . . Fiorilo," ff. 64v.-66v.

above). Other witnesses at the trial acknowledged personal debts to one of the caciques, and the means of their redemption can only be surmised. But caciques probably manipulated the terms of credit and debt among village Indians to their advantage. In their own testimony, however, they concealed their power over debtors by casting the relationship in an Andean mold: Through their alleged generosity, they were "saving" the Indians who failed to deliver the amount of tribute assigned them. The quest for colonial legitimacy forced them to try to reconcile the contradictions and conflicts between their economic power and patronage in the community, on the one hand, and their professed conformity to Andean norms of governance and authority (as sanctioned by the colonial state), on the other.

The audiencia of La Plata, and eventually the Council of the Indies, held for Liro de Córdova and reinstated his right of succession to the cacicazgo in the late 1750s.[55] Little is known of the family's activities for a couple of decades afterward, but by the 1780s, it had achieved control over both moieties. Sebastián Francisco, Juan Guillermo's son by his first wife, administered Anansaya, and Sebastián Francisco's son-in-law, Matías Quispe, was cacique of Urinsaya (see figure 9). The family had extended its holdings inside and outside the village of Tapacarí. According to private family records (which were unaffected by the need to present a favorable picture to the court), their properties included the haciendas Milloma and Casavinto in

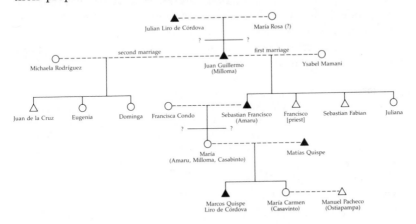

Figure 9   Genealogy of the Liro de Córdova Family of Tapacarí
Note: Shaded figures represent individuals who held the office of cacique. Names of haciendas owned by individuals are shown in parentheses.

55 Ibid., Cuaderno 1.

the parish of Las Ramadas, downriver from Tapacarí. The Casavinto estate included wheat lands and six grain mills; its assessed market value of 26,563 pesos made it one of the larger haciendas in the region. The purchase price of Milloma had been 24,000 pesos; Juan de la Cruz Liro de Córdova, son of Juan Guillermo by his second marriage, had paid it with the help of a loan of 12,000 pesos from a Carmelite convent.[56] A 1782 account book listed five other holdings: three haciendas of Sebastian Francisco Liro de Córdova and two chacras of Quispe and his wife.[57] Their total yield amounted to 541 fanegas of wheat and 47 cargas of potatoes—a poor harvest that must have suffered from the aftermath of the 1781 rebellion. Nonetheless, the estimated market value of the crop represented about three-quarters of the value of tribute owed by the originario population.[58] In addition, Juan de la Cruz Liro de Córdova owned 1,500 head of cattle that grazed on pasturelands in the estancia Aparumiri (the same estancia that Blas Condori had accused Juan Guillermo Liro de Córdova of possessing in 1758).[59] In the estancia of Amaru, María, daughter of Sebastian Francisco, owned grain mills and lands.[60] But the family's most extensive tract of land in Tapacarí was Añaguaiani. In 1782, the overseer reported that its wheat crop amounted to 253 fanegas. As was customary, he stored the grain, urging the caciques to sell it quickly because "the rebels continue to invade Tapacarí."[61]

The caciques ran their agrarian enterprises much like any other large landlord did. They entrusted management to a creole overseer, Fontanilla, who kept records of their holdings, harvests, and returns. During the harvest period, he hired between fourteen and forty-seven jornaleros for fourteen successive days to cut and gather the wheat

56 "División de la hacienda y molinas de Milloma . . .," AHMC, Leg. 1062 (1791); "Testamento de doña María Liro de Córdova," AHMC, Leg. 1090 (1792) (hereafter cited as "Testamento de doña María Liro de Córdova"); "Exp. de Juan de la Cruz Liro de Córdova . . . sobre la nulidad de la venta de tierras 'Casavinto,' " AHMC, Leg. 1256 (1782) (hereafter cited as "Exp. de Juan de la Cruz").

57 "Cuaderno de cuentas dadas . . . de las cosechas de las sementeras de los caciques de Tapacarí," ANB, EC no. 84 (1782) (hereafter cited as "Cuaderno de cuentas").

58 "Cuaderno de cuentas."

59 "Exp. de Juan de la Cruz."

60 "Testamento de doña Maria Liro de Córdova." The mills, alone carried an assessed market value of 18,000 pesos.

61 "Cuaderno de cuentas."

and between twenty-seven and thirty men for three days to load the grain on pack animals and carry it to the storage huts. To thresh and winnow the wheat on days when the wind was favorable for carrying away the chaff, Fontanilla called upon "all the people of [the estancias] Yrpuma, Guanuara, and Escalera."[62] In private, the caciques and their creole administrator viewed their properties as commercial ventures. Away from the scrutiny of rivals and oidores, there was no allusion to reciprocity between caciques and the peasants who worked on their lands.

Despite ritual gestures to nativism, this native elite was very Hispanic in its way of life. Not only did a creole look after its properties and a convent lend it money. At least two children of Juan Guillermo were educated in creole schools.[63] Several kin married mestizos or creoles, and others intermarried with cacique families of Capinota and other pueblos reales. At least one member of the family, María, had a mulatto slave as her personal servant. María's wealth also included lands, mills, herds, and all manner of textiles, including rich velvets from the capitals of Europe and *polleras* (layers of full skirts) made of fine bayeta—a luxurious amalgamation of two cultures.[64]

This, then, is the unequivocal evidence of an extraordinarily wealthy cacique family that had amassed property and power in Tapacarí between the 1740s and the outbreak of the Andean rebellion of 1781. The Liro de Córdovas had emerged from the trials with the support of the highest colonial authorities. Over the next couple of decades, the family took advantage of this legitimation to advance its economic interests. Precisely during the peak period of repartimientos de mercancías, the Liro de Córdovas extended their hold over community resources. It is not unreasonable to assume, therefore, that the processes of privatization and internal differentiation in Tapacarí accelerated in the decades prior to the 1781 uprisings.

But in the context of village society, even one like Tapacarí, which was historically weakened by ethnic fragmentation and factionalism, indigenous authority that rested on class domination and colonial legitimation was always subject to the threat of social alienation and rejection. As Hispanicized native landholders, the caciques were hardly distinguishable from other members of the colonial hier-

---

62 Ibid.

63 "Exp. de Juan de la Cruz."

64 "Testamento de doña María Liro de Córdova."

archy. Moreover, they were regarded as people who had rejected or forsaken their Andean heritage to serve their own class interests and those of the state. Their lip service to Andean ways notwithstanding, the Liro de Córdovas represented the colonizers, and thus they occupied a vulnerable position in their own society. The events of 1781 fully exposed the caciques to the scorn and hatred of their people. When rebellion finally erupted in Tapacarí early in 1781, the caciques became despised outcasts.

In the last days of February, a group of Andeans gathered together near the village of Challa, near the mountain pass where the road crossed the provincial border. One Sunday morning, as mass was being held, they swept down from the mountains and invaded San Augustín de Tapacarí, the seat of the pueblo real. The rebels killed the parish priest and several hundred other people, although Sebastian Liro de Córdova and Matías Quispe had been warned and had fled at dawn. Following the attack, the rebels retreated to the mountains, regrouped, and then attacked the Liro de Córdovas' hacienda Milloma, turning it into their fortress. The hacienda was located in the river valley, and, by controlling it, the rebels were able to cut off Tapacarí proper from the lower river basin and the central valleys of Cochabamba. Communication was also impeded by nature for it was the rainy season, and the swollen river made it difficult for troops to come to the aid of the besieged pueblo. The month of March was punctuated by bloody battles between the Andean rebels and the royalist troops. In their first foray from the provincial capital of Cochabamba, creole militiamen drove the insurgents out of Milloma and back into the mountains. In the meantime, however, other rebel bands closed in upon the village of Tapacarí and repelled the Spanish attacks. The corregidor then dispatched a second major expedition, which managed to recapture Tapacarí after a fierce and costly battle.[65]

Not a great deal is known about the alliances, tactics, or leadership of the rebels who seized San Augustín. But there is no mistaking the enmity between the rebels and the ethnic elite of Tapacarí. The caciques entrusted their valuables and 2,000 pesos in cash to a wealthy

65 "Sublevación de los indios de Tapacarí," AHMC, Leg. 1275 (1781), "Ynformación sumaria producida sobre las alteraciones de la provincia de Cochabamba en 1781," Archivo de la Biblioteca de la Universidad Mayor de San Andrés (La Paz), no. 97, f. 6; AGN, Sala 9, Intendencia, 5.8.2, Leg. 1 (July 3, 1782); Lillian Estelle Fisher, *The Last Inca Revolt, 1780–1783* (Norman: University of Oklahoma Press, 1966), 160-162, 166-167. Besides the rebellion focused on Tapacarí, there were local uprisings that same year in Arque, Colcha, Cliza, and other places.

vecino outside the village in order "to protect their property from the pillage of the Indian rebels."[66] When the rebellion had been crushed and royal inquiries began, a young mestizo woman testified boldly about the hostility that Tapacareños felt toward the cacique clan.

> Indian rebels came from Challapata and Ayopaya killing Spaniards and all white people. . . . Their first enemies were the caciques . . . who hid their possessions before they fled . . . The caciques, Don Sebastian Córdova and Don Matías Quispe, are very rich men and in all parts of this land the Indian insurgents hunt the rich to rob them and take their lives. I have heard many Indians say that the main objective of the rebels was to kill these caciques, especially Córdova, for being the compadre of the priest and for concealing the tariff [of the repartimiento de mercancías] in order to rob the Indians. It is rumored that the caciques stole from originario principales, too. They have controlled power for many generations.[67]

These observations, impressions, and rumors indicate only the shadowy outlines of this rebellion, one that articulated with the earlier and concurrent struggles that unfolded in the highlands under the legendary leadership of Túpac Catari and Túpac Amarú.[68] But they also reveal the gulf that separated the masses from the ethnic elite in Tapacarí, an elite so entrenched and so distant, with its Christian-Hispanic ways, that it could not fend off the rebels with

66 "Exp. . . . sobre la restitución de pesos pertenecientes a los caciques . . . ," ANB, EC no. 78 (1781).

67 "Sublevación de los indios de Tapacarí," AHMC, Leg. 1275 (1781), ff. 6-9v.

68 The literature on the Túpac Catari and Túpac Amarú rebellions and associated local uprisings is growing rapidly. See Leon Campbell, "Recent Research on Andean Peasant Revolts, 1750-1820," *Latin American Research Review* 14 (1979): 3-49; Alberto Flores Galindo, ed., *Túpac Amarú II: 1780* (Lima: Retablo de papel, 1976); Scarlett O'Phelan Godoy, "La rebelión de Túpac Amarú: Organización interna, dirigencia y alianzas," *Histórica* 3 (1979): 89-121; Scarlett O'Phelan Godoy, "Tierras comunales y revuelta social: Perú y Bolivia en el siglo XVIII," *Allpanchis*, año 13, vol. 19 (1983): 75-91; and O'Phelan Godoy, *Rebellions and Revolts*. Recent studies of the ideological aspects of the Túpac Amarú and Túpac Catari rebellions include Jorge Hidalgo Lehuedé, "Amarus y cataris: Aspectos mesiánicos de la rebelión indígena de 1781 en Cusco, Chayanta, La Paz, y Arica," *Revista Chungará*, no. 10 (1983): 117-138; Stern, "Age of Andean Insurrection," and Alberto Flores Galindo, "Buscando un Inca" (paper presented at the Social Science Research Council/University of Wisconsin Conference on Resistance and Rebellion in the Andean World, 18th-20th centuries, Madison, Wis., Apr. 26-28, 1984).

its own partisan defenders. Instead, the caciques moved out of the orbit of the pueblo real into Spanish territory—the only safe haven under the circumstances. The caciques became exiles, dependent on the colonial militia and state for their protection.

Thus, the earlier judicial victory of the Liro de Córdovas was a Pyrrhic one. Colonial legitimation ultimately proved their undoing in the uprisings of 1781. While it gave them a new lease on life, allowing them to accumulate great personal wealth in the village, it further eroded the traditional relationships between the ethnic elite and ordinary Tapacareños. The caciques' power and material security no longer depended upon their social prestige in the village or on their ability to command the labor and loyalty of peasants through a process of reciprocal (though asymmetrical) exchanges. Kinship and community, as defined in Andean terms, had lost their meaning in Tapacarí, and Tapacareños, both originario and forastero, saw the native elite violating traditional norms. As the pressures of repartimiento bore down harder on peasant households and stretched subsistence patterns to the breaking point, and as the Liro de Córdovas acquired title to some of the best lands and herds in Tapacarí, there seemed little the village Indians could do to block the ascent of an Indian landed oligarchy. But when Andean rebels mobilized throughout the southern Andes early in 1781, the moment of peasant reprisal in Tapacarí had arrived. The local insurgents exposed the fragility of ethnic power and authority that had come to be based primarily on class relations and colonial legitimation.

CHAPTER FIVE

Haciendas
and the Rival
Peasant Economy

Despite the ambivalence of the early colonial state toward private landownership in the maize valleys, Spanish colonists extended their control over Cochabamba's valleys and highlands until they occupied most of the fertile areas, encircling the five pueblos reales. By the 18th century, rural life in most parts of the region revolved around the hacienda, where a dispossessed and dependent peasantry worked for the landlords in return for access to the means of subsistence. Whether they worked the lands of a great estate or turned in a share of the crops they grew on a small plot, the peasants of the haciendas were bound to their landlords in a web of mutual obligations (and antagonisms) that was relatively impervious to the colonial state. Indeed, this was the source of the ambivalence of Toledo and his successors, who feared a permanent "loss" of village peasants to the private domain.

The state's perspective—that the haciendas secluded peasants from the extractive institutions of colonial society—led to an image of mute, docile, dependent people eking out a precarious livelihood under the control of an omnipotent landlord. Much of the early literature on seigneurial relations, particularly on Mexican haciendas, reinforced this view.[1] In the Andean context, the peasants appeared

---

1 This was particularly the case in the classic study by François Chevalier, *La formation des grands domaines au Mexique: Terre et société aux XVIe-XVIIe siècles* (Paris: Institut d'Ethnologie, 1952). More recent literature has challenged this interpretation. Three surveys of that literature and discussions of the research and debates surrounding the Mexican, and more generally the Spanish American, hacienda are Magnus Mörner, "The Spanish American Hacienda: A Survey of Recent Research and Debate," *Hispanic American Historical Review* 53 (1973): 183-216; Eric Van Young, "Mexican Rural History since Chevalier: The Historiography of the Colonial Hacienda," *Latin American Research Review* 18 (1983), 5-61; and Enrique Florescano, "The Formation and Economic Structure of the Hacienda in New Spain," in Leslie Bethell, ed., *The Cambridge*

to be Indians who had forsaken their rights and obligations to their own communities and the right to act or speak as members of their ethnic family. In theory, they were atomized and directly subordinated, through property and patron-client relations, to a master. They had no claim on either Andean or colonial legitimacy, such as their counterparts in Tapacarí did. There was apparently little recourse but to submit or accommodate.

Yet colonial authorities themselves contradicted their own stereotypes of the hacienda peasants when they reflected on the Cochabamba tax rebellion of the early 1730s (see chapter 3). The exploitative relations that emerged on the haciendas did not escape resistance and challenge, even when the peasants had "voluntarily" agreed to the rent or labor arrangements. Like the village peasants, tenants on haciendas sought to protect their subsistence security, but their struggle was focused on the terms of land tenure and rent. Occasionally, the conflicts were channeled through the courts, affording glimpses of the peasants' perceptions of their rights and obligations.

But it was the proliferation of a commercially oriented peasantry in the central valleys rather than direct political confrontations, that constituted the greatest threat to the landowning class. Rural smallholders who leased patches of hacienda land engaged in petty trade and crafts in addition to their agricultural activities. Periodically, they entered the market as sellers of small food surpluses or specialized commodities. The resulting myriad of economic enterprises, small in scale and precapitalist in nature, changed the contours of the regional economy. For some peasants, this diversification substantially lessened their dependence on the landlords and mitigated the effects of harvest failure. But for the landowning class, the advent of a commercially active peasantry, which increasingly controlled cereal production on the estates, undermined its economic power and challenged its monopoly of grain surpluses.

As class relations became more intricate in the eighteenth century, the social geography acquired texture and variation. Increasingly, the region seemed to be composed of two subregions: on the one hand, the central valleys, and on the other, the western highlands and river valleys that reached upland toward the altiplano. The western highlands and river valleys served as trade corridors between the altiplano and the central valleys, but they were not caught up in

History of Latin America (Cambridge: Cambridge University Press, 1984), 2: 153-188.

the economic trends that swept across the central valleys. In fact, some western areas, such as Ayopaya, seemed more disconnected from the central valleys than ever before. In contrast, the three central valleys (Valle Bajo, Sacaba, and Cliza) were the site of numerous haciendas and smallholdings, Spanish towns and pueblos, and primitive manufactories and workshops. The region's economic pulse beat there, where a growing peasant population produced, distributed, and consumed staple goods that flowed through a network of commercial arteries. Contemporary census reports reveal the subregional patterns of agriculture, industry, and trade in eighteenth-century Cochabamba.

Charting the Social Geography

The European sojourners and administrators, weary after weeks of travel by mule or horseback across the altiplano, must have been relieved and delighted upon arriving in Cochabamba valley, to find a temperate climate and a fertile land inhabited by many Spaniards and creoles. Like Vázquez de Espinosa more than a century earlier, Cosme Bueno wrote in the 1740s that Cochabamba had every right "to call itself the granary of Peru, because it produces in abundance all kinds of seeds in a benign and healthy climate. . . . Streams of good water irrigate the fields and fertilize the valleys where there are more than 300 haciendas."[2] Some forty years later, Francisco de Paula Sanz, then administrator of the royal tobacco monopoly, inspected the province and described it as "one of the most beautiful places I have seen in all the viceroyalty. [The capital city] is surrounded by country houses [*quintas*] whose lands are cultivated, ringed by fruit orchards, and bathed by the waters of two rivers, the Tamborada and the Rocha."[3] Though Paula Sanz submitted the report in 1783, he had toured the parishes of Cochabamba shortly before the western districts were convulsed by the rebellions of 1781. His report reflected an unwarranted optimism about the region's vitality and social order. Indeed, Paula Sanz discussed the state of agriculture and industry without mentioning the quality of life or hu-

2 Cosme Bueno, "Descripción de las provincias pertenecientes al arzobispado de La Plata" [1740s], in Manuel de Odriozola, ed., *Colección de documentos literarios del Perú* (Lima: A. Alfaro, 1872), 3: 123-124.

3 "Copia de la descripción de la provincia de Cochabamba que hizo el . . . d. Francisco de Paula Sanz," RAH, ML, 9/1725, tomo 70 (Sept. 21, 1783). (Cited hereafter as "Descripción de Cochabamba").

man conditions in the valleys. He was content to catalogue the economic activities of the "one hundred thousand souls" who inhabited the province.

Less than ten years later, Francisco de Viedma, the first head of the intendancy of Santa Cruz de la Sierra (which had absorbed the province of Cochabamba), wrote his well-known description of the region, a description marked by great concern for detail. Viedma spent several years traveling through the parishes and collecting data before producing his account in 1788.[4] Unlike Paula Sanz, he was deeply disturbed by the poverty and human need he had seen all around him. In the wake of the rebellions, the scandalous behavior of the corregidores, and the drought of 1784, Viedma refused to ignore the penury of peasant life, the deep class divisions, and the precarious balance of class forces in local society.

Viedma deplored the conditions he found, all the more because the region's special ecological niche in the Andean landscape seemed to have offered a happy alternative, in European eyes, to the harsh climate and austere life of puna Indians. "Upon hearing a geographic description of the entire province, who would not consider it to offer the greatest possibilities for human happiness on earth? And upon hearing of the region's abundant resources and population, who would not wonder why [the region] has suffered such calamities?"[5] It was a question that Viedma tried to answer now and again in his long report. This report was essentially a compilation of statistics and observations which, when added to Paula Sanz's report, yields a picture of zonal variations in the three central valleys of Cochabamba and the outlying western districts.

Viedma's report provided the first complete census and socioracial profile of the province. It showed that 125,245 people inhabited the five partidos of the province—about 7 percent of the total population of the viceroyalty (table 13).[6] It confirmed earlier impressions of the

---

4 Viedma, *Descripción geográfica*. There is some confusion about the year that this report was written. Although it is dated 1793, Nicolás Sánchez-Albornoz discovered correspondence from Viedma indicating that it was actually completed in 1788 (personal communication and *Indios y tributos*, 167). The intendancy of Santa Cruz de la Sierra stretched across the vast, relatively unexplored jungle lowlands east of the Andean escarpment and beyond the lowland town of Santa Cruz. However, its heartland continued to be the densely populated "high valleys" of Cochabamba and the western river valleys and highlands of Arque, Tapacarí, and Ayopaya that bordered the altiplano to the west.

5 Viedma, *Descripción geográfica*, 159.

6 Golte (*Repartos y rebeliones*, 42) has estimated that the population of Alto and Bajo Perú at the time was about 1,800,000.